Structure, Style, and Usage

Structure, Style, and Usage

K.S. Yadurajan

OXFORD
UNIVERSITY PRESS

OXFORD

UNIVERSITY PRESS

YMCA Library Building, Jai Singh Road, New Delhi 110 001

Oxford University Press is a department of the University of Oxford.
It furthers the University's objective of excellence in research, scholarship,
and education by publishing worldwide in

Oxford   New York
Auckland   Cape Town   Dar es Salaam   Hong Kong   Karachi
Kuala Lumpur   Madrid   Melbourne   Mexico City   Nairobi
New Delhi   Shanghai   Taipei   Toronto

With offices in
Argentina   Austria   Brazil   Chile   Czech Republic   France   Greece
Guatemala   Hungary   Italy   Japan   Poland   Portugal   Singapore
South Korea   Switzerland   Thailand   Turkey   Ukraine   Vietnam

Oxford is a registered trade mark of Oxford University Press
in the UK and in certain other countries.

Published in India
by Oxford University Press, New Delhi

© Oxford University Press 2005

The moral rights of the authors have been asserted
Database right Oxford University Press (maker)

First published 2005

ISBN-13: 978-0-19-566836-0
ISBN-10:0-19-566836-7

Typeset in Dante MT 11/13.2
by Eleven Arts, Keshav Puram, Delhi 110 035
Printed in Sai Printopack Pvt. Ltd., New Delhi 110 020
Published by Manzar Khan, Oxford University Press
YMCA Library Building, Jai Singh Road, New Delhi 110 001

to my parents
Anna and Challi

Contents

Abbreviations and Symbols

A.
ALD	:	*The Advanced Learner's Dictionary of Contemporary English*, 4th edn, 1989
CE	:	*Current English*, 2001
COD	:	*The Concise Oxford Dictionary*, 8th edn, 1990
DEU	:	*Webster's Dictionary of English Usage*, 1989
GCE	:	*A Grammar of Contemporary English*, 1972
LDCE	:	*Longman Dictionary of Contemporary English*, 1995
NODE	:	*The New Oxford Dictionary of English*, 1998
OED	:	*The Oxford English Dictionary*, 2nd edn, 1989
OUP	:	Oxford University Press
Wyld	:	*The Universal Dictionary of the English Language*, 1936
Zandvoort	:	*A Handbook of English Grammar*, 1962

B.
Am E	:	American English
adj	:	adjective
aux	:	auxiliary
Br E	:	British English
I E	:	Indian English
n	:	noun
np	:	noun phrase
v	:	verb
vp	:	verb phrase
pp	:	prepositional phrase

C.
*	:	An asterisk before an expression or sentence indicates that it is unacceptable/ungrammatical.
cf	:	compare

e.g.	:	for example
=	:	The equals sign is used to indicate that two expressions are equivalent in meaning.
et al.	:	and others
etc.	:	et cetera; and other things of the same kind
i.e.	:	that is
/	:	A slash is used

    1. to separate example sentences when there are more than one of them

    2. to separate two or more words or expressions heading an article in the dictionary section.

' '   : quote marks are used

    1. to enclose Indian English expressions in the alphabetical listing

    2. to enclose meanings of expressions

    3. to show that a sentence is presented as quoted material

italics   : Apart from indicating titles of books, italics are used to show that a sentence so marked is an example sentence.

sic   : Used to indicate any error of spelling or sense.

Introduction

Structure, Style, and Usage is designed as a companion volume to my earlier book *Current English* (OUP, 2001).

The present book is more comprehensive than the earlier one. Word stories are missing but in their place there is an extensive discussion of various aspects of style: the basics of good English; considerations in the choice of words; various faults of style: cliche, jargon, tautology, pleonasm, periphrasis, padding. Figures of speech and several other topics have been extensively analysed and explained. Under Structure, aspects of English structure which non-native speakers find especially difficult to understand are analysed in depth and presented in new and original ways. See, for example, the entry under 'articles'. Further, numerous Indian English (IE) constructions, many of them not even recorded in the usual books on IE, are listed and examined. As in my earlier work, I have tried to explain why the IE speaker tends to make these constructions and point out the correct Standard English equivalents. Every construction examined is authentic; in most cases I have indicated my sources.

It would be presumptuous on my part to claim that, especially in the pieces on structure, every point of interest, even for the non-native speaker, has been covered. I can only advance in my defence a remark of Chomsky's made in another context: 'Just because something has not been done, it doesn't mean that nothing has been done.' In point of fact, much has been done. But the serious student who wishes to be informed on the minutiae of English syntax should delve into that mine of information, Michael Swan's *Practical English Usage* (OUP, 2003).

'Your honour puts himself to much trouble correcting my English and doubtless the final letter will be much better literature; but it will go from me Mukherji to him Bannerji, and he Bannerji will understand it a good deal better as I Mukherji write it than as your honour corrects it.' Thus a baboo, to his British superior (as quoted by Sir Ernest Gowers in his *Plain Words—Their ABC*). The British have left India; and so the baboo is no more. But English is still with us and we continue to use it with inventive abandon. While this is so (and there is little that anybody can do about it) there are still many who cherish and value good English. It is to them that this book is addressed. I hope they will find it enjoyable and useful. (In a few cases where an example from an Indian language was called for—to explicate a point about an IE expression—I have given a Kannada example. The Indian reader can verify the point in his own language where, I believe, equivalent expressions exist.)

A word about the citations. I have in mind, particularly, citations illustrating a grammatical mistake or a fault of style. These citations are mostly from Indian sources, whether published in India or abroad. The sources have been identified to show that the example sentences are not invented. The citation may have been taken from a letter to the Editor, from a column, from an article by someone, or from a journalist's report. But it should in no way be taken as reflecting on the English of the newspaper or magazine in question.

It is now my pleasant duty to acknowledge the many sources from which I have drawn ideas and inspiration. Some readers may feel that Fowler's shadow has fallen heavily on my book. Yes, in the articles on style it has, and I make no apology for it. I cannot agree with Burchfield that Fowler's great book is now a fossil. If there are sections in it which have become out of date—and there are—they are only a testimony to the living vigour of English which has not become fossilized.

But the virtues of good writing which Fowler emphasized and defended with such vigour, wit, and animosity can never become fossilized. They are at the very heart of good writing and will always remain so. And Fowler's essays on these points: *battered ornaments, hackneyed expressions, elegant variation, metaphor, genteelism*, to mention a few, will remain classics which everyone who values good writing must study. I share with Gowers an unabashed admiration for Fowler on these and other points. I offer my own effort as a humble tribute to a great master.

At the (then) Central Institute of English (CIE; now Central Institute of English and Foreign Languages, CIEFL, Hyderabad), I had the inestimable privilege of being initiated into the study of the great European grammarians of English, Poutsma, Jespersen, Kruisinga, and Zandvoort, by that unforgettable teacher, Professor H.V. George. Subsequently I came under the influence of Chomsky and became fascinated with generative grammar. I do not view (and have never felt) these two different traditions as, in any way, contradictory. To a large extent they explore different domains of grammar and ask different questions. I am equally interested in both. The discerning reader will not fail to see these two influences in the articles on structure.

It now remains to acknowledge my indebtedness to persons and sources more immediately connected with the book. I am indebted to A. Quinn on whom I have drawn heavily in my account of Figures of Speech. (I claim, however, some originality for the analysis and classification of the figures presented in the introductory essay, 'Figures of Speech'.) I am also indebted to the publishers of *Murphy's Law* (a desk calendar) for the essay on proverbs. I hope this acknowledgment will be accepted by the publishers as adequate in lieu of a written permission by them to use some of their material.

As in the case of my earlier book, I am heavily indebted to my unseen readers across the length and breadth of Karnataka (and beyond). It is their tireless curiosity and constant encouragement which has kept my column, 'English for You', going for over fifteen years now—a record of some sort. Practically all the words and phrases discussed in this book have been taken from their letters.

In this connection I cannot thank adequately K.N. Shanth Kumar, Editor, *Deccan Herald*, I who has very graciously given me permission to incorporate material into this book which originally appeared in my columns in the *Deccan Herald*.

My wife Radha has been a source of great help and support in the preparation of this book. No person could ask for a more understanding and helpful partner. The book has greatly benefited by her scrutiny and helpful comments.

My children have helped me in transforming an illegible manuscript into orderly print for the publisher.

a

abstract words

Words like *nature, character, basis, instance, case, fact, position, situation,* and *level* should be handled with care. Some of them can appear as parts of compound prepositional phrases. They can also appear independently leading to verbosity. *Overtures of a friendly nature* are just *friendly overtures,* the empty word *nature* can be eliminated by a change of structure.

Often, omitting the abstract word leads to a simplification of structure. *There are many cases of beggars having bank accounts* (= Many beggars have bank accounts). *The candidate was admitted on a provisional basis* (= was admitted provisionally). *The office was in a mess. In many instances files could not be traced.* (= Many files could not be traced.) *It is not the case that he always comes late* says no more than: He doesn't always come late. One might argue that in a certain context, the first sentence emphatically denies some assertion made by another person or corrects an impression given earlier by the writer/speaker himself. If so, they are very special cases. Usually the first sentence is only an expanded version of the second. The force of negation in *doesn't always* is expanded into *it is not the case that.*

In other cases, the structure with the abstract word can be replaced by a simpler equivalent. *In spite of the fact that he had been warned* (= Though he had been warned). *May I call your attention to the fact that* (= May I remind you that).

Even when the abstract word does not lead to a sentence becoming longer, an alternate construction without it may be more direct. Untouchability is no longer practised in temples *as was formerly the case* (replace the italicized portion with: *as it used to be*).

The words now being discussed as leading to verbosity do have their legitimate uses. *Fact,* which is the source of much wordiness, has its legitimate uses in such phrases: *the fact is, in point of fact, the fact that.*

Basis is legitimately used in: *There is no basis for your suspicion. Case* is required in: *Two cases of hepatitis B have been reported.* There are other legitimate uses. Consult the COD.

The verbosity examined till now should be distinguished from cases where a word or phrase is totally redundant and omissible; for example, the bracketed words in the following: *Weather (conditions) improving; temperature (levels) are rising; the question (as to) whether,* etc.

This brief discussion should act like a trigger and warn the student against redundant vacuities. For a fuller discussion, consult *The Complete Plain Words* (Gowers, revised edn, 1986).

I will close this section with a few citations to show how easily writers embrace these empties.

1. *It is fortunate* (= Fortunately) *the ties between them have acquired a certain level of stability*—New Indian Express, 18 March 2004. (Replace *a certain level of* by *some*.)

2. *I don't go around campaigning but help out at home. This usually involves attending to various files and letters*—Deccan Herald, 17 March 2004. (Put comma after *home*; omit *this usually involves*.)

3. *People from all walks of life with a level of dedication needed to serve the country*—The Hindu, 16 March 2004 (Replace *with a level of dedication needed* by *dedicated*.)

4. *High level contacts on a frequent basis have become the norm*—New Indian Express, 18 March 2004. (Change to *Frequent high level contacts have become*.)

I will end with a citation from no less an authority than *The New Oxford Dictionary of English*: '*A network of consultants in all parts of the English-speaking world has assisted—by giving information and answering queries by e-mail, on a regular, often daily basis*' (Introduction, p. XVI). *On a regular, often daily basis?* This may be sought to be justified by considerations of rhythm, balance, etc. But *answering queries regularly, almost daily* is more compact with no loss of information.

accede–concede

Both the words have some points of meaning in common. In both cases there are two parties involved, A and B. And in both cases, one party, say A, gives in. But with *accede* A agrees to do something that B has been demanding. With *concede* A accepts B's point of view though, initially, he might have been opposed to it. Consider this imaginary dialogue:

PM: The prices are rising and we must do something to contain them. I concede your point.

MP: Will you then roll back the proposed hike in rail fares?

PM: No. I cannot *accede* to that demand.

So one can *concede* a point without *acceding* to a related demand.

'according to me'

Sentences like *According to Harry it's a good film / According to Joan the people across the road are moving* are correct. But *According to me, she is sick* is not. Why?

Michael Swan (*Practical English Usage*) from whom these sentences are taken explains: 'We do not usually give our own opinion with *according to*.' Why?

According to may be used to give the opinion of an authority (on a subject). *According to Aristotle, the best course in life is to observe the golden mean. According to Einstein, nothing can travel faster than light.* Or the phrase may be used to introduce an opinion which you neither support nor condemn. You just report it. *According to Harry, it's a good film.*

Neither of these conditions obtains where the person quoted is the speaker himself. Modesty precludes the speaker from taking on the role of an authority; nor can he take an entirely neutral role while giving an opinion. It is his opinion, he is offering it. Necessarily he must believe in it.

For these reasons it is best to avoid *according to me*. You should introduce your statement with something like: *In my opinion / I feel / If you ask me*, etc.

It is this requirement that the speaker exhibit a becoming sense of modesty which accounts for *John and I* (instead of *I and John*). And, if an opinion has to be expressed which conflicts with what has been put forward by others, the phrase *I should have thought* is often used (especially in formal situations). *I should have thought that the matter required further examination.*

ache/pain

Have you ever considered why we use *ache* in some cases and *pain* in other cases? The dictionary says that *pain* is a more sustained, severe affliction: apparently *ache* is not so severe.

Really? what about a toothache? Only those who have had it know what it is. (Incidentally even if more than one tooth hurts, it is still *toothache* and not *teethache*) But nobody says *tooth pain*.

We have *stomach ache, toothache, headache, backache;* but *chest pain*. It would seem that with organs (functional body parts), the word is *ache*. In other cases it is *pain*. *Heartache* (*My heart aches...*) can only have a metaphorical meaning. In the layman's perception, pain is felt in the chest, not the heart.

This said, in other cases it is *pain*. We have *labour pains, muscle* (or *muscular*) *pain*. Outside the context of the body parts mentioned above, it is true to say *ache* is a less severe form of suffering than *pain*. Thus: *My feet have begun to ache* (after a long walk).

affect/effect

One would have supposed that the distinction between *affect* and *effect* was clear enough. But apparently it is not so. Here is a citation: *Chocolate kills dogs! True. Chocolate effects a dog's heart and nervous system, a few ounces is enough to kill a small sized dog* (The Times of India, 15 January 2001, 'Education Times', p. 4).

Effect as verb means 'to bring about', 'to cause to occur'. It is a transitive verb. So what is brought about must be mentioned. *The prisoners effected their escape under cover of darkness. / In mild cases of feverishness Crocin effects a cure.* When such is the case, what does *chocolate effects the heart* mean? It is nonsense.

The word required is *affect*. This means 'to have an influence on'. Chocolate has an influence on a dog's heart. So we can say *chocolate affects a dog's heart*.

It is best to remember that *affect* is a verb; *effect* is usually used as noun. Both mean pretty much the same. But the grammatical structures are different. With *affect*, the structure is: *affect* + noun (noun phrase); *affect the heart/lungs/trade*, etc. With *effect*, the structure is: *have an effect on something/somebody. Bright sunlight has a bad effect on sensitive skins. / The Gujarat earthquake will have a tremendous effect on the nation's economy.*

The rule given till now has been: use *affect* as a verb and *effect* as a noun. Now for some modifications.

Effect also can be a verb but the usage is somewhat formal. See the examples given earlier. Here are some more sentences illustrating the correct use of *effect* as a verb. *Government plans to effect some changes in the Constitution. / Over the last few years we have seen many changes effected in our economic policies.*

aftermath of success'?

Basking in the *aftermath* of the success of her latest film...(Sunday Herald, 11 November 2001). Is *aftermath* the right word here?

Aftermath is generally associated with unpleasant, even disastrous situations. A stock phrase is the *aftermath of war. Epidemics usually follow in the aftermath of an earthquake. Food prices soared in the aftermath of the drought* (NODE).

What, then, is the right word here? A suitable candidate would be *sunshine.*

Initially *aftermath* referred to the new grass that grows after a field has been mowed or harvested (*after* + *math* = mowing). This meaning still survives. The current meaning (consequences or results of an event, especially an unpleasant one) is a later development.

Here is another word used in the wrong context. *Infosys spreads IT tentacles to Mangalore* (*The Times of India*, 20 September 2001, p. 6). *Tentacles* is another word with negative associations: *the tentacles of an octopus*, for example. What is the point in speaking of Infosys as spreading its *tentacles*? Is it some monster out to gobble up the whole state?

The correct use of a word depends on the proper appreciation of a whole lot of dimensions. (See DIMENSIONS OF A WORD.) Here we need emphasize only the association of a word which is determined by the textual context in which it appears.

Logicians speak of connotation and denotation. Connotation has to do with meaning; denotation with reference. The word *dog* has a certain meaning (a four-legged animal, etc.). It also refers to an object (in this case, an animal) in the external world. But beyond this it has many associations captured in such phrases as *to lead a dog's life, to die like a dog,* etc. (All words and phrases do not necessarily have both a connotation and a denotation. The sentence: *The present king of France is bald* connotes something; it has a meaning. But it has no reference, no denotation, as there is no king of France today.)

The proper use of words calls for a knowledge which goes far beyond the brief 'meanings' given in a pocket dictionary. Learner's dictionaries like the ALD and LDCE give a good deal of guidance on these matters.

'agog villagers'

A report from Gajanur—the village from where Dr Rajkumar was kidnapped—says, 'Questions like, *Has Gopal met Veerappan?*, *What are his demands?*, and *When will Annavaru return?* continue to haunt the agog villagers.'

To be agog means 'to be eager, expectant, excited'. The word can describe a person's state or condition both before and after some news, event, happening, sight. *We were all agog at the sight of Manhattan from Liberty Island.* This describes the tourists' state after an event has taken place. (They have now seen the New York skyline.) *As the plane touched down at JFK we were all agog at what we were going to see.* This describes the tourists' excited state of expectancy. They are now going to see the world's greatest city.

But the important grammatical point to note is: *agog* cannot appear before a noun. In other words, *agog* cannot be used attributively; it can only be used predicatively, i.e., after the verb.

Agog is not the only adjective of this type. Common adjectives like *asleep, alone, afraid, aghast, alive,* and *awake* can only appear in the predicate. You can say: *He is afraid,* but there is no *afraid man; the baby is asleep,* but not *the asleep baby.*

[The behaviour of these *a*-adjectives is paralleled by the behaviour of some *a*-adverbs. *Many of our brightest students are abroad.* But there are no *abroad students.*]

The typical adjective (some grammarians call them central adjectives) can appear both in the attributive and predicative positions: *the tall boy— the boy is tall; the old woman—the woman is old.* These adjectives denote a characteristic, more or less permanent or significant feature (*the dashing young man, the cranky old fellow, the lucky dog*). Not so the adjectives which are restricted to the predicate position. The contrast can be brought out quite strikingly by considering the pair: *timid, afraid.* 'Timidity' is a more or less permanent quality of some persons. Hence we have *a timid person.* Not so *afraid.* Even a bold man may be afraid sometimes. So *He is afraid,* but not *an afraid man.*

Agog is like *afraid.* A person who is agog is not naturally and physically always *agog.* So we can't have the *agog public.*

'a good knowledge of English'

(classifying 'a')

The English article system is a fairly complex network of subtle meanings. Without an understanding of these meanings, it is just impossible to see how the articles are used. Most grammar books still continue to give mere lists showing where an article is used, noting exceptions along the way. Naturally this does not (and cannot) guarantee success in the use of the articles.

The distinction between countable and uncountable nouns (or count and mass nouns) is the first step in understanding the behaviour of English nouns (more strictly, noun phrases) not only in respect of number (singular vs plural) but also article usage. Uncountable nouns (*rice, gold, air*) have no plural form; also, they can't be preceded by *a* (see 'AN INFORMATION'). Thus there is no plural for *information*; nor is there a phrase like *an information*. But surprisingly (and to the confusion of the learner) some uncountable nouns are found with *a* in certain phrases. *Knowledge* is an uncountable noun. It has no plural form and no numeral can appear before it. The phrase *a knowledge* is also not possible. But *a good knowledge of English is a must* (from an advertisement). Is this correct English? Or, has the copywriter stumbled?

The copywriter has not stumbled. The phrase is well-formed. How come?

To understand the usage here we should know that the article *a* has not only a weakly numerical meaning and is the principal mechanism to convey a sense of indefiniteness, it is also the means of classifying. It has a classificatory function. The school grammar sentence *This is a pen* should be understood as saying: This belongs to the category of objects called pens. It is a specimen of that set of objects. That is, the article *a* has here a classifying function.

The difference in meaning between the two uses of the so-called indefinite article *a* in the two sentences: *I met a boy/This is a pen* can be clearly seen if we examine the two sentences with the nouns in the plural. The first sentence will be: *I met some boys*; the second sentence: *These are pens. Some* is the plural equivalent of the weakly numeral *a*. There is no plural equivalent of the classifying *a*. Now back to the phrase: *a good knowledge of English*. The function of *a* here is classificatory. We can grade/classify competence in English: *a poor knowledge, a fair knowledge, a good knowledge, an excellent knowledge*.

Notice now that *knowledge* still remains an uncountable noun in the phrase *a good knowledge of English*. No numerical can appear anywhere in the phrase.

This explanation in terms of the classificatory function of the article *a* accounts for the use of the article in the following expressions: *a good education, a bad cold, a mild fever*. Without the adjectives, these nouns cannot appear with *a*. *She has fever*, not *She has a fever*.

Consider the word *distrust*. This can be used as a verb: *I distrust him.* It can also be used as a noun: my *distrust of him*. But can you say *She had a distrust of him*? I don't think so. But: *She had a distrust of strangers.* Better still: *She had a deep distrust of strangers.* These are fine. Why?

Precisely for the reason discussed earlier: *a (deep) distrust of strangers* has a classifying meaning: what type of distrust?—*a distrust of strangers.* So the classifying article *a* can be used. But *a distrust of him*—is not a type of distrust. No classificatory meaning is possible.

agreement puzzles

A fundamental rule of English syntax is that the subject and verb of a sentence agree in number. Actually the rule is stated in much wider terms: that the subject and verb agree in number, gender, person, and case. But in modern English, the verb shows no inflection for gender and case. That is, regardless of whether the subject represents a noun in the masculine, feminine, neuter, or common gender, the form of the verb remains the same. Contrast this with our own languages where the gender of the subject noun is reflected in the verbal inflection; in Kannada, for example, *avanu bandanu/avalu bandalu/adu banthu.* As for case, while all subjects are supposed to be in the nominative case, it is only the personal pronouns (*I, we, he,* etc.) and the relative pronoun *who* which show case distinctions. The verb shows no inflection (= change in form) for case. Person, again, is a distinction noticed only in the personal pronouns. Here, too, the modern English verb shows no distinction in form for person.

Agreement, then, boils down to agreement in number. And the scope of this agreement is quite limited. With first and second person subjects, the English verb shows no change: *I speak./You speak.* It is only with third person singular subjects (all nouns are in the third person) and that, too, in the present tense, that agreement is seen. *She speaks French* vs *They speak French./You speak French./I speak French.* But: *She spoke to me./They spoke to me./I spoke to them* etc.

But this extremely restricted phenomenon causes endless problems to the non-native speakers of English. Some are under the impression that, regardless of the number of the subject, the verb must end in *-s*. *They thinks/speaks,* etc. Some others are under the impression that a subject in the singular must *always* have a verb in the singular: *You seems/looks happy....* (Surprisingly they don't say: *I thinks/speaks,* etc. The pronoun *you* always requires a plural verb, even when it refers to one person only.)

Still others, who know the rule well, land in trouble because of a failure to identify the subject correctly. In this article I will confine myself to this last group.

Consider this: *The association submitted a memorandum to Governor V.S. Rama Devi...on their demands,* which *includes an anti-quackery bill.* Although *which* is the nominal subject of the relative clause, the real subject is the noun phrase referred to by *which.* And this noun phrase is: *a memorandum...on their demands.* There are two nouns here: *memorandum, demands.* With *which* noun should the verb in the relative clause agree? Should the verb be *include* or *includes*?

To settle the problem, ask yourself this question: Does the memorandum include an anti-quackery bill or do the demands include an anti-quackery bill? Clearly the anti-quackery bill is one of the demands. It is included in the set of demands presented in the memorandum. Agreement is, therefore, with *demands,* i.e., the verb should be *include.*

Similar problems arise when the phrase *one of* + *N* is the head of a relative clause. Here quite contradictory results can be obtained. *One of the doors which were damaged is locked. / One of the doors which was damaged is locked.* In the first sentence, more than one door is damaged. Of them (i.e., the damaged doors) one is locked. In the second sentence, only one door is damaged and that is locked. (Of the doors, one, which was damaged, is locked.) (I owe these examples to a friend who has very kindly passed on to me a letter received from the Oxford English Dictionary Word and Language Service (OWLS) clarifying some points of agreement.)

These options—depending on the interpretation of the *one of* + *N* structure—are available only when there is a following relative clause. Otherwise *one of* + *N* agrees with a singular verb. *One of the doors was locked.* (Of the doors, one was locked.) Note, however, that the noun in *one of* + *N* must be plural: *one of the doors;* not *one of the door.* Obvious as this is, you will encounter sentences like: *Chennai is one of the biggest city of India.* See also: AGREEMENT: NP + PP STRUCTURES.

How does agreement work when the subject is a clause? There is compelling evidence to show that a clause is not a noun phrase: it has none of the grammatical properties of nouns (which are 'heads' of noun phrases). Number, gender, case, and person, features applicable to nouns, don't apply to clauses.

Still, when the subject is a clause, the verb cannot be in any form—

singular in one case and plural in some other case. By convention, a clause is assumed to be singular and the verb (in the case of sentences with subject clauses) must be in the singular form. *That prices are rising is not good news for the government.* The plural subject *prices* requires the plural verb *are.* But the subject of the sentence is *that prices are rising,* a clause, and so necessarily singular. Hence the verb *is* in the predicate. Cf also: *That the Western powers are piqued at India's nuclear capability is now clear.*

Speaking of the ban on coaching classes, a professor of English is reported to have said (according to *The Times of India*) *What benefits the ban will have are not clear.* The professor seems to have been misled by the presence of *benefits.* But the subject of the verb *are* is not *benefits.* The subject is *what benefits the ban will have*—a clause. And a clause is taken to be singular for purposes of agreement. The sentence should have read: *What benefits the ban will have is not clear.* Cf *It is not clear what benefits the ban will have.*

agreement: NP + PP structures

Agreement with the head of a noun phrase seems to present problems to native speakers and others alike. First an Indian example: *a stream of self-proclaimed nationalists insists that her birth alone must disqualify her* (Sonia Gandhi) *from becoming PM, (India Currents,* 3 December–4 January 2004, p. 8). *Insists* would be correct if agreement is with *stream.* But is that the head of the noun phrase? Can a *stream* insist? Or is it self-appointed nationalists? If it is the latter, the verb must be in the plural: *insist.*

Now for a similar mistake in 'native' writing. *Fries is just one of the many original supporters of Microsoft's X-box effort who has left the company or the game team.* (Fries was the Vice President of games publishing in Microsoft.)

What is the antecedent of *who?* Is it Fries or the many original supporters of Microsoft's X-box effort? If the latter, as I think it is, then the verb should be plural *(have).*

agreement: Some special cases

A.

1. Some nouns referring to groups of people, though plural in meaning, can be used with singular or plural verbs. *Government have/has decided to accept the report.* The singular form is used when the noun is viewed as standing for a single, impersonal body; the plural draws attention to the

group as composed of individuals. The distinction in reference is reflected in the choice of relative pronouns (if the group noun is the antecedent). In the impersonal view we find *which*: *The government, which faced stiff opposition over the bill*.... Contrast this with: *The government, who are pinning their hopes on a good monsoon*.... Similarly with: *Shekar's family, which is a powerful one*.... *Shekar's family, who are into steel and cement*...

Some other words which can be used in this way are *class*, *committee*, *firm*, *staff*, *jury*, *party*, *team*, *minority*, *union*. Notice they are all collective nouns.

2. Plural nouns indicating quantities and amounts take a singular verb.

Four miles is not much of a distance.

There is just two litres of petrol in the tank.

3. In calculations involving numbers either singular or plural verbs can be used. *Three times six are/is eighteen*.

4. The expression *more than one* is followed by a singular head and takes a verb in the singular. *More than one reporter has said*.... But *one of* is always followed by a plural head and takes a plural verb. *One of the reporters said*...

(One *one of* + N in relative clauses see below.)

5. Nouns/noun phrases joined by *and* take a plural verb.

Tendulkar and Dravid are great batsmen.

Deccan Herald and *The Times of India* are the leading papers in Bangalore.

But where the nouns joined by *and* stand for a single idea or refer to a single person or object, a singular verb is used.

Bread and butter is my regular breakfast.

The Secretary and correspondent of the school has resigned.

Nouns/noun phrases joined by *or* take a singular or plural verb depending on the number of the second noun (phrase).

Either Shekar or Suman knows Rahul's address.

Either Ravi or his friends have told the Principal about the incident.

Neither–nor show the same behaviour as *either–or*.

With phrases conjoined by *as well as*, agreement depends on the first conjunct: *The elephant, as well as a number of other wild animals, is found in the Kabini forest*.

6. Agreement is with the head of a noun phrase. Hence, regardless of the number of any noun in a prepositional post-modifier, a singular head noun is followed by a singular verb.

A story of angels and daemons is always interesting.

None except his family is aware of his future plans.

7. Uncountable nouns, even when involving a notion of plurality, require a singular verb.

All his hair is gone.

The traffic is very heavy on this road.

Too bad, your luggage is held up at Bombay.

Some other nouns of this type are: *news, scenery, poetry, furniture*.

B. Indefinite pronouns

1. The indefinite pronouns are (a) *some, any, every, no*, and their compound forms *someone, somebody, anyone, anybody, everyone, everybody, no one, nobody;* (b) *all, both, each*, and *none, either, neither* which have no compound forms.

The compound forms can only be used substantively; the simple forms can be used either attributively or substantively.

2. The compound indefinite pronouns are singular and agree with a singular verb.

Everyone is welcome.

No one was selected.

Someone has blundered.

Does anyone know where she lives?

Everyone thinks that he knows best.

Forget it. Nobody is to blame.

3. Of the 'simple' indefinite pronouns *each, either, neither* agree with a singular verb.

All the fingers are not the same. Each is different.

We questioned both of them. Neither was willing to speak.

These are two expensive pens. Take what you like. Either is as good as the other.

4. *All, both*, and *some* (where number is thought of) are necessarily plural, agreeing with plural verbs.

All are welcome.

'How are the newborn twins?' 'Fine. Both are doing well.'

Some are wise; some otherwise.

All and *some* can be used in an uncountable sense.

All is well.

All is as it should be.

In the uncountable sense *some* indicates an unspecified amount and implies a partitive sense; i.e. 'some of x'.

Some of the milk has turned sour.

5. *None* can have a singular or plural reference depending on the context.

None are so deaf as those that will not hear.

Why should I bother? It's none of my business.

When *none* is followed by an *of*-phrase, the noun in the *of*-phrase will necessarily be plural: *none of the boys/books/children*. Grammatically, agreement should be with a singular verb. *None of the children was inoculated* (of the children, none, not one). But in informal styles a plural verb may be found. *None of the children were inoculated.*

Similarly with *neither, either. Neither of them is/are dependable.*

allusions

A reviewer in the *San Jose Mercury News* (SJMN) reviewing Merriam Webster's *Dictionary of Allusions* remarks: 'As classical learning slips [such references] may leave all but the few confused. Perhaps that's just as well, since there's no cliche worse than a 2000-year-old cliche'—SJMN, 16 January 2000.

Really? Let's examine the question a little closely. Two questions arise: What should be the attitude of the well-informed writer towards these expressions vis-a-vis his reader? What is the likely fate of these expressions?

Plainly the two questions are related. If nobody uses them, they will die. But that is unlikely. It is only in certain types of communication that one takes care to see that no terms/expressions are used which the reader is unlikely to understand. In other cases, in literary (and even business), communications where an element of surprise or sophistication is intended, the entire resources of the language as embodied in its history, literature, and myths, may be put into use. And expressions like *a gargantuan appetite* and *the sword of Damocles* are likely to be pressed into service.

Because they are part of the English lexicon, its vocabulary, they encapsulate a certain set of complex ideas into a concept. *A gargantuan appetite* is a huge appetite, as of a giant; *the sword of Damocles* signifies a situation of great and imminent danger in the midst of apparent luxury and prosperity. Even as the common nouns of the language (*chair, table, house, joy, fear, melancholy*) stand for certain entities, physical or mental, these expressions also stand for certain concepts which have been identified. Like other words, they are listed in the dictionary with their meanings. A good writer who wants to express himself briefly and precisely will find them indispensable. They are exactly like the non-classical expressions of the type *Hobson's choice* (no choice at all; take it or leave it).

We can now broaden the scope of our discussion. Instead of just *classical allusions*, we can discuss the question of *allusions in general.*

Many of these expressions involve a personal name, whether historical, fictional, or mythological. *Hobson's choice, Freudian slip, Occam's razor, spoonerism, bowdlerize, platonic love, Parthian shot, pyrrhic victory, jerrymander* involve names of historical persons. *Midas touch, Achilles' heel, Herculean task, quixotic, Pickwickian* involve names of fictional or mythological figures.

A second (and large) set of expressions of this type involves no personal names. They are usually figurative expressions having their origin in mythology, fiction, history, or daily life: *dog in the manger, to cross the Rubicon, cold shoulder, to eat the humble pie, to draw a red herring, a basket case, curate's egg, catch 22*, etc.

All these will be found listed in good dictionaries with their meanings. As you learn the other words, you have to learn them, too.

A third set of expressions has to do with quotations. Most quotations are appreciated best in the context in which they occur. In that context, they sum up a set of ideas, feelings in a memorable way. Some achieve a wider application. But how long they have this privilege depends on the extent to which they are free of local, particularizing elements.

There was a time when *Even the ranks of Tuscany could scarce forbear to cheer* was a journalistic cliche. But not any longer, because of the local element *ranks of Tuscany*. Not many today are aware of the Tuscan invasion of Rome and what happened then. On the other hand, quotations like *to err is human* (Pope) and *to be or not to be* (Shakespeare), being completely free of a local element, enjoy a wider application.

Still very few quotations have achieved the status of concepts. Among the few which have achieved this status are: *hoist with one's own petard* (having one's plans to cause trouble to others backfire on one); *caviare to the general* (a good thing unappreciated by the ignorant); *the buck stops here* (the responsibility for something cannot or should not be passed on to someone else). (All meanings from NODE.)

Allusions of the type discussed here are part of the vocabulary of English. And, as with words, some of them get replaced by newer ones, though only very rarely. Actually they are far more durable than hundreds of slang and colloquial expressions that are 'in' today and 'gone' tomorrow. No coinage to come is likely to replace *the sword of Damocles* or *to cut the Gordian knot*. *A dog in the manger* will continue to be in use as long as there are dogs and mangers.

Scylla was a she-monster with six heads dwelling on the Italian side of the Straits of Messina, opposite the whirlpool, Charybdis. It was nearly impossible to pass through the Straits without being caught by one or the other (as described in Homer). Hence the phrase *between Scylla and Charybdis* (= between two dangers such that an attempt to avoid one increases the risk from the other). A more readily intelligible phrase giving the same meaning is *between the devil and the deep sea*. The Americans have come out with their own version of this situation: *between a rock and a hard place*.

Here is a case of a classical allusion giving place to a more easily understood, self-explanatory modern phrase. But the classical phrase has not died. It continues to be listed in dictionaries. Perhaps it is less frequently encountered than the other two. (The Americans seem to be more comfortable with their coinage.)

As a rule, in 'cultivated writing' (e.g., the *Time* magazine), classical allusions are frequently encountered. One is more likely to see Hercules mentioned as a model of superhuman strength than Schwarzenegger; Croesus as symbolizing great wealth and opulence than Bill Gates; Cleopatra as the ultimate woman than Elizabeth Taylor.

Now for some citations. *The company's [Novell's] big vision now is technology's Holy Grail, a unified electronic world that connects servers and laptops* (SJMN, 27 April 2003). *His Achilles' heel won't be his lack of familiarity with Sacramento* (SJMN, 9 October 2003). *It is tempting to see Rumsfeld as a symbol of war itself, like Achilles or Ajax, lost in the calm, found in the fray* (Time, 29 December 2003–5 January 2004). *Since October, Iran has spun more tales than Sheherzade to explain bits and pieces of nuclear research it had neglected to mention* (The Economist, 28 February–5 March 2004, p. 10). *The dispute that Nehru had first internationalized now hangs over India's head like the proverbial sword of Damocles.*

Tharoor, p. 165, '... *if the government decides to call for a review of the Supreme Court order, it could open a pandora's box of issues* (India West, 10

October 2003). *This massive leviathan* [Indian bureaucracy] *has become an albatross round the neck* (*The Hindu*, 5 February 2002).

These direct references apart, classical allusions appear in subtle ways not recognizable by the ordinary reader. *Abandon all cell phones, Ye who enter here*—one cell phone company proclaims, echoing Dante (*New York Times*), or, they are neatly fitted into a modern context, literally. *Achilles had his heel; women have the A.C.L.* (anterior cruciate ligament in the knee, which tears easily in women sportspersons—heading of an article in the *New York Times*).

When one encounters an allusion one is not familiar with, one tries to guess the meaning from the context. Generally we can get at the meaning, in a way. But not always ... *the UTI became a favourite hunting ground of well-connected carpetbaggers* (*India Today*, 16 July 2001, p. 10). What does one make of this? Or of this: *Most of us bite the bullet if we are unsure of what someone means*....

Guessing meanings and making some sense may take us some distance but not far enough. We cannot use an expression correctly unless we have understood it fairly well and studied the contexts in which it is used.

Discussing the phrase *hoist with one's own petard*, the reviewer in the *San Jose Mercury News* (referred to above) asks: 'Shall we describe today's suicide bombers as 'hoist with their own petard?' Of course, not. The expression is correctly used when something devised for the destruction of others backfires and destroys the schemer. This is not so in the case of suicide bombers. Even before the mission starts, they know they are going to die. There is no 'unexpected backfiring' here. No one has cleverly trapped them in their own machines.

Here, as elsewhere, there is no shortcut to success. Diligent study is the only solution.

An understanding of the stories behind words and phrases sharpens one's appreciation of their meanings and makes for the correct use of these words and phrases. Unfortunately dictionaries barely give the meanings of words and phrases, with little or no indication of how they came to mean what they do. The older dictionaries were certainly better in this respect than the more recent ones. Still, *The Concise Oxford Dictionary* is, perhaps, the best affordable one, all things considered.

One can also consult with profit Merriam-Webster's *Dictionary of Allusions*, and, of course, that classic Brewer's *Dictionary of Phrase and Fable*.

The Oxford Dictionary of Phrase and Fable is the most recent authoritative book available on the subject.

also

Also is traditionally described as an adverb. It is said to be used as in *He had spent a good deal of his life on the continent. He had also lived for a year or so in India.* (Not: He had spent a good deal of his life on the continent. *Also* he had lived for a year or two in India.) *She sold her diamond ring and also a pearl necklace.* (Not: She sold her diamond ring, *also* a pearl necklace.) The examples are from Flavell and Flavell (1981), who take a strong conservative view on this topic. This view was first stated by Fowler (1926). It has been strongly supported, more recently, by Burchfield (1998).

Others have taken a more liberal view: Kingsley Amis, for example (Amis, 1997), and *Webster's Dictionary of English Usage* (1989), after examining the question concludes: 'This is entirely a matter of style and has nothing to do with grammar.'

More careful analysts have admitted one case of *also* opening a sentence: where *also* 'refers to the whole clause' (Swan, 2003). *It's a very nice house, but it's very small. Also it needs a lot of repairs.* The NODE identifies *also* in this use as a sentence adverb: *also a car is very expensive to run.* Trask (2001) admits the front-shifting of a phrase beginning with *also. Also in the last eight is Kournikova* (= Kournikova also is in the last eight [KSY].Cf. also: *Also troubling are the somewhat vague and sweeping charges brought against Mr Skilling (The Economist,* 28 February–5 March 2004, p. 58).

DEU notes that the construction (using *also* as a conjunction) is quite rare. This seems to be correct. But it is likely that the usage is more evident in certain types of texts than in others. I have noted it quite often in Chomsky's writings on linguistics. He is particularly fond of *also* as an additive conjunct. You can also find it on every page of what is perhaps one of the best one-volume English grammars ever written, R.W. Zandvoort's *A Handbook of English Grammar* (1962). I will quote just two examples: Note, though, that *will* in 'You will have your way' expresses a different shade of meaning from that of the same auxiliary in 'I will be obeyed'; also that; 'He will get in my light' expresses the annoyance of the speaker (p. 75). In similar cases, English often uses a definite article when the person is not the subject of an active sentence; also in a number of idiomatic phrases (p. 139). As for *also* opening a sentence there are several examples in the footnotes (e.g., pp. 104, 292) as also in the text.

(See for example, p. 256, line 8 from the top.) And, finally, here are some examples from Quirk et al., GCE. 'The omission of the preposition is optional with deictic phrases...; also with phrases which identify a time before or after a given time in the past or the future' (p. 319). For an example of *also* opening a paragraph, see p. 319.

In India, the national dailies carefully avoid the use of *also* discussed here. But columnists and contributors are quite at home with the usage. See, for example, *The Hindu*, 4 January 2005, edit page: 'Information: an inviolable right', column 3, para 2.

After these citations from authorities on British English, perhaps it is unnecessary to point out that the *American Heritage College Dictionary* (1993) admits the conjunctive use of *also. It is a pretty cat; also friendly.* Here is a quote from the SJMN: *Smith is a ranch hand who works...outside Houston. Also he has a live-in partner back home* (20 October 2003). For an example of *also* opening a sentence (and a paragraph), see the article by Robert M. Gates in the *New York Times* (8 June 2004, p. A25).

'a matter of public concern'
(English usage and the native speaker)

The study of language (or should I say languages?) in our country seems to go on in a remarkably unremarkable way. There are, of course, clashes, usually physical, over the study of this or that language, especially English. But informed debate over matters of grammar, style, and usage is, it seems to me, non-existent.

The situation is quite different in the English-speaking world. They have always taken a keen and lively interest in their language. Several volumes can be written on the views of English writers and the general public on the use of English. It is a continuous and on-going debate. Practically every major newspaper has a column discussing English usage, and the response of readers (as seen, for example, in Safire's books; his columns are collected and issued in book form every two years) is breathtaking. What makes for this lively debate about this language? For one thing, it is the in-built peculiarities of English, which puzzle native speakers and foreign students alike. The story is told of the owner of a small zoo who lost two of his animals in a fire. He wrote to a company supplying animals: *Dear Sirs, Please send me two mongooses.* This didn't sound well. So he began again: *Dear Sirs, Please send me two mongeeses.* This sounded even more terrible. So he made a third draft: *Dear Sirs,*

Please send me a mongoose. And while you are at it, please send me another mongoose. (The plural is mongooses.) As with matters of etiquette, the plural of many English nouns has to be individually learned. A fertile field for discussion and instruction. For another (look back for the other part of this correlative) there are numerous constructions in English which have become debatable either because popular usage has gone ahead blissfully ignorant of the correct form (example: *like* in place of *as*) or scholarly pedants have found fault with perfectly normal constructions (example: the *split infinitive*).

And then there is always the question of the choice of words. In what contexts can a word be used? Can you say, for example, *an inveterate scholar*? Can *gay* be any longer used in the sense of 'merry, jocund'? Has *meticulous* any negative associations? In short, English exhibits the bewildering complexities of a vigorous, growing language. There is no academy (as in France) to regulate the language and pronounce with official authority on what is correct and what is not. Hence the lively debate in the press and elsewhere on English usage.

Here is what a columnist had to say to his editor on ending a sentence with a preposition: *What do you take me for? A chap who doesn't know how to make full use of all the easy variety the English language is capable of? Don't you know that ending a sentence with a preposition is an idiom that many famous writers are fond of? They realize that it's colloquialism a skilful writer can do a great deal with. Certainly it is a linguistic device you ought to read about.* (See also Churchill's comment on this topic in END PREPOSITION.) The irrepressible Shaw lashed out at a copy editor in the London *Times*: *There is a busybody on your staff who devotes a lot of time chasing split infinitives. I call for the immediate dismissal of this pedant. It is of no consequence whether he decides to go quickly or to quickly go or quickly to go. The important thing is that he should go at once.* James Thurber, the celebrated cartoonist and humourist who wrote for the *New Yorker* burst out: *When I split an infinitive it is going to damn well stay split.* I can go on with stories of this type. I will end with the outburst of a member of the Harper Usage Panel on *hopefully*. 'On my backdoor, there is a sign with large letters which reads: THE WORD HOPEFULLY MUST NOT BE USED ON THESE PREMISES. VIOLATORS WILL BE HUMILIATED'.

Fowler's *A Dictionary of Modern English Usage* took both sides of the Atlantic by storm; Safire's column 'On Language' (in *The New York Times Magazine*) elicits hundreds of letters from adoring, agitated, argumentative readers (as witnessed in his books where his articles are periodically collected); Burchfield's revision of Fowler (1996) received such worldwide notice from native speakers (and others, too) that he had to add a supplement about it in the third edition (1998).

Such is the interest the English-speaking people have in their language.

ambiguity

An expression is ambiguous if it admits of more than one interpretation. *The lamb is ready to eat.* In isolation and without further context, it may mean either the lamb is ready for us to eat (it is properly cooked) or the lamb is now ready to eat something.

Speech (or writing) should be clear and precise—unless one has reasons to be intentionally vague, imprecise, and ambiguous. Now let us examine in some detail the ways in which ambiguity can arise.

1. At the level of words, ambiguity may arise because of polysemy: a word may have more than one meaning and these meanings may be available in a given case. *I saw him near the bank* (a financial institution? the bank of the river in the locality?) Ambiguities of this type are usually resolved by further context in a given situation. Another example: *Certain remedies are available for this malady.* (Some remedies? Sure remedies?)

2. At the level of structure, ambiguity will arise in the following cases: (a) Where a pronoun can be understood in respect of more than one noun: *John talked to Bill about himself.* (Who does *himself* refer to: John? Bill?) *Ravi discussed with Raju his plans for the vacation.* (Whose plans? Ravi's? Raju's?)

(b) Where a relative pronoun can be interpreted in respect of more than one antecedent: *The mother of the child who was missing has been traced.* (Who was missing? The mother? The child?). *The secret police terrorized Iraqis working for international press services who were courageous enough to try to provide accurate reporting* (NYT, 11 April 2003). (To whom does *who* refer—Iraqis? Press services?)

(c) A modifier may refer to different heads: *a little used car*: a (little used) car? or a little (used car)? (Hyphenated, there is no ambiguity: a little-used car.); *a new car salesman*: a new (car salesman)? or a (new car) salesman?; *some more suitable clothes*: some more (suitable clothes) or some (more suitable clothes)?; *old men and women*: old (men and women) or (old men) and women?

(d) Negation in the context of certain structural words: A *because*-clause following a negative main clause creates ambiguity. Fowler (1926) noted that the sentence *He did not oppose the motion because he feared public opinion* could be interpreted in two ways: (a) He was afraid of public opinion, so he did not oppose the motion. (b) He opposed the motion. It was not because he was afraid of public opinion. Here is another example (authentic) of the same type: *I am not unhappy because I am not in the executive committee.* (I am happy—because I am not in the executive committee. I am unhappy—but that is not because I am out of the executive committee.)

A similar ambiguity arises in the case of a negative main clause followed by *so that*: *The child has not yet learnt to express a thought fully so that only one meaning is conveyed* (Fowler, 1926). Is the child conveying only one meaning because he has not yet learnt to express fully? Or is he conveying many meanings because he does not know how to express himself properly?

(e) Ellipses can sometimes result in an ambiguous construction. We will consider two cases.

(i) *He loves his dog more than his wife.* (Is the dog dearer to him than his wife or does the wife love the dog less than he does?) (ii) With the infinitive of some verbs which can be understood in an active or passive sense. One such example has been already given: *the lamb is ready to eat* (= for us to eat / to be eaten.) There are not many verbs with which this can happen. So this type of ambiguity is rare. Anyway here is another (constructed) example. A cannibal might say: *The priest is ready to cook.*

(f) An adjunct phrase (of time / location) can make it possible to interpret a sentence in more than one way. *John did not speak to Mary at the party.* This leaves open the possibility that John spoke to Mary at some other time. *He could not catch the flight on Monday.* (Perhaps he caught the flight next day or some other day?)

3. In the cases considered till now, the same structure could be understood in two ways. In the examples to be given now, only one interpretation is possible but we see that the writer had in mind quite a different meaning. Here is a classic example: *Piano for sale by a lady going abroad in an oak case with carved legs.* And here is one from Lederer's collection: *The patient was referred to a psychiatrist with a severe emotional problem.*

It was this sort of thing which Cobbett had in mind when he wrote (1823). 'Of all faults to be found in writing, this [i.e., the wrong placing of words] is one of the most common, and perhaps it leads to the greatest number of misconceptions.'

Fowler (1926) endorsed Cobbett's comment. But Burchfield curtly remarks: 'There is an air of unreality and implausibility about these old precepts and about the examples given in support.' Copy editors and proofreaders remove the great majority of such crudely ambiguous constructions at the pre-publication stage. This may be so. But misplaced adjuncts continue to provide unintended mirth. Here is an example cited by Burchfield himself: *A youngster woman, married to a Kuwaiti and about 20 Asians were among those flying.*

Unintended meaning can also arise more subtly. In the context of pronoun reference: *Superstar Amitabh Bacchan receiving the prestigious Satyajit Ray Lifetime Achievement award from his son Sandeep Ray during the 66th Bengali Film Journalist's Association award ceremony in Kolkata.* (Whose son?). *Spring cleaning? Why kill your wife? Let us do it for you. / Guilt, vengeance and bitterness can be emotionally destructive to you and your children. You must get rid of them.*

Unintended meaning can also arise in the context of negation and ellipsis. Writing about books—They are much better than sweets as gifts—a well-known columnist says: *It* [the book] *will not affect the recipient's digestive system, illumine his or her mind and last the rest of his life.* In the absence of *but will* (after digestive system), the negative force is carried across the sentence: *it will not illumine his mind and will not last the rest of his life.* (See also: 'BEING A TAMILIAN').

We have distinguished ambiguous constructions (which yield more than one interpretation) from constructions where the reader gets a different meaning from the one the author intended. Some ambiguities are naturally resolved in speech (*old men and women*); others in the context of situation. But the careful writer/speaker should not depend on these saving devices. The analysis presented above should help him to be on guard against all types of miscarriages arising from ambiguity.

amidst/among

In some contexts, the two are practically interchangeable: *He stood amidst/ among the ruins.* But in: *amidst rumours of war* we can't have *among.* Similarly in: *Among all the men I have known,* we can't have *amidst.*

Amidst is a variant of *amid* and means in 'the middle of'. *Among* is the current form of *amongst*. It has more meanings than *amidst*. Besides 'surrounded by' 'in the middle of' it can mean: (1) in the number of (something) included (see the example given above: also, *I was among the first to arrive*). (2) between: *They are always fighting among themselves*. (3) have a distributive sense: *Distribute these copies among the class*.

'among the firsts'

'[She] was among the firsts in the advocate fraternity to plead for safeguarding the name and dignity of women lawyers...' (The Times of India, 18 November 2002).

The word *first*, as a pronoun, has no plural form. So although *among* suggests a plurality, we can't have *firsts*. It should be *among the first*.

First in the sense of 'something that someone has been the first to do' is a countable noun and has a plural form. *Russia has many firsts to its credit in space exploration*.

and
(opening sentences)

Is it correct to begin a sentence with *and?* It is an old problem brusquely dismissed in usage manuals with the short reply that there is nothing wrong in beginning a sentence with *and*.

Any number of examples can be cited from standard authors. But let us understand the problem and try to show why it is possible to begin a sentence with *and*.

School grammars describe *and* as a conjunction which can join words to words, phrases to phrases, and sentences to sentences. Where words and phrases are concerned, the use of *and* is obligatory. *We had bread, butter for breakfast. / That's a nice cup, saucer*. These are impossible with or without a comma. The two nouns must be connected by *and*. Even when the phrases are not so closely related in meaning *and* is required. *The company has hired a new Manager and a Senior Accountant*.

With sentences, the use of *and* is not obligatory. *Mary dropped the children at school. She then went to the store to buy some sugar*. Combining the two we get: *Mary dropped the children at school and* (then) *went to the store to buy some sugar*. The events are connected, sequentially. So we can, if we want, join them. Using or not using *and* here is a stylistic choice.

In all the cases discussed till now, the use of *and* is as described in school grammar books. What is the justification for beginning a sentence with *and?* (A point not discussed in school grammars.)

Consider a real example. *This gave me hope that Vajpayee would take a firm stand with his party and* (1) *tell them that what happened in Gujarat was shameful and* (2) *wrong. And* (3) *that the only way to make up for the disgraceful incompetence of the BJP government in that state was for heads to roll and* (4) *for the party to get down to some serious rehabilitation and* (5) *reconstruction.* (*India Today*, 29 April 2002. I have numbered the *and*s for convenience of reference.)

Cases (1) and (4) are like the sequential case discussed earlier; (2) and (5) are like the examples of the conjoined noun phrases examined earlier. Case (3) is what we should now look at.

This sentence presents a new idea different from what is found in the previous sentence. The earlier sentence is concerned with condemnation; this one with rehabilitation. But the two ideas are related in the sense that they are concerned with the same subject, namely, Gujarat. In short, the meanings here are distinct enough to be separated but close enough to be connected. The problem is solved by putting a full stop and beginning with *and*. The writer could have put a semicolon and continued with *and*. The effect would be the same.

Finally note that *and* can begin a sentence only when it is part of a discourse. It cannot begin a discourse with no previous context.

The point about *and* discussed above could also be raised about *but*. *But* also can connect sentences. *Bruce Lee was thin but he was very strong.* It can also be used to begin a sentence. *I had my misgivings about the journey. But it turned out to be quite pleasant and enjoyable.* Surprisingly, the problem is not so hotly discussed as with *and*.

Whether discussed or not, the problem is the same as with *and,* and the answer in both cases is the same. It is a matter of style.

'an information'?

There is a distinction in English between nouns which represent objects which can be counted (or which people generally are in the habit of counting) and those which cannot be counted. Nobody counts rice or wheat or sugar. We don't ask for *a million rices*. We ask for *a kilo* (or *a quintal*) of rice. Similarly with wheat, sugar, coffee, etc. As against nouns of this type, there are nouns which represent objects which people are generally in the habit of counting: *one boy, two girls, three chairs*, etc. The distinction, then, is between countable and uncountable (or mass) nouns.

Only countable nouns can have a plural form; and only they can be preceded by the indefinite article *a* or a numeral: *a boy, two boys.*

Uncountable (or non-count/mass) nouns cannot be preceded by the article *a.* Instead they can be used with expressions indicating quantity: *a grain of sand, a particle of sand, a pound/kilo of sugar, a glass of water, a cup of tea....*

Quite possibly, the distinction between count and non-count noun is found in other languages as well. It stands to reason that only birds would (if they could) count rice or wheat and not human beings. Nevertheless it is not the case that what is uncountable in English is uncountable in other languages also. *News* is an uncountable noun in English. But in vernacular languages, it is a countable noun. Kannada, for example, has *vaarthegalu.*

This can lead to surprising ungrammaticality at times. A reader asks whether *an information* is correct. He says he heard this (the full expression is: *an additional information*) in an English lesson broadcast by AIR, Bangalore. Even those who don't say *an information* may be trapped into saying *an additional information.* But here, too, *an* goes with *information* and that is not possible. The correct expression is: *an additional piece of information* (or something like that).

The article *a* in expressions like *a boy, a chair* has, in addition to the meaning of 'indefinite' (i.e., unspecified), the additional meaning of *one.* This numerical sense becomes more prominent in examples like *a dozen oranges; a bat and a ball....* Still *a* is not the same thing as *one.* You would rather say: *I'll pay no more than one rupee for this* than *I'll pay no more than a rupee for this.* (See *a* or *one.*)

antithesis

We want peace, not war. Life is a blessing, not a curse. Flowers bloom in sunlight, not in darkness. This way of emphasizing an idea by presenting it in a contrasting frame is a figure of speech known as ANTITHESIS.

In these cases, a point is emphasized by contrasting with its opposite. In other cases, the contrast may not be so extreme: the contrasting term may not be an opposite but a limiting term. *The cup that cheers, but not inebriates.* (Tea as described by the poet William Cowper.) *Be thou familiar; but by no means vulgar.* (Polonius advising his son Laertes in Shakespeare's *Hamlet,* 1.3.61.)

There are also cases where a complex event (or events) is presented in terms of opposites. Biblical prose is replete with such cases. *God hath chosen the foolish things of the world to confound the wise; and God hath chosen the weak things of the world to confound the things which are mighty....*

The antithetical construction, as noted above, is witnessed much in religious prose and it was quite in fashion in the eighteenth century. Dr Johnson was a great master of this. His famous letter to Lord Chesterfield bristles with pointed sentences in this style. The Lord, who had ignored Johnson when he was poor and struggling, offered his patronage after Johnson had become successful and famous. Johnson wrote back: *The notice which you have been pleased to take of my labours, had it been early, had been kind; but it has been delayed till I am indifferent, and cannot enjoy it; till I am lonely and cannot impart it; till I am known and do not want it.* Here is another gem from Johnson. *Marriage has many pains, but celibacy has no pleasures.*

Today, the antithetical construction is much in favour with copywriters. Some current examples: *Small cars are in big trouble. Again* (advertisement for Tata Indica). *Take TV technology to the top. And bring price down* (Phillips). And newspapers which are out to exploit tricks of language to grab attention, naturally go for this construction whenever they can. *Start saving today for a comfortable tomorrow.*

Time now to give a proper definition of antithesis as a figure of speech: 'A rhetorical or literary device in which an opposition or contrast of ideas is expressed by parallelism of words which are the opposite of, or strongly contrasted with, each other' (NODE).

Antithesis should not be confused with oxymoron. In an oxymoron, a single concept is expressed by a conjunction of opposites: *civil war, virgin mother, a modern classic.* The opposites define the concept. In an antithesis (or antithetical construction), the opposite is used to emphasize a concept (peace, not war); to clarify it (the cup that cheers but not inebriates); or to present an event/situation in contrasting terms. *Small cars are in big trouble. Again.* There is no single concept here parallel to *civil war, virgin mother.*

a/one

School grammars introduce pronouns as replacing nouns. This is good enough when you consider pairs of sentences like: *Arvind is in class 5. He plays cricket. / Sheila is my neighbour's daughter. She works in a convent school.*

But given a pair like *The old man was tired. He sat down,* we notice that *he* replaces the whole phrase *the old man.* But this is a problem for the grammar writer. No student is likely to say: *The old he sat down.* But I have noticed another case where the rule that pronouns replace nouns has, in fact, led to a strange, ungrammatical construction. *Do you have a knife? I have a one at home but haven't got it here.*

One here should replace the noun phrase *a knife* and not just *knife.* So you cannot say *a one* meaning 'a knife'. The noun and the idea of single are both covered by *one.*

Now here is an expression where *a* is used in place of *one.* A reader has drawn my attention to an expression which, he says, he frequently hears in his office. (He is a copywriter with an advertising firm.) *I can't do two or three jobs at a time.* What the speaker wants to say would come out better (and more grammatically) with: *I can't do two or three jobs at one time* or *at the same time.* (Both these phrases have other meanings as well. *At one time* can mean at some unspecified time in the past: *At one time he was an insurance salesman. At the same time* is used to introduce a thought or suggestion at variance with what has been said before. *You have got to be firm but at the same time you have to be sympathetic.*)

At a time is normally used in contexts where some periodicity is implied. Thus a doctor may say: *Take these tablets, two at a time.* There is also a notion of specified groups separated in time (in our example, groups of three). In the absence of these meanings, you cannot use *at a time.*

a or one?

The indefinite article *a* has a numerical sense in cases like *He has a Santro and a Qualis.* The meaning of *a = one* can also be seen in contexts where other numerals appear. *He has a cow, three buffaloes, and two oxen.* You can also say: *a hundred rupees* or *one hundred rupees.*

Nonetheless it is not the case that *a/one* are freely interchangeable. There are several cases to be discussed. Let's begin (and perhaps confine ourselves to) the case of numerals.

Informally you can say: *a hundred rupees* or *one hundred rupees.* But in a strict financial/business context it is only: *one hundred rupees.* That is why on a cheque you will find: *Pay Mr so-and-so Rs One hundred* (and not *a hundred*).

A second dimension has to do with what follows *a/one: a/one hundred;* but: *two thousand, one hundred and ten* (not *two thousand, a hundred and ten*).

Cases of this type are sometimes explained by saying that *a* (in the context we are examining) can only appear at the beginning and not in the middle. But this is hardly an explanation.

The fact seems to be that *a* can be used (in place of *one*) only when what follows is the name of a number, a word in the language. *Hundred, thousand, million,* etc. are names of certain numbers. They are words in the language. So we can have *a hundred/thousand/million.* But 2,110 is not the name of any number. It is a number. So you can only read it (or write it in words) as: *two thousand one hundred and ten.*

This 'rule' has an exception. When a 'number name' is followed by tens (e.g. 1022) we can write either *one thousand and twenty-two* or *a thousand and twenty-two.* Possibly because in the speaker's mind *thousand and twenty-two* are dissociated and not felt as one number.

There are other cases to be considered—with terms of quantity, measurement, distance, temperature, etc. But this will do here.

anyone/any one

The compound indefinite pronouns should be distinguished from the same words written separately. In *any one, any* is a determiner and the group means 'any single person, thing, etc'. *You can withdraw only Rs 5000 from this ATM at any one time. Anyone* is an indefinite pronoun meaning 'no matter who'. *Anyone will tell you that this can't be done. Some body* can only refer to a corpse. *Everybody (everyone)* is an indefinite pronoun. But in *every body, every* is a determiner and the group means 'every organization, institute, etc. We have a number of elected boides at the district level. Every body/each body has a three-year term.* Only with *none* are the groups *no one, none, no body* equivalent.

The adverbial *sometimes* ('occasionally'); *Sometimes the temperatures goes beyond 40 degrees (Celsius) in parts of Andhra Pradesh* should be distinguished from *some time* (='a considerable time') where *some* is a determiner. *War and Peace is a very long novel. It will take you some time to go through it.*

Sometime refers to an uspecified time in the future. *I'll call you sometime next week.*

articles

The English noun must be preceded by a determiner, i.e., a possessive (*my book*), or a demonstrative (*this book*) or an article (*a book*). Cases like *man is mortal* or *books are expensive* contain a zero article.

1. The articles are *a*, *the*, and *zero*. (In certain contexts *some* also functions like an article.) *An* is not a separate article. When the following word begins with a vowel sound, *a* becomes *an*: *an orange, an eye, an image*. It is the sound that matters, not the spelling. Hence *an M.P., a university.*

With words beginning with the letter *h*, in some cases the *h* is silent. Hence *an honest man, an heir, an hour.* In other cases, the *h* is pronounced; hence *a history lesson, a hotel.*

The has a strong, stressed form and a weak unstressed form. In the weak form, the final sound [i] is not pronounced.

Non-native speakers of English have great problems with the use of the articles. Although grammar books give long lists of the uses of the definite article and the indefinite article, with no explanation as to why the articles are used the way they are, the student is reduced to memorizing usages and is hopelessly confused when he has to use them on his own.

A great deal of article usage can be explained. Once the rationale behind article usages is understood, success in the use of the articles comes more easily.

2. The articles convey certain meanings. The correct use of the articles depends on the type of noun and the article meaning to be conveyed.

For this purpose, nouns can be classified as at Figure 1. PROPER nouns are names of persons (*Ram, Nikita*), places (*Delhi, London*) and things (*Kohinoor, Excalibur*). All other names are COMMON nouns.

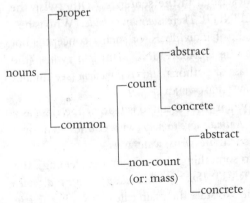

Figure 1: Noun classes

Common nouns can be divided into COUNTABLE (or COUNT) nouns and UNCOUNTABLE (or MASS) nouns. Countable nouns stand for things which can be (and usually are) counted: *one boy, two girls, three flowers*. Uncountable nouns stand for things like *rice, sand*, and *water*. Both count and non-count nouns can be ABSTRACT: *A penny for your thoughts* (count, abstract); *ripeness is all* (non-count, abstract) (see AN INFORMATION).

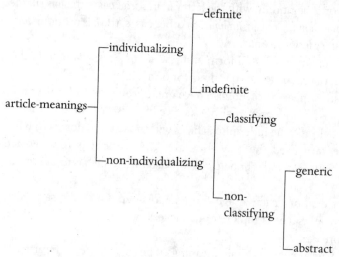

Figure 2: Article meanings

3. Now for some classification of article meanings:

We speak of a meaning as DEFINITE when the hearer knows what you are talking about; he can identify it. *Get me the book on the table.* (Not any book but a book as described in the sentence.) Otherwise the meaning is said to be INDEFINITE. *There is a man outside.* (Who is he?)

When there is no thought of individuals (or such a concept is not possible), the meanings can be CLASSIFYING. *This is a python* (the serpent is assigned to the class of pythons); *this is a modem* (see further below. See also: A GOOD KNOWLEDGE OF ENGLISH).

Or it can be GENERIC when what is stated is true of the class as a whole. *Boys are mischievous/Animals love to play* (with countable nouns) or true of the substance as such: *fire burns; water wets*.

When the reference is to something abstract (an idea, feeling), the meaning is said to be ABSTRACT: *Don't give in to despair. Life is a game.*

4. We are now in a position to state the main rules governing article usage in English.

(a) A countable noun, on the first mention, must be preceded by *a*. *One night a wolf met with a dog*. The reader, at this point, has no way of identifying these animals.

(b) On second and subsequent mention (i.e., if the noun is repeated), it must be used with *the*. *The wolf was all skin and bones; the dog was fat and well-fed*. The reader now knows what wolf and dog we are talking about. It is the wolf and dog mentioned in the previous sentence. The sense, therefore, is definite.

(c) If we begin with a plural countable noun, *a* cannot be used. We have to use *some* (or some other word indicating plurality). *I met some children and women on my way to work this morning*. In subsequent reference, a plural pronoun—if the nouns are not repeated—may be used. *They were all carrying bouquets*. But if the nouns are to be repeated, we have to use *the* (as the meaning is now definite): *The children were all carrying bouquets and the women were all wearing a feather in their hats*.

(d) As the examples at (2) and (3) show, a noun becomes definite once it has been introduced. It can also become definite when there is a post-modifying phrase: *the girl next door; the story of Helen, the reign of Ashoka*. The reader knows what the reference is: not any story but of Helen, not any king's reign but of Ashoka, not any girl but the girl next door.

(e) In some cases, the identity of what is being talked about is situationally clear: *the fan has stopped* (= the fan in the room we are in). Similarly, *The roof is leaking/Turn off the tap/Close the door*. For the same reason we speak of *the sun, the moon*, and *the stars*. Although there may be many suns in the universe, *the sun is behind the clouds* can only refer to our sun; *the clouds*, too, can only be in our atmosphere.

(f) What is situationally clear is unique in a particular context. Some other objects are unique in themselves—*the Bible, the Vedas*, epics like *the Ramayana, the Mahabharata,* and *the Iliad*. Hence the definite article.

(g) Countable nouns can also be used in the plural, with no article: *Books* are expensive. *Termites damage wood. Locusts destroy crops.*

There is no thought of any individual here, no particular book (or books); no particular locust (or locusts). The reference is generic.

The structure of the underlined nouns may be analysed as: zero article + plural N. Since the absence of an article makes for a different meaning, we speak of a zero article here. Further, this makes it possible to state an important, distinguishing property of nouns in English: they are always used with some article in the absence of any other determiner.

Certain countable nouns can be used in the generic sense in more than one way.

Zero article + plural: Tigers are ferocious animals.

The + singular noun: The tiger is a ferocious animal.

A + singular noun: A tiger is a ferocious animal.

It can be easily verified that these usages are not possible with all countable nouns. (*The book is expensive* can only have a definite meaning.) Names of animals, professional groups/classes (among human nouns) can be generally used in this way: *Philosophers pursue truth/The philosopher pursues truth/A philosopher pursues truth.*

The generic sense need not always cover the whole class. In *Invitees should be in their seats by 5 p.m.*, the sense is generic, although there is no class of 'invitees'. The same meaning may be seen in *Members should pay their dues by the 15th of August.* We may, if we wish, speak of a 'limited generic' sense in these cases.

(h) Countable nouns can also be used in a CLASSIFYING sense. *This is a python.*

The article *a* does not give an indefinite sense here. If the noun is in the plural we get *These are pythons.* Contrast this with the case where *a* is used to convey an indefinite sense. *I saw a python this morning.* In the plural, this would be: *I saw some pythons this morning.*

The difference between a classifying sense and the generic sense should be obvious. In the former, the object is assigned to a class; in the latter, some property of the object is stated.

The classifying sense is found with predicate nouns as in *He plans to be an engineer/I hope to be a Major soon.*

The sense is classifying also in such expressions as *What a stupid fellow. You are an ass.*

The article *a* in this usage is not found when the predicate noun normally denotes an office, position generally held by only one person at a time: *He was appointed Principal/She has taken over as Director General of AIR.*

5. Uncountable nouns are used:

(a) in a classifying sense, or (more often) in a generic sense:

(i) *This is mercury/This is nitric acid/This is spinach.*

There is no need to mention that there are no corresponding plural forms here.

(ii) *Diamond is the hardest substance in nature/Oxygen supports combustion/Water becomes steam when heated.*

Notice the difference between countable and uncountable nouns in this usage. With uncountable nouns, there is no *a* in the classifying sense; in the generic sense, there is no *a* or *the*. In both the senses, only the *zero* article is possible.

(b) Contextually limited, an uncountable noun can be used in a definite sense:

The water in this city is polluted/The gold I bought from that jeweller turned out to be of a poor quality/The milk supplied by the local dairy is not always pasteurized.

(c) The article *a* is not possible with uncountable nouns: **a paper, *a gold, a water* are not possible. However, they can be used with *a* when preceded by a numerative, i.e., a word indicating measure or quantity: *a glass of water, a grain of sand, a cup of milk, a gram of gold, a breath of air.*

(d) Some other nouns which can have a countable sense are generally used in a non-countable sense. Thus, while we can speak of *the literatures of different countries,* literature itself is an uncountable noun. Such nouns are generally used with no article: *The study of Art is fascinating/Literature broadens one's view of life/Agriculture is still the major occupation of millions in India/Life is a journey of discovery.*

When qualified by an adjective, they still have a generic sense: *English literature is a subject in most universities in India/Indian agriculture is still primitive.*

6. Proper nouns—1
(personal names)

(a) Personal proper nouns take no article. *Einstein was once a clerk in a patent office.* When speaking of living persons, it is customary to use an appropriate title—Mr, Mrs, Ms—if no other title like Dr or Professor is admissible. No titles are used with names of dead persons other than royalty: *Queen Elizbeth the First; King James; Emperor Ashoka. Dr Johnson* (the lexicographer) is an exception by common consent.

(b) The article meaning with a proper name is definite (though no *the* appears). When you use a proper name, it is understood that the hearer knows who you are referring to. You can't say: *Surender called* unless the other person knows who Surender is. (If he didn't know who Surender is, you would say: *A certain Surender called.* This use of *a* is possible even when the name is used with a title: *a Mr D'souza.*

(c) A phrase like *the brave Horatius* is understood as: the brave warrior (or fighter, etc.) Horatius. The article goes with the common noun *warrior*. But in *the sly fox*, the article goes with *fox* (the fox who was sly). But where the adjective is part of the name, no article is found: *Little Tommy.*

(d) Family names in the plural can be used with *the*. The reference can be to (i) a particular family, or (ii) the clan: (i) *The Mohans cordially invite you....* (ii) *The Nehrus originally came from Kashmir.* In (i) the sense is definite; in (ii) generic.

(e) The sense is also definite in such constructions as: *Kalidasa is often said to be the Shakespeare of India.*

The proper noun *Shakespeare* is now turned into a countable common noun. The reference is to one particular *Shakespeare*—that of India. (Definiteness achieved by a post-modifying phrase.)

(f) In constructions like *Narayan? You don't mean the 'Narayan'?* The sense is again definite—among so many who bear the name Narayan, reference is to a particular, well-known one, say *Narayan, the writer.* The construction bestows on the noun a measure of uniqueness. So the sense is something more than just definite.

(Note: The same use is found in cases like 'The verb is *the* word in a sentence' [= the most important]; 'that is *the* point', etc. In these cases, the meaning of being unique, the most important, is even more prominent.)

(g) We have examined till now the definite, indefinite, and generic senses of noun phrases with proper nouns. It remains to show that a classifying sense also is possible. *A Daniel came to judgement!* (For further details, see CE, p. 1.)

7. Non-personal proper nouns—1

(a) Names of days of the week and of the months are proper nouns. They are used without an article: *Come again on Monday/December is a cold month.*

The second sentence is a generic statement, not so the first. Still there is no article with Monday, although a particular Monday (the one to follow at the time of speaking) is meant. In the context of a sequence, *the* would be used: *the following Monday.*

These comments also illustrate how the days of the week, although proper nouns, are also used as common nouns.

(b) Similarly, names of the seasons can be used as proper nouns or as common nouns: *We usually go on a holiday in summer/I was in Botswana in the summer of 1994.*

(c) The parts of the day are used without an article. *Morning broke fresh and clean.* This is not a case of morning being used as a proper noun. It is a case of the word being used in an abstract sense (= a period of the day). But in: *I met him in the morning,* the sense is definite (= the morning of today; this morning). Similarly with *night, evening, dawn, dusk, nightfall* but *in the night.*

(d) Nouns like *heaven, hell, fate, fortune,* and *parliament* are often used as proper names without an article: *Fortune favours the brave/All good souls go to heaven.*

(e) Names of subjects and languages (*Mathematics, Medicine, French, Hindi*) are treated as proper names: *Mathematics is a fascinating subject/ Hindi is India's national language.*

Non-personal names—2

Some types of non-personal names have *the*; the use is mostly systematic, though in some cases it is a matter of convention. Otherwise, as with personal proper names, no article is used.

(a) Names of cities and countries are proper nouns. No article is used with them: *Bombay is the financial capital of India/India is often referred to as the subcontinent.*

Cases like *the Sudan* and *the Hague* are exceptional.

Descriptive proper names like the USA (the United States of America), the UK (the United Kingdom) are preceded by *the.*

Names of rivers, seas, and oceans are preceded by *the*: *the Ganga, the Thames, the Atlantic, the Mediterranean.* It is possible to explain the use of *the* in these cases. *The Ganga* is understood as the river Ganges, *the Atlantic* as the Atlantic Ocean.

In the same way, names of hills, mountains, and peaks are used with *the*: *the Alps, the Himalayas, the Andes, the Everest, the Matterhorn.* But: *Rocky Mountains* (or *the Rockies*).

Some geographic names have a descriptive word preceding them. These act like titles; no article is used with them: *Lake Michigan, Lake Chad, Mt Everest, Mt Vesuvius, Cape Cod.*

But: *the Cape of Good Hope* (or: *the Cape*), *the Bay of Bengal* (descriptive proper names).

(b) Usage varies with the names of buildings and streets: *Washington Monument, the Carnegie Hall, Buckingham Palace, (the) Brighton Road.*

8. Special cases

(a) Parallel to *The philosopher pursues truth*, adjectives denoting a state or quality common to a group of people can be used with *the*, in the generic sense. *The poor were oppressed by the rich, and no provision was made for the old and infirm* (quoted in Zandvoort, p. 26). (See also: the RICH.)

(b) In *Man is mortal*, the sense is generic. But the structure here (*zero* + singular noun) is an exceptional one. It is found with *woman* (*woman thy name is frailty*), *mankind*, and *humankind*.

(c) The classifying sense is found with some nouns used in the singular with no article. In *dinner is ready*, the sense is not indefinite; nor is it definite. It does not mean the dinner you were expecting or anything of the kind. It can only mean: the meal called 'dinner'. *Lunch, breakfast, tea* are also used in this way.

(d) Certain groups of nouns are used in an abstract sense, with no article. Among these are *school, church, jail, hospital, bed*. These are concrete nouns but they are associated with certain activities: getting instructed and educated in a school, for example. When reference is to an associated activity, these words are used with no article: *School begins at eight. / She was in hospital for less than three days. / Shobraj was convicted and sent to jail.*

These same nouns are found with the relevant article when the reference is to the building: *The church needs repairs. / The school is close to where I live. / You will find a parking lot next to the hospital. / A new jail is coming up outside the city limits.*

(e) In direct contrast to the usage noted above, words like *radio, bottle,* and *pen* are found with *the* when reference is to use. Names of musical instruments are also used with *the: I listen to the radio every evening. / My sister plays the veena / the violin. / In my time, people would flock to the theatre as they now do for the cinema. / Some people take to the bottle as others take to the pen.*

But TV has no article. *What's on TV this evening?* And as with the nouns discussed in (d), *the* is used when the instrument is meant. *I have to take the TV for repair.*

(f) Names of games and sports are used without an article: *Ravi plays golf. / Neethi wants to play tennis.*

(g) Names of diseases and illnesses usually take no article: *People over forty should check themselves for diabetes/blood pressure*, etc./*Ranjan was down with flu/malaria.*

But: *I have a cold/a headache.* No article with *toothache*! *Can't eat. I've got toothache.*

(h) The use (or non-use) of the articles in certain prepositional phrases is more a matter of idiom than grammar. It would be pointless to distinguish whether the absent article should have been *a* or *the* or what the precise article meaning is.

Some phrases with no article: *On demand, in hand, in debt, at home, to lose heart, to call a thing to mind, in case of, by way of.*

Some phrases with and without the article: *in (the) presence of, under (the) command of, in (the) face of, in (the) light of.*

Some phrases with the article: *in the event of, for a change.*

8. Some other uses of the articles:

(a) In some phrases, *a* has a numerical meaning (= one) *not a word, one in a hundred, five rupees a kilo, a penny saved is a penny gained, in a moment, one at a time.* (See *a/one*)

(b) In some phrases, *the* is found instead of a demonstrative: *He is rather busy at the* (= *this*) *moment./I didn't have the money at the* (*that*) *time.*

(c) A superlative is preceded by *the*: *the best boy in the class; the tallest building in the world.* But: *at best, at (the) worst.* (See also: BEST FOOT FORWARD?)

The is also found in some comparative phrases: *the more the merrier/ the tougher they come, the harder they fall.*

(d) *The* is also used before numerals in dates and titles, though usually suppressed in writing: *Queen Elizabeth II* (read: *the second*)/*July 29th* (read: *July the 29th*).

article with USA/US

Used as a noun referring to a country, the article would be required in both cases: *the USA/the US.* We have here what is called 'a descriptive proper noun'. As such, the article *the* is used with it: *the United States of America;* exactly as in *the United Kingdom/the* (now defunct) *Union of Socialist Soviet Republics* (*the USSR*).

Note, incidentally, that *the US* is far more frequent than *the USA. The United States* (or *the US*) has come to mean *the United States of America,* much as *the Continent* stands for the continent of Europe.

Used as an adjective, naturally *US* will not take any article. But the noun following it (that is, the noun modified by *US*) may require an article. Thus *the US forces in Afghanistan/a US helicopter/US marine*. But the noun modified may be an abstract noun not needing an article: *US intelligence/US foreign policy*; or the adjective and noun may define a class used in a general sense: *US veterans/US officials/US ground troops*. In these cases naturally there will be no article. (These same phrases when used in a specific sense would, of course, be found with *the*: *the US ground troops involved in the attack; the US officials on the inspection team*, etc.)

As can be seen, there is nothing special about the use of the article in any of the cases considered so far. But there is a tendency among us to use the abbreviation without any article. *My brother is leaving for the USA next week.—Raju's sister? Well she is in US*. We tend to use the abbreviation as a regular proper noun.

Note finally this point. In *George W. Bush, President of the USA*, the name of the individual appears with his official designation. There is no article before *President*. But in: *George W. Bush, the President of the USA* the title is used to identify a certain individual. The article *the* is necessary in this case. If an announcement is to be made without giving the name, it would be, for example, *Ladies and Gentlemen, the President of the USA* or *the President*.

assent/consent

Both the words indicate agreement. But *consent* has the additional suggestion, in some cases, that the person giving his consent has some legal/constitutional authority which makes his assent significant. Thus a bill, although passed by both the Houses of legislature, can become law only after it has received the President's assent (in our country; in Britain, the Sovereign's assent is required). Outside this special situation, the two words can be used indifferently in many contexts.

There is a subtle difference between the two worth noting. *Assent* is largely a matter of approval; *consent*, a matter of expressing your willingness (to do something). *He consented to make a speech* (= expressed his willingness to...). *He asked the girl to marry him and she consented* (examples from ALD, first edition, thirteenth impression). The line between giving approval and expressing willingness is not always clear and, in fact, may not matter. In such cases, it doesn't matter whether we use *assent* or *consent*. *I can never assent/consent to such a proposal*.

Used as verb, these words are followed by a prepositional phrase (see the examples above); used as nouns they require, usually, the verb *give: to give one's assent/consent*. (But: *to receive the President's/Royal assent*). They can also be used absolutely, that is, without an object: *I assent/consent*.

These are formal words. In informal situations there is a range of words and phrases: *Ok/Ok. Fine/I agree*. To the suggestion: 'Shall we go to a movie?' The answer (if positive) could be, for example, *Ok*. Not *I assent*. That would be ridiculous.

'a suspecting finger'?

Commenting on the predicament in which a minister found himself, a columnist wrote, '...his future in politics looks very bleak. His butter-wouldn't-melt-in-my-mouth appearance before the TV cameras did not fool anyone.' (*Deccan Herald: Sunday Spotlight*, 8 September 2002).

Some might have thought that the expression *butter-wouldn't-melt-in his mouth* is an Indianism. I have a feeling that a similar, if not the same, idiom exists *in some of our languages. In any case, the idiom is in Standard English. The expression has been hyphenated here* because it has been used attributively (= as an adjective modifying *appearance*).

Another expression worth commenting on in this context is: *the finger of suspicion. Quite some years ago, the phrase the needle of suspicion came into* prominence in the country. I can't remember now who used it in what context. Perhaps it came into prominence during the investigation into the Bofor's case. We now have *the finger of suspicion*. It makes sense. Cf *to point a finger at someone* (= to blame). But *to point a suspicious finger* makes little sense. A reporter in *Sunday Spotlight* (25 August 2002) writes: '...with the arrest of Sri Bhagwan Sharma of Gurgaon whose revelation led to some more persons who pointed a suspicious finger at the IPS officer, the prime accused [now absconding]....' The writer goes on to ring another variation on the phrase: '...*police have not questioned* [the Minister] *against whom a suspecting finger has been raised ever since Shivani was murdered'*.

The admissible phrase is: *the/a finger of suspicion*.

'as well as'

The earth's atmosphere *lets the sun's rays enter and warm the surface as well as retards the escape of heat* (*India Today*, 12 August 2002, p. 47).

Does the sentence sound odd to you? If it does, your feel for correct English is excellent.

What is wrong with the sentence is the use of *as well as*. This phrase can be followed by a noun (phrase) *John as well as Mary*. It can also be followed by a verb (as in the sentence cited). But if it is a verb, it must be in the *-ing* form:...*lets the sun's rays warm the earth as well as retarding the escape of heat*.

To the rule that the verb after *as well as* should be in the *-ing* form, there is one exception. When the main clause (i.e., the structure before *as well as*) contains an infinitive with *to*, the structure following *as well as* can contain an infinitive: *I have to write a column every week as well as work on a book*.

There is another point about *as well as*. The structure preceding *as well as* presents new information; the structure following *as well as* gives old information, i.e., information already known to the hearer (or assumed to be known). *Tamil is spoken in parts of South Asia as well as Tamil Nadu*. It would be odd to say: *Tamil is spoken in Tamil Nadu as well as parts of South Asia*. It can't be new information that Tamil is spoken in Tamil Nadu. If this is so, what is the new information in the context of the earth's atmosphere and the sun's rays? That it lets in the sun's rays is pretty obvious. So it has to be the given (= old) information. What is new is that it retards the escape of heat. The sentence should, therefore, read: *The earth's atmosphere retards the escape of heat as well as letting the sun's rays enter and warm the surface [of the earth]*.

One last question. Why should *as well as* be followed by the *-ing* form of the verb (except in the one case indicated above)? Perhaps the answer lies in the character of the *-ing* form. If it is a preposition (as indeed it is likely; see GCE, p. 619), then the *-ing* form is a gerund, as it should be. Cf *Smoking, in addition to being disgusting, is dangerous*.

atheist/agnostic

An atheist is one who does not believe in the existence of God. He is the opposite of a theist. The atheist is convinced that there is no God. The universe is governed by natural forces and that's that.

An agnostic takes a less rigid stand. He only maintains that it is not possible for the human mind to say anything about God. It is a subject beyond the competence of the human mind. No knowledge of God, one way or the other, is possible. You can neither prove nor disprove the existence of God. A scientist may have his personal views about God. But, as a scientist, he can only be an agnostic.

Gnosis is knowledge, especially positive knowledge about spiritual matters. The negative particle *a* negates this. It is this same word, in a more general sense, which appears in *diagnosis*.

at/in

School grammars characterize the use of *at* and *in* when referring to places as follows: *in* is used with names of countries and large towns; *at* is used when speaking of small towns and villages. *Rajesh is in California./Shekar lives in New Delhi./Sabir lives at Tondanur in Andhra Pradesh.*

But this analysis explains only a fraction of the cases where *at* is used in connection with places. Regardless of whether the place is big or small, when the place is viewed as a *point*, the preposition is *at*. *The plane landed at Frankfurt before taking off for New York.* But when the place is viewed as having dimension, *in* is used. *Tara lives in Frankfurt./He was in the club when the police arrested him.*

The distinction between a place viewed as a point or as one having dimension explains these cases as well: *Clinton studied at Oxford. For Nirad Choudhary it was a dream come true to live in Oxford./I met her at my uncle's./ I can never forget the time I had in my uncle's house as a boy.*

A second distinction governing the use of *at/in* has to do with whether the place is viewed as associated with a characteristic activity or not. Thus we have: *at the club, at the theatre, at the clinic, at a party, at a meeting....* Contrast these with *in the hall, in the house, in the garden....* Notice also that this usage overlaps with the usage described earlier. In *at the club* we have the sense of the club as a meeting place, that is, it is viewed as a point, not as having 'dimension'.

Names of commercial establishments are usually indicated by *in*: *She works in a departmental store/in a hospital/in an insurance company* regardless of the size of the establishment. But when such establishments are denoted by a name, we find *at*: *Many Gujaratis work at Macy's, Bridgewater, in New Jersey/I bought this scarf at Harrods.*

How do we explain this usage? The answer lies, perhaps, in assuming that in the absence of a name, the establishment is viewed as a three-dimensional object; with the name it is viewed as a point, much as in *I met her at my uncle's.*

at large'

The cheetah which escaped from the zoo is still at large. / Veerappan, wanted by two state governments for his criminal activities, is still at large. As these examples make it clear, *at large* is used of persons and animals which should be in confinement but are not.

Now consider this sentence from a newspaper report: *A look at these areas leaves no doubt that a health risk is at large.*

What is this supposed to mean? That there is an imminent danger of some disease breaking out? We have to put this meaning on these words; they don't bear it. Only if 'health risk' is viewed as something which should be kept in restraint, confined, but now has got loose (escaped) can any sense be made of the sentence. But that would be putting too much poetry into journalistic prose.

authority and usage—1

The French have an Academy which pronounces on what is acceptable or not in the use of the French language. Bulletins are periodically issued decreeing that such and such an expression is correct or incorrect. The Italians and Spaniards, too, have similar academies keeping a watchful eye on their languages.

English, however, has no such academy to regulate the use of the English language. Some attempts were made in the eighteenth century (by John Dryden first and then by Jonathan Swift) to set up an English Academy on the lines of the French Academy. But these efforts came to nothing. There is now a British Academy (founded in 1902) but this learned body only claims to promote 'the study of the moral and political sciences, including history, philosophy, law, political economy, archaeology and philosophy.' It does not pronounce on what is acceptable or not in English usage.

The absence of an authoritative academy does not mean that in the case of English 'anything goes'. In the early days—and even in the days of Shakespeare and Milton—English spelling was pretty fluid. Shakespeare himself would spell his name in more than one way. Milton has both *me* and *mee, she* and *shee* (among other variably spelt words). The early typesetters would add (or cut) an extra letter or so to 'justify' the right margin (i.e., to keep the right margin straight). But with the coming of the dictionaries, especially *Dr Johnson's Dictionary of the English Language*

(1755), spelling became more or less fixed. No formal authority but a great dictionary began to act as an arbiter of correct spelling.

The advent of English grammars has had a similar effect on what is 'correct' or 'acceptable' usage. Although the great English grammars— from Henry Sweet's *A New English Grammar, Logical and Historical*, in two volumes (1892, 1894), to the comprehensive grammars of H. Poutsma, Etsko Kruisinga, and Otto Jespersen—all claim to record, and not pronounce on, usage, they have all had a stabilizing and controlling effect on how English is to be used. Keeping in mind the usage of the best writers, the great grammars have laid down implicitly, and sometimes explicitly too, what is correct usage; a tradition continued, in recent times, by Quirk and his associates in their comprehensive grammars. (See, e.g., *A Grammar of Contemporary English* by Quirk, et al. 1972.)

The prescriptive approach became more pronounced with the publication of that remarkable book, Henry Watson Fowler's *A Dictionary of Modern English Usage* (first published in 1926; revised by Sir Ernest Gowers in 1968, and by R.W. Burchfield in 1996). Fowler was not a trained grammarian or linguist. But he had plenty of common sense and a strong aversion to illogical, confused, ambiguous, pompous, and (yes, he did not hesitate to use the term) illiterate use of words. The book, as Gowers notes, quoting *The Times*, 'took the world by storm'.

It is now common practice for dictionaries to add 'usage notes' on certain constructions and phrases and declare whether they are acceptable or not. The reader need only look up such entries as: *hopefully* (*hopefully the situation will become clear by next week*), *like* (*like I said...*), *back* (*I met him two days back*), the split infinitive (*I request you to kindly grant...*), to see how the dictionary has become an arbiter of usage.

The basic structure of a language (word order, structure of phrases and clauses, internal rules holding across certain elements, e.g., the rule of subject-verb agreement in English; rules interpreting the reference of pronouns, etc.) is unchanging. In a fundamental sense these are independent of the speakers of the language. There is no question of 'usage' here.

In certain other cases, largely vocabulary, which is the most fluid part of a language, fashions come and go. Some 'unacceptable' usages (e.g., the use of *like* in place of *as*) stick on. There is little that anyone can do here to stem the popular tide. In such cases we should remember the old Roman saying: Usage is mightier than Caesar. The informed user will not try to correct but will himself observe the distinction in the use of these words depending on time, place, and circumstance.

authority and usage—2

When, in 1961, *Webster's Third*, purporting to describe actual usage, listed *ain't* and, in the usage note, added: 'Used orally in most parts of the US by many cultivated speakers especially in the phrase *ain't I?*', it caused a furore. James H. Sledd, a professor of English and a grammarian, is reported to have burst out: '...any red-blooded American would prefer incest to *ain't*' (DEU, 1989, p. 62).

But *Webster's Third* was, in fact, describing actual usage. Notwithstanding James Sledd's outburst, the usage continued. One of the most famous instances of it was when Ronald Reagan kicked off his campaign on Labour Day with: 'You ain't seen nothing yet', a remark echoed years later by Margaret Thatcher when she, as British Prime Minister, visited the US and called on Reagan.

So here we have an expression in wide use, instantiated in the speech and writings of some of the most famous people. Has this given *ain't* total legitimacy? Far from it. *Webster's Dictionary of English Usage* concludes with this remark: 'a stigmatized word in general use; in ordinary speaking and writing tends to mark the speaker and writer as socially or educationally inferior' (p. 64). The *Concise Oxford Dictionary* (10th edn, 1999) says: 'In modern English the use of *ain't* is non-standard, despite being widespread in many dialects and in informal speech'. And Michael Swan (*Practical English Usage*, 2003) notes its use as confined to 'non-standard English'.

This is how dictionaries and grammars try to regulate usage.

Now coming to our own brand of English, IE, what should our stand be on such matters?

On matters of divided usage in Standard English we go with the view accepted/recommended by the standard British grammars and dictionaries. This also means that typical 'Indianisms' like *What he said?* (lack of inversion); *You only told me* (wrong use of *only* in place of the emphatic reflexive expression *you yourself*); the universal question tag *Isn't it?* (*He is coming tomorrow, isn't it?*); *the book which you gave it to me* (the 'resumptive' pronoun in a relative clause); *All his friends will be there to meet him when he will come on the 16th* (*will* in subordinate temporal clauses); and a host of other incorrect expressions like *discuss about, called as, pick up a quarrel, lot of luggages, boarding and lodging*, etc. must be condemned as simply bad, incorrect English. There is no justification for these things. Those who know better don't use them and those who use them should know better. To justify these and claim them as part of Standard Indian English would be to make a laughing stock of our English.

But in lexis, in the coinage of new phrases and expressions, we can be legitimately proud of our contribution to the development of Indian English. I am particularly impressed by such expressions as *Lakshman Rekha, the creamy layer* (as applied to SCs and STs), *Mandalization of the Indian society, the glass struggle* (in Andhra Pradesh). Other equally authentic and original expressions provoke a smile: *relay fast, eve-teasing, suitcase culture*, etc. And then there are the quite numerous words and expressions deriving from Sanskrit or originating from the colonial days, many of which are now part of Standard British English: *ahimsa, dharma, bungalow, satyagraha*, etc.

In this area of lexis, too, one comes across expressions which are direct translations from the mother tongue: *father's property (What do you think it is, your father's property?), a head-going business*. There are adequate Standard English equivalents in these cases. No justification can be found for using these expressions.

To conclude: British usage is regulated by the standard dictionaries and grammars. These same instruments control and regulate the use of English in India. But educated, informed Indians have shown great creativity and enriched the vocabulary of Indian English. These coinages, whether recorded or not in British dictionaries, are part of Standard Indian English (SIE).

avoid, prevent, avert

For quite some time Pakistani and Indian troops were confronting each other on the LOC in Kashmir. But thanks mainly to American diplomacy, a war has been... What is the word needed to fill the blank here? *Avert*, of course. Why?

Actually all the three words listed at the beginning can be used but with different subjects. *We have been able to avoid a war with Pakistan. America has prevented a war flaring up between India and Pakistan. Thank God, a war with Pakistan has been averted.*

But change the subjects and you will find that the verbs, too, will have to change. *We have been able to prevent a war with Pakistan?* No. *America has averted a war flaring up between Pakistan and India?* No, again. We *avoid* (= try not to meet, get away from) somebody, something. Obviously we have avoided a war with Pakistan.

You *prevent* something from happening. So *America has prevented a war flaring up between India and Pakistan.*

Speaking in grammatical terms, with *prevent* the subject is doing something which affects the object (in this case, *war*); with *avoid*, he merely gets away from it.

Now what about *avert*? Notice first that *avert*, in the sense we are considering now is usually found with events. Secondly, the subject of a sentence with *avert* is logically its object. *War has been averted.* That is, *avert* is usually found in passive constructions.

These facts are easily explained. With *avert* we don't do anything to what is averted. We take steps to see that the factors or circumstances which would bring about the event are eliminated. Hence, *thanks to American diplomacy, a war with Pakistan has been averted.*

To sum up: with *avoid* the subject's action in respect of the object is merely negative; he does not directly act upon it. With both *prevent* and *avert*, it is more positive; with *prevent* even more so than with *avert*. *He prevented him from entering the room.* With *avert* it is indirect.

award/reward

'*...people are upset with the failure of the police to nab the fugitive on whose head police have declared an award of Rs 50,000....*' Is it *award* or *reward*?

Award can be judicial: *the Cauvery Tribunal award;* it can be a token of recognition of merit: *award of a scholarship.* The first sense is technical; the second can be generalized as some form of recognition of excellence, superior work/achievement.

Reward is compensation for some work done. And in one of its senses it specifically refers to a sum of money offered for the capture of a criminal, return of lost property, etc. Clearly the word needed in the present context is *reward* not *award.*

awarded/honoured

'Noted theatre personality honoured'. This is fine as a headline. A 'function' might have been arranged when speakers eulogized his contribution to the theatre and the organizers presented him with a shawl (or whatever).

In short, *honour* can be used as a verb without any further details of how a person was honoured.

The same usage is not available with *award*. *Noted artist awarded* does not make sense. You can say *X given an award*. Now we are using *award* as a noun. But as a verb it can't be used by itself.

To see the point better, consider a parallel verb (with a similar grammatical structure). *Noted artist given a cash prize*. Fine. But *Noted artist given*?

Award and *give* are verbs which take two objects. A direct object (= thing given) and an indirect object (= the person to whom something was given). *They gave him a prize. / They awarded him a scholarship.*

These verbs make no sense when used alone and by themselves even in a headline. These are verbs taking two objects. The direct object must be mentioned when the verb is used. (You may omit the indirect object, the person.) Thus of the two following sentences (authentic), the first one is incorrect: *Shimoga social worker awarded. / SP gets Sangeeta Ganga award* (DH, 21 August 2001, p. 9).

In North India they have gone one step further. In the Jaipur City Palace you can see artisans advertising themselves as: *Ram Singh—National awarded / Balbir—State awarded* (names fictitious).

Parallel to *honour* (*They honoured him*) we have *reward*. *Courageous boy rewarded*. Like *honour* (v), *reward* (v) takes an object and a prepositional phrase. *They honoured him with a citation. / They rewarded him for his services / with a medal.*

In general, transitive verbs taking one object can be used as illustrated with *honour* and *reward*. Constructons like: *So-and-so honoured / rewarded* are, in effect, passive construction, where the original object appears as the subject (and the passive verb stands alone). *They honoured Semmangudi* or *Semmangudi honoured*. But transitive verbs taking two objects must have the direct object mentioned. *Boy awarded a gold medal*.

b

'Bangalore's any pub'

'A visit to Bangalore's any pub or restaurant will prove that all of this is true' (*Sunday Herald*, 8 September 2002).

How does this sentence strike you? To help you decide, let me give you two more sentences. *The Captain's all men fought bravely. / All the Captain's men fought bravely.* You will agree that the second sentence is better. Here *all* precedes the possessive expression; in the first sentence, *all* appears between the possessive and its head (*men*).

Does this mean that nothing should intervene between a possessive and its head? No. *John's second son/the school's cricket team/the officer's well-considered, carefully drafted report*—all these are well-formed. What is not permissible is an intervening quantifier (an 'indefinite pronoun' to use traditional terminology); specifically, *any, all, both, some.* They cannot be placed between a possessive and its head: *John's both sons/ Baldwin's some students/the canteen's all the workers....* These have to be rephrased as: *both the sons of John/some students of Baldwin's/all the workers of the canteen.* Note, however, that numerals and *many* can appear between a possessive modifier and its head: *his two sons/Gulliver's second adventure/Vajpayee's many admirers.*

In the light of this discussion, you will see that the sentence we started with should read: *A visit to any of Bangalore's pubs or restaurants will prove that....*

We have yet to explain why numerals and *many* can appear in the position where *any, both, all,* and *some* cannot appear.

Vajpayee's many admirers implies that Vajpayee's admirers are many; *Gulliver's second adventure* means 'the adventure referred to is the second one of Gulliver'. A similar acceptable (idiomatic) translation is not possible for *his two sons.* We cannot say: *His sons are two.* But this is so for other reasons. In place of the *candidate's two supporters* we can have *The candidate's supporters were (just) two.*

The point is: the quantifiers which can appear between a possessive and its head are just those which can appear in the predicate (*His many admirers = His admirers are many*). *All, both, some, any* are not of this type. They cannot appear in the predicate. *All his friends* cannot be rephrased as *His friends are all; any of Bangalore's pubs* cannot be reframed as *Bangalore's pub is any.*

before/earlier

He is an insurance agent now. Earlier he was a car salesman. This is correct. But *Before he was a car salesman is incorrect.*

Before can refer to an 'earlier time' only when this earlier time is explicitly mentioned. *Before becoming an insurance agent, he was a car salesman.* He is an insurance agent now. Before that he was a car salesman. The demonstrative *that* refers to the time prior to his being an insurance agent. Without this *that*, *before* by itself cannot make such a reference. In this, American English seems to differ from British English. Here is a citation. *These young women are being very creative, finding a way to continue being Muslim in the American context. Before, young Muslims may have stuck with the traditions of their parents or rejected them totally to become completely Americanized'* (*New York Times*, 9 June 2003).

before/in front of

Before is the opposite of *behind*. *There is a park behind my house*. But: *No parking in front of the gate*. Why?

Before as a preposition of place is restricted to a few very special contexts. Its more general use is as a preposition of time, meaning 'earlier than': *the day before yesterday / two days before Christmas / He taught English as his father had done before him / Something ought to have been done before now* (ALD).

In the sense of *in front of*, *before* is found where position is to be indicated in a series. *A comes before C in the alphabet. / Your name comes before mine in this list. / She stood before me in the queue*.

It is also used in contexts involving persons of consequence, authority or importance. *He was produced before the magistrate for reckless driving. / The court has directed the Home Secretary to appear before it on the 7th of next month*. The persons need not be necessarily judicial officers. The speaker addressing the chief guest at a formal meeting may say: *Sir, I stand before you....* Then, of course, *you kneel or prostrate before the deity in a temple*.

In a figurative sense we have: *The task now before us is....*

Before can also function as an adverb. *I think I have seen this film before. / Have we met before?* (When introducing yourself to somebody).

Counting back from a point of time in the past we use *before*. *When I went back to the town I had left ten years before I found everything had changed.* (A common mistake here is to say: *the town that I had left before ten years*.) Counting back from the present we use *ago*: *Three days ago I heard that....*

'being a Tamilian'
(free adjuncts)
'*Being a Tamilian', Dr Kalam is a chronic bachelor.* This was how a paper wrote about Dr Kalam when his name was being considered for the office of the President. This is surprising, to say the least. I did not know that Tamilians were confirmed (or 'chronic') bachelors.

Or is it that the reporter has unwittingly used a construction which means what he never intended it to mean?

Obviously the reporter wanted the sentence to be understood as: *He is a Tamilian and a bachelor,* i.e., he expects the reader to interpret his statement as involving a coordination by means of *and.* But we don't get that interpretation.

Structures of the type we are now examining (*being a Tamilian*) are called FREE ADJUNCTS. They are part of a sentence but grammatically stand apart. There is a clear break, marked in writing by a comma. Usually (but not always) they open with a participle, as in our example.

When the free adjunct has no subject of its own (as in the present case), the subject of the main clause is interpreted as the subject of the free adjunct. This can lead to unexpected (and amusing) results as in *Lying in a pile of dust for years, the Secretary finally found the club records of 1950.*

There is no misreading of this type in the present case. Quite clearly (and correctly) Dr Kalam is the subject of the free adjunct. But the fault here is the ridiculous semantic relationship suggested between the adjunct phrase and the main clause.

A free adjunct which mentions some activity which took place prior to the main clause action is generally equivalent to a coordinate construction. *Entering the room he switched on the radio.* (He entered the room and he switched on the radio.) This is also the case where the free adjunct is a nominal phrase and no specific connection is suggested or implied between it and the main clause. *A retired teacher, he opened a grocery shop.*

But where the free adjunct is introduced by a conjunction, interpretation in terms of coordination with *and* is impossible. *Though an orphan, he rose to become a college Principal* (= in spite of being an orphan; not: *he was an orphan and*). The same is true of cases where some connection is *perceived* between what is said in the free adjunct and what is stated in the main clause. *A brilliant physician, he chose to lead the life of a farmer* (= although a brilliant physician).

Now what about the reporter's sentence we began with?

The participle *being* has the effect of conveying the meaning of cause or reason. Cf *Being a man of independent views, he couldn't remain long a follower* (because he was a man of independent views). *Being a man of understanding, he built up a large circle of friends.* So no wonder we are more than puzzled when we read: *Being a Tamilian, he remained a chronic bachelor.*

A free adjunct with a subject of its own is an ABSOLUTE FREE ADJUNCT. The point about misreading the subject (*Lying on a pile of dust...*) does not arise in these cases. *The Minister arriving, the meeting began.*

'best foot forward'?

Is the Boy Scout movement still alive in our schools and colleges? I don't know. In my time it was. And it was from a scoutmaster that I heard phrases like: *to pull one's weight, to put one's best foot forward, to take it* (whatever it was) *in your stride.*

To put one's best foot forward has a literal meaning when, early in the morning, you are faced with the prospect of a ten-mile trek across fields and hills. Indeed, one dictionary gives the meaning of the phrase as: *to go as quickly as possible.* The COD gives a more general, figurative meaning: *make every effort, proceed with determination.* However, the point of interest for us now is the use of the superlative *best* in the phrase. When there are only two feet, how can you talk of 'the best foot'?

The matter has not gone unnoticed. Usage pundits have hotly discussed the issue. The construction, sometimes called 'the superlative of two', (Jespersen) has been in existence for centuries in serious, literary work. And yet one cannot but wonder how one can talk of 'best' (or any superlative form) where only two objects are involved.

Jespersen (*Essentials of English Grammar*, 1969) says: 'Apart from such set phrases as *the lower lip, the upper end, the lower classes,* the natural tendency in English is to use the superlative in speaking of two'. He cites these examples: *Put your best leg foremost; Whose God is strongest, thine or mine* (Milton); *We'll see who is strongest, you or I* (Goldsmith). But Fowler (1926) says: 'This use of *-est* instead of *-er* where the persons or things compared are no more than two should normally be avoided'; the *raison d'être* of the comparative is to compare two things, and it should be allowed to do its job without encroachment by the superlative.'

Here we have two diametrically opposed views, each held by a formidable authority. Jespersen is, perhaps, the greatest grammarian of English; Fowler, the last court of appeal in matters of usage. What should lesser mortals do in a situation like this?

Clearly Jespersen has overstated the case. No one will ever use the superlative in cases like: *He is the taller/* or *the shorter of the two/this is the heavier of the two boxes.* In all such cases, a more explicit comparison involving *than* is possible. *John is taller/shorter than Bill; this box is heavier than that box.*

Even when no such explicit construction with *than* is possible, there are cases where only the comparative can be used: *the upper/lower lip/ the upper window.* You can't say, *this lip is upper than the other* or any such thing. That would be nonsense. But you can see the form is *-er* and not *-est*.

What, then, are the cases where, as between two objects, only the comparative can be used (and not the superlative, contrary to Jespersen)?

They are precisely those cases where the point of comparison involved is a single 'quality'—height, weight (in our examples).

As against these, the cases cited by Jespersen involve not just a single point of comparison but a set of such points. This may not be readily apparent. But a little analysis will show this to be the case.

When you are urged to put your best foot (leg) forward, you are asked to put forward that foot (leg) which, as tested on numerous occasions in the past, has proved most reliable and strong. It is not just a comparison between two feet (or legs); it is a comparison based on an estimate of a whole set of previous performances.

An analysis on these lines will account for most cases of 'the superlative of two'. But one or two hardy specimens refuse to submit to any such analysis and stand out as incontrovertibly irrational but well-established. One such is '*the eldest of the two*'. 'We cannot agree as to *which is the eldest of the two* Miss Plumbtrees'' (Jane Austen, 1811).

'bin Laden's assassin'
(*possessive interpretation*)

bin Laden's assassin visited Delhi airport (news report). What? bin Laden assassinated? When?

As it turned out, he had not been assassinated. One of his men had visited Delhi airport.

The relation between a genitive modifier and its headword is not always straightforward. Broadly speaking there are two kinds of genitive constructions: (1) Where the noun in the 'possessive' form stands for a person or thing: *my mother's picture, John's overcoat*; (2) where the genitive refers to a class or kind to which the person or thing denoted by the headword belongs: *a giant's task* (work fit for a giant), *child's play* (something easily done), *a fool's errand*.

There is no problem with the second type of phrases. The meaning is often idiomatic but that is all. The first type of phrases, however, pose problems of interpretation.

The meaning can be one of *possession*, e.g., *my uncle's car.* The headword may denote an action and the genitive may denote the agent: *the new MP's maiden speech* (The MP made the speech); or the headword may denote the agent (or agents): *Caesar's murderers* (They murdered Caesar). There are other possible meanings but we will not go into them.

The way in which we understand *Caesar's murderers* is the way phrases of this type are usually understood. We understand the headword as denoting the agent(s) and the word in the genitive as denoting the object / persons undergoing the action. *Vajpayee's tormentors* are the persons tormenting Vajpayee, not the persons employed by Vajpayee to torment others: *Sonia's detractors* are persons like Uma Bharati, not Jaipal Reddy.

Since this is the only way such phrases are normally understood, we take *bin Laden's assassin* to be the man who finished off bin Laden.

Words like *murderer, assassin* denote persons who have actually done some deed (of killing). As against these words, a word like *hit man* describes a person who will do a certain type of deed: he can be hired to kill. So *bin Laden's hit man* would only mean the person who executes bin Laden's orders to kill (and not kill bin Laden himself).

'bleak chances'

'What is the possibility of a major earthquake rocking Karnataka?' 'Well, the chances are very bleak.'

I'm sure many must have been surprised to read this, as I was, when it appeared in a newspaper (28 January 2001).

Bleak is a word used in negative contexts only. *A bleak mountain top* is bare, exposed, windswept. We can speak of *bleak hills and mountains.* Applied to weather, we have such expressions as: *a bleak winter morning* (cold and dreary). In a figurative sense, *bleak* means 'not hopeful or encouraging, dismal.' *For the Gujarat victims, the future is pretty bleak.* It is in this sense that the word is used in respect of events which are, in themselves, desirable but very unlikely to happen. *He is now working as a door-to-door salesman. His chances of being absorbed as a management trainee are bleak / The Dalai Lama is an optimist. But the chances of Tibet securing autonomy in the foreseeable future are bleak.*

In the light of this analysis, consider the remark on the earthquake. Is an earthquake something to be welcomed and are we supposed to be depressed and dejected that the chances of a major earthquake in Karnataka are pretty remote? The use of *bleak* in this context suggests just this.

The opposite of *bleak* is *bright; a bright day, a bright outlook, bright prospects.*

A neutral term to refer to the unlikely chance of something happening (good or bad) is *nil. The chances of a major earthquake are nil./ His chances of being appointed Chief Secretary are nil.*

border/boundary

The Kannada Sahitya Sammelan at Belgaum (2003) brought to the fore the dispute between Maharashtra and Karnataka. One paper referred to the acerbic views [of the Sammelan President] 'on the Belgaum *border* dispute'. Others spoke of 'the *boundary* dispute' between the two states.

What's it anyway? Is it a *border* dispute or a *boundary* dispute?

The two words are, as hinted above, frequently used interchangeably in IE. The same paper which, on the first day had used *border dispute* came out next day with *boundary dispute* between Karnataka and Maharashtra.

Strictly speaking, *border* is used in connection with countries. It is the official line that separates two countries. It can also refer to the areas close to the official line. The *Mexican border* is the line separating Mexico from the US. *The Rio Grande forms part of the US border. Jeumont is a small town on the border between France and Belgium. India is facing infiltration across the border in Kashmir. Our border with Bangladesh is very porous* (i.e., there is large-scale illegal immigration into the country from Bangladesh). *Border* as a verb can be used of states within a country. *Wisconsin borders on Illinois.*

For historical reasons, *the border* (in England) refers to the territory between England and Scotland. Though part of one country now, the United Kingdom, the two were, for centuries, separate and hostile countries, frequently fighting with each other.

Boundary is the word in connection with units other than (and smaller than) countries. The Mahajan Commission did a fine job in drawing the *boundaries* of the states in the Indian Union. When you draw a *boundary* line, you create *boundary* problems. More generally *boundary* can refer to the limits of any area, big or small. *You can play anywhere within the boundary of the park.*

So we have a *boundary* dispute with Maharashtra and Kerala. The country as a whole has a *border* dispute with China and Pakistan.

brain/brains?

Is it *brain* or *brains*?

The word *brain* can refer to the organ in the head which is the centre of the nervous system and controls thoughts, feelings, and emotions and directs all motor activity. In this sense, it is used in the singular form only: *The study of the brain is a fascinating subject. / Some drugs can induce severe brain damage / brain surgery / brain fever.*

Brain can also be used in the sense of 'intelligence', 'mental power'. In this sense, in some cases it is used in the singular and in some other cases in the plural.

In the attributive position (i.e., used as a noun modifier), it is used in the singular. (This is in line with the general rule that nouns used as modifiers are generally in the singular form): *a brainwave* (a sudden, clever idea); *a brain-teaser* (a difficult problem); someone's *brainchild* (a person's original plan, invention, idea. *I wonder whose brainchild it is—the new one-way rule on most roads in Bangalore*).... But we have a *brains trust*, possibly because, by definition, it is made up of a number of people, not just one. (The Americans have simplified matters by using the singular form here also.)

Otherwise (i.e., when not used as a modifier), the word is found in the plural: *He is the brains of the party; pick someone's brains* (get some good, useful ideas from somebody); *rack one's brains* (to remember something, to solve a problem, etc.). *Have you any brains?* (have you any sense?) Here, too, an occasional singular form may be found. *Don't tax your brain too much.* But the plural form is always possible.

Now we come to the case where only the singular form is required: *She has brains* (= She is very clever, intelligent). But: *She has an excellent brain.* In this case, with a modifier, it is singular; otherwise plural.

brood

Brood as a noun is normally used to refer to a family of young birds all born at the same time. With reference to humans, it can only be used jocularly: *She has a large brood of grandchildren.*

But many Indian English users are under the impression that 'brood' can be used in connection with humans without any hint of hilarity. Here is a *hakim* speaking: 'Any man who goes for a morning walk, breathes fresh air and remains fit shouldn't hesitate if he desires to extend his brood.'

The hakim was speaking in the context of a report that daughters born to men above 50 would have a reduced lifespan.

C

'can be able to'
If you can be able to go to Portland....

The correct form, of course, is *If you can go* or *If you are able to go.* How does *can be able to* get in?

We get a clue to this when we look at some other cases of modal + *be able to* structures (*can, will, may,* etc. are called MODAL AUXILIARIES). We have *I may be able to help you/Perhaps Rani will be able to come next Sunday.* These are possible because *may, will* have different meanings from *be able to. May* suggests a possibility; *will* a certainty (tempered by *perhaps*). Because these structures are possible, some think, mistakenly, that *can be able to* is also possible. But *can* has the same meaning as *be able to,* resulting in a bad tautology. The point can be made clearer by another structure, *be likely to.*

You can say: *He may come.* You can also say: *He is likely to come.* But you cannot say: *He may be likely to come.* It is a hopeless tautology. If you say *He will be likely to come,* it is contradictory; *will* indicates some certainty contradicted by *likely. He can be likely to come* is pretty nonsensical.

Conclusion: A modal construction with *be likely to* is not possible; with *be able to* you can have it with *will, may,* but not *can.*

Now consider the phrase *That can be possible.* Why does this sound odd?

You can say: *That can be done.* Does it mean that only a past participle can occur in the frame *can be*? No. *That can be true. True* and *possible* are both adjectives. How come *true* is good but not *possible*?

Analysing further you can see that *That may be possible* is correct. So what is wrong with the sentence is the modal *can.* But why can't we have *can* while we can have *may*?

The modal meaning required here is: 'possibility coupled with some uncertainty'. It would seem that *may* expresses this meaning better than *can.* Cf *It may rain/It can rain.*

'can't help but'

Pointing out that the sentence *I cannot but do it* means 'I cannot do otherwise' and the sentence *I cannot help doing it* means 'I cannot stop myself from doing it', Safire asks, 'What then does *I cannot help but do it* mean?' He invokes Jaques Barzun, the usage pundit (he edited Wilson Follett's *Modern American Usage*) to give the answer. 'It means that one does not know the existence of two distinct idioms.'

Safire continues: '*Cannot help but*' is confusing, redundant and sloppy. I hope today's kick in the mouth will curtail its use, though I cannot help but think that the diatribe won't rid the world of this squared idiom' (*On Language,* 1981).

Much the same opinion was current in Britain at the time. Thus Flavell and Flavell in their revision of F.T. Wood's *Current English Usage* (1926) say: '*I could not help but laugh at what he said*: A confusion of two constructions'. *I could not but laugh* (now somewhat archaic) and *I cannot help laughing*.' Their recommendation: 'Use the latter'.

But more recently Robert Burchfield in his revision of Fowler (1996) asks: 'Should *help* be followed by *v-ing* or can you have *help but*?' His answer: 'The matter remains unresolved and both types are still in use.' The prescriptive *Practical English Usage* (Michael Swan, 2003 edn) notes the *can't help but* structure as 'common in American English'. But the usage-oriented LDCE (1995) treats the construction without any restrictive comment.

What does one make of all these varying judgements?

Let's have a fresh look at the facts. The first point to note is that the construction has been in use for more than a hundred years. The first recorded use goes back to 1894. *She could not help but plague the lad* (H. Caine). Almost a hundred years later we have *She could not help but feel that all the passengers on the bus were pensioners* (1984, cited in Burchfield).

Next the three structures do not have the same impact: *I can't help admiring him./I can't but admire him./I can't help but admire him.*

The first one suggests that, in spite of some possible reasons for not doing so, the speaker admires him. This reservation is absent from the second sentence. The man is such you can only admire him. There is no other option. The third sentence combines these two meanings. There is a suggestion of reservation noticed in the first sentence but there is also the suggestion of there being no other option. You can only admire. It is a more emphatic form of the first one.

These distinctions will become clearer if we supply some more context to our example sentences: *I can't help admiring him although he is a scoundrel./I can't but admire him—he has done so much for his people.*

I can't help but admire him. He has his weaknesses but look how much he has done for his people.

Speakers have intuitively felt that there is something distinctive about the *can't help but* structure. Far from being a solecism, it is a well-constructed phrase.

capable/competent

Speaking about the date when the construction of the Ram temple at Ayodhya would begin, an RSS spokesman is reported to have said:

'Dharm Sansad is the only capable body which can decide anything on it' (*The Times of India*, 13 January 2001, p. 1).

When the ability (physical, mental as measured in terms of power, knowledge, skills) to do something is in question, *capable* can be used. *He is capable of running the marathon/India is capable of landing a space vehicle on the moon.* In cases like this, we can also use *can*: *He can run the marathon./ India can land a space vehicle on the moon.* There are subtle differences in meaning here, nuances. *Can* makes a plain assertion; *capable* emphasizes the ability. Grammatically *can* is followed by a verb in the stem form (*can run, can land*); *capable* is followed by a preposition and a verb in the *-ing* form (*capable of running/landing*).

In respect of activities (as indicated above), a person can be assessed as *competent* (or otherwise). *He is a competent runner/swimmer/driver.* Notice that the reference is to individuals. India may have the ability or capability of sending a rocket to the moon. But you don't say that India is a *competent space power.*

Competent (again in respect of individuals) when applied to a piece of work does not suggest excellence. A *competent* piece of writing is just that: it will pass but nothing more. A *competent* detective is not a super-sleuth.

Now for a meaning of *competent* entirely different from the one we have been considering till now. *Only the Vice-Chancellor is competent to order an inquiry into the matter./The Deputy Commissioner is competent to assess land-tax.*

In these cases, the meaning is: 'has the required authority or power under the law'. In other cases, the authority or power may be derived from a rule/regulation of the body/society/organization in question. The secretary (of a club) is *competent* to issue notices to defaulting members about their dues.

It will now be seen that, in the citation we began with, the word required is *competent*. 'The Dharm Sansad is the only body *competent* to decide....'

'cards' and 'covers'

Six cards and three covers, please, I heard a gentleman say the other day at the Sadashivnagar post office. The clerk had no difficulty in understanding the request and duly handed the gentleman the required articles.

I don't know about north India but all over the south, the terms *card* and *cover* are freely used. But what we call a *card* is a *postcard* (in USA a *postal card*). I remember an uncle of mine—a gentleman educated in the old days—frequently writing *Received your p.c. of the 15th.... P.c.* was the abbreviation for 'postcard'.

Card as such is understood in English speaking countries as a *greeting card*, a *birthday card*, an *anniversary card*, etc. *I sent her a card on her birthday. She hasn't yet got it.* The picture postcards that you see at a tourist spot are also cards. *She is now holidaying in Paris and has sent us some lovely cards.*

These senses apart, a *card* can be *a business card, a visiting card,* (in America *a calling card*) or *a credit card.* Only with us it is also a *postcard.*

If the use of *cover* is on the decline, it is not because we have discovered that it is not correct English but because it now costs Rs 5. *Cover* in Standard English is anything which 'covers': *Please put a cover over the bowl;* it can refer to the covers of a book, magazine: *Will Vajpayee make it to the cover of Time or Newsweek?* It can be part of the expression: *a dust cover* (which you find on some books—a (usually) coloured, removable flap; in British English *a dust jacket*).

And then there are transferred or figurative senses as in: *an insurance cover, to take cover* (to hide in some safe place), *to break cover* (to come out of hiding).

The postal 'cover' is *envelope.*

'car of John'?
(possessive)

A grammar book widely in use in schools has this: *This is the dog of the boy. The dog of Peter is called Spot. The boy is holding the chain of the dog.* The author goes on to say: 'It is better to write these sentences as: *This is the boy's dog. Peter's dog is called Spot. The boy is holding the dog's chain'.*

It is not that the second set of sentences are better. They are the only way to express the ideas in question. The first set of sentences are impossible. *The dog of Peter* is simply ungrammatical.

Here is what Quirk et al. (*A Grammar of Contemporary English*) have to say on the question: 'Although we may say either *the youngest children's toys* or *the toys of the youngest children*, the two forms of the genitive are not in free variation. We cannot say, for example, *the roof's cost* or *the hat of John'.* (Quirk et al. put an asterisk on these phrases to show that they are 'unacceptable'.

The point is not whether an '*of-* phrase' cannot be used as an equivalent of the 'apostrophe and *-s*' construction. It can be, with certain restrictions.

The point is whether phrases like: *the dog of Peter / the hat of John* are possible. They are not.

Very few grammar books discuss this question at length; one of the most authoritative which does discuss this question at great length is *A Handbook of English Grammar* (R.W. Zandvoort).

As Zandvoort points out: '*John's father*, but the *father of John and Mary*;... *Shakespeare's plays*, but, on a title page, "*The Works of Shakespeare*".' (p. 113).

Zandvoort comments: 'With proper names, the genitive [apostrophe and *-s* construction] is commoner than the *of-* adjunct, the latter being chiefly used for the sake of balance.'

There is no need to go further into this question of the choice between the '*of-* adjunct' (as Zandvoort calls it) and the 'genitive' (apostrophe and *-s* form). The interested reader can profitably study the elaborate and scholarly discussion in Zandvoort (sections 300–17).

For present purposes, it is enough to note that with personal proper nouns (*John, Mary, Roopa*, etc.) where the meaning is 'possession' or 'belonging', the construction is just with an apostrophe and *-s*. It is *John's car* and not *the car of John, Mary's frock*, not *the frock of Mary*. Another way of saying these things would be by the use of *have, belong. Neethi has a cat = Neethi's cat; the book belongs to Pranav = Pranav's book.*

It is important to note that what is ruled out as unacceptable is the construction with a personal proper name. '*The handbags of the ladies*' is fine. There is no personal proper name here. But if we substitute *Mary* for *the ladies* we get the odd-sounding: *the handbag of Mary*. Cf also: *the saree of Sita*.

Grammar books, especially the ones intended for young learners, cannot be overburdened with too many rules and fine distinctions. That would be self-defeating. The way out is to be careful in the data presented: the example sentences and the sentences appearing in the exercises. This will enable the student to have an intuitive grasp of what is acceptable and what is not. If he does not encounter *the hat of John* but sees only *John's hat*, he is unlikely to produce *the shirt of John*. He will say *John's shirt*. The cases where a genitive construction can alternate with an *of-* phrase (the '*of-* adjunct') need not be specifically discussed. Permissible examples should be introduced gradually (in higher classes). Perhaps at the degree level, the stylistic and other considerations involved may be discussed.

cause/reason

Dictionaries bring in *cause* in their definition of *reason* and *reason* in their definition of *cause*; yet, the two are not synonymous. In the sentence: *The cause of the accident is being investigated,* we cannot use *reason*. And in the context: *Why is she angry?—I don't know,* we understand the second sentence to mean: *I don't know the reason.* It cannot be: *I don't know the cause.*

And yet there are cases where *cause/reason* seem to be interchangeable. *What is the cause/reason for the downturn in the economy? / What is causing the delay? What is the reason for the delay?*

Let us begin with cases where only *reason* would be used. *He has good reason to be satisfied. / Why is she upset? I don't know (the reason). The reason he withdrew from the contest is....* These are cases where events/actions are viewed or analysed in terms of personal motives, intentions, feelings or actions of other persons. In these cases, even when we are talking about something which has caused the result, we speak of reasons, not causes.

Now for some cases where only *cause* is in order. *The moon's gravity causes high tide. Exposure to heavy doses of radiation causes leukaemia* (= blood cancer). In these cases, an event B is analysed in terms of another event A; B because of A. We establish a causal relationship between A and B.

If we stopped just at this point, it would appear that when personal interactions are involved, we use *reason;* in other cases (i.e., when there are no persons involved) we use *cause*. This is true to some extent but not entirely so. The facts are more complex. In particular, the situations where *reason* is used are more complex.

Why do we see lightning first and then hear thunder? / Why does water boil when heated? There are no motives, intentions or personal interactions here. And yet in the answer to these questions, *reason* would be used. *The reason we see lightning first is light travels faster than sound. / The reason that water boils is the air dissolved in water gets heated.* (As a matter of fact, the answers in these cases may begin with *because*. But *reason* is not ruled out.)

Notice now that in all these cases we are trying to 'explain' an event in terms of internal occurrences/changes or some external factors.

Explanation is different from assigning a *cause* (although finding a *cause* is a great step towards explanation and quite often nothing more can be done). One may observe that heat melts ice and say *Heat causes ice to melt*. But why? How does it happen? An answer to this question would be in terms of *reasons*.

In the light of the above discussion consider now this sentence (an authentic one)...*its* [Down's Syndrome, a disease] *reasons are not known....* Should we use *cause* or *reason* here?

Of course, *cause*. It is not known what *causes* Down's Syndrome. That is what the writer wants to say. If there had been a question: 'Why does a child with Down's syndrome perform poorly at school?' The answer could be: *The reason is: the disease affects brain cells*. Notice how the explanation of a result (its features) is in terms of *reasons*. But the result itself (e.g., damaged or impaired brain cells, which is one aspect of Down's syndrome) would be traced to some *cause*. Perhaps an extra copy of chromosome 21 *causes* Down's Syndrome.

Cause and 'effect' are relative terms. A may be the *cause* of B. But A itself may be the result of X. So when we try to analyse A and explain how it brings about B, we have to give *reasons*.

Finally when the *cause* also explains the result, *cause* and *result* can be interchanged. *What is the cause of the delay in implementing the airport project? / What is the reason for the delay?* 'The government has not yet cleared the project'.

To sum up: In personal situations even when we are looking for *causes* we speak of *reasons*; in all cases where a result is being analysed or explained, we use the word *reason*. And then there are some cases where the *cause* also explains the result. In such cases, *cause/reason* are interchangeable.

cleft and pseudo-cleft

What we have done in Indian English is to give the word concern....

Should the infinitive here be the 'bare infinitive' (*give*) or the '*to-*infinitive' (*to- give*)? (The structure exemplified by the sentence is what is called a *pseudo-cleft* sentence. It is called pseudo-cleft because we also have *cleft* sentences.)

Given the sentence, *John declined the invitation*, we can give prominence to *John* by reframing the sentence in this way: *It was John who declined the invitation*. This sort of highlighting or focusing is possible with elements other than the subject. We can, for example, highlight the object. *It's Mary that John is going to marry* (from *John is going to marry Mary*). Focusing helps clarify matters. *It was John (not Henry) who declined the invitation*. Sentences of this type are cleft sentences. They begin with the word *it*.

With cleft sentences, it is not possible to highlight (or focus) the verb. Given: *John tore up the letter,* we would have to say: *It was to tear up the letter that John did.* But with a *pseudo-cleft* structure we can properly highlight the verb. *What John did was to tear up the letter.*

In this structure (i.e., the *pseudo-cleft*), the main verb appears in the second part of the sentence. It can be a *to-* infinitive or a 'bare' infinitive. Perhaps the *to-*infinitive is more frequent. *What you have done is (to) spoil the show.*

In terms of the information content of the sentences (*cleft, pseudo-cleft*) notice an important difference. In *It was John who declined the invitation,* the structure beginning with *who* presents 'old' information, i.e., information already known to the hearer. He knows that somebody has declined the invitation but not who. The new information is given in the first part of the sentence: it was John.

In a *pseudo-cleft* sentence, the sequence is reversed. The old (or 'given') information is in the first part of the sentence; the second part of the sentence gives the 'new' information. *What John did was to decline the invitation.*

cliche

A cliche is a well-worn expression. It has been so often used as to have lost whatever point or freshness it once had. It is now a dead counter popping up (if one is not careful) at the appropriate triggers.

A housebreak in the neighbourhood? *Ah, crime is raising its ugly head.* / More buses to handle the peak hour traffic? *That's the crying need of the hour.* / Fencing the border to stop illegal immigration? *More easily said than done.* / A South Asian free trade zone? *A consummation devoutly to be wished for.*

The italicized expressions are all cliches. They run into thousands. Among these are:

1. Similes such as *stupid as a mule, sly as a fox, vain as a peacock, hungry as a wolf, dead as the dodo, sick as a parrot, timid as a hare, busy as the bee. In case you think these are confined to names of animals, have a look at these: safe as houses, clear as a bell, green as grass, hot as hell, pure as the driven snow, pretty as a picture, spread like wildfire, tough as nails.*

2. Metaphors such as *leave no stone unturned, explore every avenue, a tower of strength, wheels within wheels, calm before the storm, to let the grass grow under one's feet, to pour oil on (or fish in) troubled waters, to sit on the*

fence, to play second fiddle, to feather one's nest, a bee in one's bonnet, a bolt from the blue, (at the) crack of dawn.

3. Quotations such as *the cup that cheers but not inebriates, more sinned against than sinning, born to blush unseen, sadder but wiser.*

4. Adjective + noun combinations such as *tender mercies, high dudgeon, burning issue, blissful ignorance, crass stupidity, acute crisis, acid test, grave emergency, integral part, filthy lucre.*

5. Miscellaneous phrases such as *ways and means, in this day and age, at this point of time, climate of opinion, time frame, (not for) love or money, add insult to injury, well but not wisely, the powers that be, the high and mighty.*

6. Discourse phrases such as *be that as it may, last but not least, to make a long story short, without rhyme or reason, not to put too fine a point on it, to declare without fear of contradiction, suffice it to say, in the last analysis.* See also SIAMESE TWINS, OMISSIBLE PHRASES.

This should give a fair idea of what cliches look like. The reader can doubtless supply many more examples himself.

Understandably, cliches have been condemned. The writer who indulges in cliches is not thinking for himself. If he did, he would ask himself why it is always *under active consideration.* Can there be *a passive consideration?* Why not say: *The matter is under consideration? Acute pain* is understandable; there can be *mild pain.* But an *acute crisis?* If it is always an *integral part,* what about a mere *part?* Is it a *spare part* (as Gowers asked)?

It is not only the adjective + noun cliche which is seen to be mechanically misused; the other types of cliches, too, are misused. Is it only the bee that is busy? What about the ant? Why always *at this point of time* and not just *now?* For the reader, the encounter with these familiar ghosts is not exhilarating; it is boring.

The only context where it is fun to encounter cliches is in a piece of humorous writing, as in P.G. Wodehouse, where they are deftly used, often with a slight twist, or just hinted at. You can also make fun of the use of cliches. It can be quite entertaining. See, for example, Art Buchwald, *The cliche expert testifies on love.*

But there are many expressions which, no matter how frequently they are used, cannot be condemned as cliches. They are like the words of the language; they are the counters of thought. *Swan song* and *Achilles' heel* (both condemned by Orwell and others) cannot be replaced by any other expressions as compact and meaningful. The stories behind such expressions have imparted them a precise, specific meaning. Not to use them would force one into a totally unnecessary, long-winded explanation. To this group belong (among others) *crocodile tears, cat's paw, dog's life, lion's share, sour grapes, dog in the manger, as the crow flies, the last straw* (based on animal fables); *Draconian measures/laws, the sword of Democles, Barmecide's feast, pyrrhic victory, a Herculean task,* and a host of other expressions based on classical mythology and legends (see ALLUSIONS).

Besides these two groups of expressions, there are other phrases which are also irreplaceable: eponyms like *Hobson's choice;* quotations like *Knowledge is power* and phrases like *the thin end of the wedge.* These too embody a concept much like the words of a language. They are not just a way of looking at things (like the similes and metaphors referred to earlier).

The banality of cliches is not recognized in IE. On the other hand, it is considered a mark of one's mastery over the language to use them. *How is Raju? Fit as a fiddle. And Deepti? In the pink of health and peak of perfection. What about your brother? The less said about him the better.*

I am sure, many will vouch to having heard these (and similar) expressions from persons known to them. Besides these well-worn phrases from standard English, we have created our own stock of IE cliches: *fortunately or unfortunately; all in all (Mr Raman is all in all in that organization; he is whole and sole); have a heart-to-heart talk* (a frank, open discussion, usually while negotiating a dowry deal before marriage); *safe and sound* (when you arrive at a place, the first thing you do is to write home '*a safe and sound arrival*' letter); *as luck would have it; rough and ready, rough and tough (He is a rough and tough fellow); get tensed (Why you getting tensed Sir? What has happened?)* (no inversion; it is how they speak); *straight and simple (Ramu is a straight and simple man); do one thing (Do one thing, Sir. You come tomorrow*—the usual reply one gets when one goes to a government office seeking some information or to get some work done); *cheap and best; not your father's property (Shut up. This is a public bus, not your father's property).*

I will close this piece with a few citations from Indian newspapers and magazines: *The* callous indifference *and* criminal neglect *of public safety on the part of those running the so-called public utilities (Deccan Herald,* 27 August 2003), *Today society is crying hoarse berating* the powers that be *for failing to protect his life (The Hindu,* 13 January 2004). *Now the Left faces an acid test of keeping economic growth from becoming demonical (Statesman,* 16 July 2004)*...unable to come to grips with the stark reality of what went wrong.... (Hindustan Times,* 3 July 2004). *The tragedy of Indian aviation lies*

in *the fact that we are having the worst of all options* at this point of time
(*Hindustan Times*, 14 January 2004).

Note also these expressions are fast developing into cliches. *Personal
integrity, it seems, has become an* endangered species (*San Jose Mercury News*,
13 November 2003). *His speech was full of words of wisdom for the youth
with anecdotes from his personal life experiences for a* road map *to success in
the real world* (*India Tribune*, 3 July 2004).

Cliches can also be regional. An observer has noted: 'People do not
die in Pakistan newspapers. "They *breath their last*." And sometimes if it
is early in the morning "*they breath their last in the wee hours*"' (italics added).

climax

'A figure in which a number of propositions or ideas are set forth so as
to form a series in which each rises above the preceding in force or
effectiveness of expression' (OED). The point is well illustrated by a 1553
citation given by Burchfield (1998): *Of sloth cometh pleasure, of pleasure
cometh spending, of spending cometh whoring, of whoring cometh lack, of
lack cometh theft, of theft cometh hanging, and here an end of the world.*

During World War II, when Hitler's armies were poised to cross the
English Channel, Churchill made a memorable speech stirring his people
to fight the invader. Here is a passage from that speech: '*We shall fight on
the beaches, we shall fight on the landing grounds, we shall fight in the fields and
in the streets, we shall fight in the hills. We shall never surrender.*' Note how the
passage rises in a crescendo to the final, emphatic, defiant assertion. See
FIGURES OF INDIRECTION.

Outside of rhetoric, climax refers to 'the most intense, exciting, or
important point of something, a culmination or apex' (NODE). Thus
we can speak of the climax of a speech, an event, etc.

'coffee is liked by me'?
(*passive*)

A retired English teacher from Rajasthan has written a long letter seeking
clarification on the use of the passive voice. He wants to know whether
sentences like these can be passivized: (1) *I take milk in my breakfast.* (2)
You eat eggs. (3) *I have a cow.* (4) *You have some bats, balls, etc.* (5) *The elephant
has a trunk*...(there are many more, fifty in all).

Of course none of the sentences cited can appear in the passive. *A
cow is had by me./Some bats and balls are had by you./A trunk is had by the*

elephant are simply impossible. More generally a sentence with *have* as the main verb rarely admits the passive. A standard exception is *A good time was had by all*. Try passivizing: *I have a bad toothache*. The passive is worse than the toothache.

As for the first sentence, *Milk is taken by me in my breakfast* is simply ridiculous. Another point: you generally take *medicine* (in the sense of *take* required here). (See TAKE CARE).

The English teacher's problems arise because he firmly believes (what he must have been taught at school) that, if a sentence has a subject and an object, it can be turned into the passive. In the passive, the object becomes the subject (*He killed the tiger—The tiger was killed by him*). So, if there is an object, it should be possible to make it the subject by 'passivizing' the sentence.

But it is not so. The object can become the subject only when there is some justification for doing so. If we are talking about Newton we would say (among other things) that *Newton formulated the law of gravity*. But if we are talking about gravity, we would say: *The law of gravity was formulated by Newton*.

A sentence is not merely a sequence of words ('making complete sense'); it has an information content distributed in a certain way. Generally, the subject is what is 'given' or 'known'. In our example above, 'Newton' is what is given. Perhaps the announcement said: *A talk on Newton*. The predicate contains 'new' information.

A moment's reflection will show that this is as it should be. The sentence, as a unit of discourse, is concerned with the organization of information. The most sensible way to organize information is: to begin with what is known (the 'given') and to proceed to what is not known (the 'new'). In *Chandrashekar propounded the theory of black holes*, what is given is *Chandrashekar*. That is the topic of the lecture. What is presented as new is: *he propounded the theory of black holes*. 'Black holes' have been around for quite some time. If someone should give a talk on them, he might well say: *Black holes were first posited by the Indian astrophysicist Chandrashekar*. In cases of this type, the point of interest (or the starting point) can be either the subject or the object.

As against these, there are cases where the point of interest can only be the subject. These are cases where we talk about, for example, a person, his tastes, attitudes, and preferences. *I get up at 5 in the morning. I have a cup of coffee. Then I go on a brisk walk for about forty-five minutes. I then have my breakfast....* These sentences must remain in the active. They cannot be turned into the passive.

This does not mean that, say, *coffee* can never be the subject of a sentence. All that is being said is that, in a sentence like: *I have coffee in the morning, coffee* has to stay where it is. We cannot form a new sentence with *coffee* as subject. But there can be a talk on *coffee. Coffee is grown in parts of Karnataka....* But even in this discourse it will be impossible to say; *Coffee is liked by me.* It is not one of the facts of *coffee* worth mentioning that it is liked by me. I can only say, parenthetically, as it were, *Well, you know, I like coffee.*

Let's examine this a little further.

Snuff was introduced in Europe in the eighteenth century. Soon it became a rage. It was patronized by the high and mighty. Napoleon was particularly fond of it. Even at Waterloo, it is reported, the Emperor was observed opening his silver snuff box and taking a pinch of the invigorating stuff. (He had lost the battle by then.)

Such being the case, if there is an occasion to talk on (or write about) snuff, a sentence like: *Snuff was patronized even by Napoleon* is very likely to occur in the discourse. Because it is a point about snuff that even a great man like Napoleon was fond of it. But it is not a point about coffee that I like it. Who am I?

This is the reason why sentences about a person's individual tastes and preferences cannot generally be turned into passive. *I watch TV in the evenings. I admire Pierce Brosnan. I like Brazilian coffee...*must all remain in the active form only. But suppose it is a fact that Madonna admires Brosnon, then there is nothing wrong (grammatically) about *Brosnan is admired by Madonna.*

So, in teaching the passive, this point should be made clear. The object (of the active sentence) can become the subject of a passive sentence only when there is some significance attached to putting the original subject in the predicate position. With verbs like *write, discuss, kill, discover...*, which are 'actional' in a very basic sense, the passive is possible as there is always some significance attached to putting the original subject in the predicate position. *Amundsen discovered the magnetic South Pole.* Here 'discovering the South Pole' is the 'new' information: *The magnetic South Pole was discovered by Amundsen.* Here 'Amundsen' is the new information. It is a piece of relevant, significant information about the South Pole. In this case, either of the noun phrases can be presented as 'new' information. And this is so with sentences containing the other verbs mentioned above. In fact, it is in cases of this type that the usual active–passive interchange occurs.

With verbs expressing personal tastes, preferences, attitudes, etc. while the object can be presented as 'new information' about the subject (*I like coffee*), the subject cannot be presented as 'new information' about the object—except in cases like the ones discussed earlier (Napoleon—snuff; Madonna—Pierce Brosnan). That is why sentences like *I love you, I hate you, I prefer coffee to tea*...are in the active form only.

It is important to understand that it is not that these verbs don't ever appear in the passive; they can't appear in the passive when the subject is I, you,...or any common/proper noun like man, boy, girl, Joseph or Sridhar. But in: *Diana loved Dodi*, the passive *Dodi was loved by Diana* is quite natural. Both the nouns can appear as significant, new information about each other.

Finally consider the verb *have*. A sentence with *have* cannot appear in the passive. Reason? The verb denotes not an 'action' but a 'state' (possession). Hence *the elephant has a trunk* (my Rajasthan reader's example) has no passive. Other verbs which describe a state (and not an action) like: *resemble, marry, lack* (= be deficient in), and a few others, also don't passivize.

We have now distinguished three classes of transitive verbs. The basically 'actional' verbs like *write, explore, discover, destroy*...where there is some action 'which passes over from the subject to the object' readily admit a passive; verbs of personal taste and preference admit a passive only when the subject is of some consequence, significant enough to be presented as 'new information' about the object; transitive verbs, which express a state or condition (e.g., *have, resemble*, etc.) do not passivize.

collocations

This is the *plain* truth. It is *utter* nonsense. I am *dead* certain. You are *hopelessly* mistaken.

The adjectives in the above sentences are what naturally go with the nouns after them; *utter truth* or *plain nonsense* would sound strange (especially *utter truth*). *Plain truth* is matched by *damned lie*. *Great brilliance* can be described as *sheer brilliance*. We can also say, surprisingly, *sheer nonsense*. But not *sheer truth*.

Both wind and rain are everyday natural phenomena. To describe an excess of these, English has *strong wind, heavy rain*. You don't say *heavy wind, strong rain*.

Good English is more than correct, grammatical English. One of the things that marks good English is what I have been illustrating till now: the choice of the right word; more specifically, in the present case, a knowledge of the right collocation, i.e., what goes with what.

You *slip on* a dressing gown, a jacket, a robe, shoes; but you *slip into* something more comfortable. You *take* a pill, medicine but you *have* coffee, tea. You *catch* a cold, a cough, flu, measles, mumps, a whooping cough; but you *develop* an allergy, arthritis, heart/liver trouble, high blood pressure; you *go down* with appendicitis, bronchitis, diarrhoea; you *contract* AIDS, conjunctivitis, pneumonia; and finally you *suffer* a heart attack, a stroke. You may *be on/be given* antibiotics, drugs, medication. You may *undergo* a surgery, a transplant; you may *have/be given* acupuncture, an anesthetic, a blood transfusion.

These are cases of verb + noun collocations taken from one 'field': illness. To continue with some more common examples (from another field): a meeting may be *called, convened*. It may be *adjourned* for want of quorum. In the case of a body like parliament, it may also be *prorogued* (bring a session of parliament to end without dissolving it). A House— Assembly, Parliament—may also be *dissolved*. Fresh elections will have to be held.

'Collocation' may be defined in a broad way or in a narrow way. In a broad definition, every case of 'fixed' (or generally occurring) expression would be a collocation—with the exception of idioms, e.g., *kick the bucket, make both ends meet*...and phrasal verbs with an idiomatic meaning, e.g., *put up with somebody*. It would include prepositional groups like *agree with* (a person), *differ from* (somebody), etc. This is how the *Oxford Dictionary of Collocations* defines the term. In a narrow definition, only lexical items which go together (*adjourn a meeting, execute a contract, terminate an agreement*...) would be collocations. The narrow definition takes the view that collocation is purely a matter of lexis; items like phrasal verbs and expressions with 'fixed' prepositions belong to syntax.

A good knowledge of collocations makes for English as it is used by the native speaker. It achieves clarity and precision resulting in economic and effective communication. *He was waylaid by two masked men and looted* leaves us in no doubt as to what happened. But it is not proper English.

As there were not enough members present, the Chairman said they would meet again later and left is not proper English either.

Collocations should be distinguished from cliches. The point is best understood by comparing a collocation like *heavy drinker* with a cliche like *acid test*. *Acid test,* when first coined, had a point. Gold can be identified and distinguished from all other materials by an acid test. So *acid test* became a new, striking metaphor. But overuse has deadened the metaphor. It is now a cliche.

In *heavy drinker* there is no original insight. It just happens that *heavy* is being used with drinker. It is not any one man's choice: it does not provide any particular view of drinking which can be questioned, as we can, for example, with another cliche *busy as a bee*. Why not busy as an ant? A similar lack of explanation, apart from the fact of co-occurrence, is found with a *proper rascal, a thorough scoundrel* (both collocations).

Some collocations can be explained, e.g., *illegal immigrant, illicit liquor*. (For more on this and some other collocations, see my *Current English*.) But in general, a collocation is what it is; no explanation can be given. It embodies no original insight which can be deadened by use.

'concerned clerk'

This famous Indianism exemplifies a strong tendency in IE to use as a noun modifier any participle, including those which can only occur in the predicate. *The clerk who is concerned*...can be shortened in standard English to *the clerk concerned*. In IE it can undergo a further transformation and end up as *the concerned clerk*.

It follows that *the concerned clerk* is not the only such expression. I have noted in my *Current English* (OUP, 2001) another such phrase, *the dealing clerk*. I have now come across an even more astonishing (and amusing) expression. The arrest and subsequent release of an industrialist in Hyderabad made big news. The sub-inspector who arrested the industrialist was placed under suspension *'for not following the laid-down procedure'* (as reported in *New Indian Express*, 29 October 2002). My most recent collection is: *On the leaving day she said she would come back in October.* See also 'AGOG VILLAGERS'.

'conjugal bliss'

'When a man sees a woman in a deserted field, the first instinct to surface is the basic desire for conjugal bliss'. (The District Magistrate of Muzaffarpur as reported in a recent book on management.)

Conjugal bliss is the joy and happiness associated with the holy state of matrimony (though some may feel that this is a contradiction in terms). Mere sexual desire cannot be equated with *conjugal bliss*. Perhaps the DM felt that the appropriate terms in this context ('lust', 'sexual desire') were too crude. In any case, *conjugal bliss* is quite inappropriate in this context.

consider/regard

These two words as verbs have some meanings which are quite distinct from each other; e.g., you can say: *I have considered your proposal*. But not *I have regarded your proposal*. And '*she regarded him* (= looked at him) closely'. Not *She considered him closely.*

But in the sense of 'viewing something/somebody as something' the two are near synonyms. Dictionaries, ALD and LDCE, for example, have this as a common meaning under *consider* and *regard*. But if you examine the illustrative sentences given, you will find that there are cases where only the one or the other can be used. *We consider that you are not to blame./Do you consider it wise to interfere?* In these cases we cannot have *regard*. *He will be considered a weak leader*. Here we can have *regard*. *He will be regarded as a weak leader.* What is the explanation?

Where 'view as...' has the meaning of 'perception' *consider* and *regard* are interchangeable. Actually in such cases you can replace *regard*, *consider* with *look upon*. *He will be looked upon as a weak leader.*

But where 'view as' is interpretable as 'be of the opinion', only *consider* can be used, not *regard*: *We consider* (= are of the opinion) *that you are not to blame./Do you consider it wise to interfere?* (Are you of the opinion that it is wise to interfere?)

This apart, there is a point of syntax to be noted. Where *regard* and *consider* are interchangeable, *consider* is generally found without *as*. (But see below.) *I consider him a genius. Regard* is always found with *as. I regard him as a genius.*

In passive constructions, *consider* is found with *as: a painting previously considered as worthless.* (All examples from the ALD, 1989.)

consign a person?

Has Veerappan been consigned to Sri Lanka with all honours? (*The Times of India*, 17 November 2000)

Consign (v) in commercial usage is 'to transmit, send goods specifically addressed, to be delivered to a person or trading company'. In this sense what is sent is a *consignment*. The person sending is a *consignor* and the person receiving the goods is a *consignee*.

In the non-commercial sense, *consign* means 'to hand over, commit or deliver to a person's care': *consign a child to its uncle's care/consign one's soul to God.*

Figuratively we have such uses as *consigned to the flames.* A variant of this sense is one with strong negative associations: *consign to the dustbin* (a government report), *consign to oblivion, consigned to years of misery.*

But in a purely neutral sense of sending something to somebody or, somewhere, only goods can be *consigned*. You cannot *consign* a person.

'content man'

He is a self-proclaimed content man. But is the 43-year-old Sunil Shetty really content? (Biz India, September 2003)

Content is a predicate adjective, i.e., it can appear in the predicate after a form of BE. *He is quite content with his present position.* Like most adjectives it can also qualify a noun. But in this function, the form is *contented. He is a contented man.* So the first sentence should read: *he is a self-proclaimed contented man.*

cost/price

An advertisement for the [Hyundai] Accent says: *Ultimate luxury at an unbelievable cost (The Times of India,* 24 September 2001). *Cost?* Or is it *price?*

The distinction between *cost* and *price* is a subtle one. Leaving out the figurative uses, let's see how the terms are used in connection with things/objects.

In terms of what one has to pay to get an object, the word is *cost.* Thus a manufacturer may say: *It will cost us Rs ten million to produce this model.* A person who has bought something may say: *It cost quite a bit; it put me back by several thousands./That's a fine vase. Oh, yes. It cost me quite a bit.*

Anything offered for sale comes with a price. There is a price tag on everything, as they say. Looking at a new sound system you may ask: *What's the price of this?* (Not *What's the cost of this?*) But for the manufacturer to produce it, it would have *cost* him Rs X. And once you have bought the sound system, you may say, to an admiring (or envious) neighbour: *Oh, it cost me quite a bit.*

To summarize: Things are offered for sale at a *price*; for the manufacturer (or the buyer) they *cost* Rs X.

To go back to the Hyundai advertisement. Clearly it should read: *Ultimate luxury at an unbelievable price.*

Now for the figurative usages: *You will have to pay a heavy price for this* means: 'You will have to suffer a lot, experience severe setbacks', etc. And not in terms of money. Similarly, a costly (mis)adventure has no reference to money, or at least no primary reference to money. *Cross-border terrorism will prove a costly misadventure for General Musharraf.*

These distinctions apart, *cost* has a wider range of uses than *price: the cost of living*, for example.

costly/expensive

'Expensive' is usually used in connection with consumer goods and services. In these cases there is invariably a choice. *The Sony flat TV is more expensive than many other brands. / The LG microwave is more expensive than a Kenstar with similar features. / A Parker ball pen is more expensive than....*

But in cases where absolute costs are involved—and it is not a question of choosing between alternatives goods/services—the word is costly. *Repairing this leaking roof will be quite costly. / Putting up an additional bathroom will cost you a lot of money.* But: *A granite flooring is very expensive.*

This apart, *costly* is often found in figurative expressions (*a costly mistake/ a costly misadventure*). *Expensive* is not used in these cases.

d

dangerous/serious

Decades ago G.K. Chettur in his (then) much used book, *College Composition*, deplored the use of *dangerous* in the sense of *dangerously ill*. *I hear so-and-so is dangerous. / Both my father and uncle have been dangerous for more than a week.* A possible explanation for this use of *dangerous* may be found in the phrase 'out of danger'. Thus a doctor may announce (of an accident victim): 'Thank God, he is out of danger.' But in point of fact, dangerous does not mean 'dangerously ill'. It can only mean 'likely to cause great harm—to person, property, etc.' *It is dangerous to swim in this river. / Cigarette smoking is dangerous to health.*

A parallel (inadmissible) usage is found with the word *serious*. I quote:...*the injured, four of them serious, have been identified....* What the writer (in this case a reporter) means is that four of the injured were in a serious (or 'dangerous') condition. But *serious* can have this meaning only when used attributively with an appropriate noun: *a serious illness/situation.*

'Appropriate' because, with other nouns, the meaning may be different: *a serious person* (= solemn and thoughtful); *a serious essay on the pollution problem* (intended to provoke thought); *a serious mistake* (having serious consequences), etc. In any case, used predicatively (i.e., after a form of the verb BE), the meaning can only be: the speaker is not joking but means business and expects you to consider what is being said as important and act accordingly. *Look here. I'm quite serious about it./Be serious. This is important.* It cannot mean that someone is critically ill.

In informal conversation where people freely mix English with Kannada—or the other way around—*serious* is used in the sense of *dangerously ill* even by those who don't use it in that sense when they are speaking English.

'deplore the PM'

'We deplore the Prime Minister for not facing Parliament—', said a prominent Congress politician, as reported in the papers.

There must be some mistake in reporting here. You cannot deplore a man. You can deplore a situation. You can deplore the PM's refusal to allow a debate (under Rule 184) but you cannot deplore the PM.

'did you know/do you know?'

These two sentences are not synonymous. *Do you know* merely asks a question. *Did you know* suggests a certain degree of surprise on the part of the speaker. He has come to know of something which has surprised him (he didn't expect it to be like that) and he is now passing on that information to his friend. The speaker expects the listener to be equally surprised. *Did you know that a tortoise takes just one breath or two per minute?* (We normally take 12–16 breaths per minute.)

'different size shirts'

The question of what expressions can modify a noun is an interesting, tricky one. Adjectives, by definition, modify nouns. There is no problem with them. *A black shirt, a white cap, a brown belt*...the list can be endless. And not just single adjectives. More than one adjective can occur, though here a question of order arises. *A tall, dark, young man* but not: *a young, dark, tall man*. There may be some question as to whether this should be considered 'ungrammatical'. But it is certainly not the favoured (or usual) order of these adjectives.

And then there is the case of nouns acting as adjectives, that is, modifying another noun: *a stationmaster, a railway engineer, a customs officer, a silver coin, an iron bar.*

Possessives, too, by definition, can precede a noun: *Neethi's admirers.* And this possessive can even be marked on a phrase: *The Queen of England's crown.* Here we have what is called 'the group genitive'. Some other examples: *The Museum of Modern Art's new Director, / The Director of the Museum's books* (= books of the Director of the Museum). The phrase in this construction can be quite long. An American grammarian has asserted that he finds nothing odd about: *the man who came yesterday's hat.* Some might feel that this is going too far. *Star News* the other day, went even further when it spoke of *Union Minister of State for Home's brother-in-law* (9 o'clock evening news, 30 October 2001).

At this point one may note the tendency of English to permit whole clauses and sentences to act as noun modifiers: *a never-to-be forgotten story, / that what-do-you-call-him scoundrel....* But for all this, there are restrictions on what can appear as noun modifiers: *shirts of different sizes, books on different subjects, carpets of different designs.* How does it sound if we made these phrases precede the noun?—*different size shirts, different subjects books, different design carpets.* Quite bad, I think.

It is not just the word *different* that creates a problem here. *A man with a peculiar accent, a child with a charming smile, a story of unbelievable courage and endurance*—in every case the phrases are as they should be: after the noun.

Notice now that the phrases which resist being placed before a noun, i.e., phrases which are uncomfortable in the attributive position, are mostly prepositional phrases. But when you examine a larger range of prepositional phrases, you find that some of them are not bad in the attributive position; actually quite acceptable: *a man with a bad temper—a bad-tempered man; the man with the gold tooth—the gold-toothed man; the man in the red turban—the red-turbaned man.* But *the man with strange ideas—* **the strange ideas man; the leader with the largest following—** *the largest following leader.* In short, the cases where a prepositional phrase can be converted into a phrase in the attributive position are just those where the phrase can be converted into adjectival expressions in *-ed*.

Returning now to *shirts of different sizes,* we see that we can't turn this into: *different sized shirts,* because there is no expression like *different sized/different size.* The same goes for the other expressions like *a child with a charming smile, a man with a peculiar accent*.... But, because there are many cases where a prepositional phrase following a noun can also be used attributively, we tend to think that in every case this is possible. We then produce specimens like *different size shirts*. Additionally, the influence of the mother tongue may be at work here. In our own languages, such constructions are freely possible.

dimensions of a word

Several considerations must be kept in mind while choosing a word. Among these are:

    (a) its lexical properties,

    (b) its usage status,

    (c) its context of use,

    (d) its collocational properties, and

    (e) its field (or subject) restrictions.

Now for some brief explanatory comments:

1. The first thing about the lexical properties of a word is its etymology. You should know whether it is a native English word or a foreign word absorbed into English.

Foreign words far outnumber native words in English today. One should have a general awareness of this for the proper use of words. To illustrate: *go* is a native word; *proceed* is from Latin. In everyday conversation, you would say *Let's go*. Not *Let's proceed*.

Lexical properties also include meanings. The word selected must be such as to express your meaning precisely; not some near synonym, or even some seemingly similar (but different) word: *an emergency meeting* is not *an emergent meeting; an officious person* is not *an official; to infer* is not *to imply; to reject* is not *to refute*.

Note also: There are no synonyms, i.e., no two sets of words which can be interchanged in all contexts.

I should also add (perhaps I should have made it the first point): make sure that the word you want to use *exists* by consulting a good dictionary. *Amputed, expectedly, strengthy, costed, thusly*, are some of the non-existent words sometimes found in Indian English. They are not in Standard English, nor are they used by most educated Indian speakers of English.

2. Usage status indicates restrictions on the use of a word (apart from field or subject restrictions). Usage restrictions may be (a) geographical and (b) registral.

(a) Geographical restrictions

Apart from purely dialectal words which are peculiar to a particular region, many words may be found in one variety of English but not in another. Among native varieties of English, British and American are the most important. There is considerable difference in the vocabulary of these two major varieties of English. To illustrate briefly, the words in brackets in the following are American, for the British English words preceding them:

pavement (sidewalk), petrol (gas), railway (railroad), return ticket (roundtrip ticket), vest (undershirt), chemist (druggist), hoarding (billboard), note (money; bill), sweets (candy), cupboard (closet), dustbin (garbage can), queue (line), public school (private school), post (mail), lorry (truck), level crossing (grade crossing), torch (flash light)

There is a rising tendency in India today to use American words: *face off, stand off, gridlock, downside, flipside,* are among the many words that have come to use in the last decade. By and large American equivalents haven't replaced their British equivalents. In some cases, e.g., *TV*, IE may seem to have adopted American usage. But *telly* (British) was never in use in India. We just seem to have hit upon the same term as the Americans. This is so in quite a few cases. See my CE.

(b) Registral restrictions

'Formal' words are appropriate to a professional, scholarly writing or public speaking in a ceremonial context, characterized in grammar by complete syntactical constructions. The opposite of *formal* is *informal*. In the following illustrative pairs of words, the first one is formal, the second informal or colloquial.

adumbrate—outline, cease—stop, endeavour—try, proceed—go, obtain—get, visualize—foresee, transmit—send, summon—send for, complete—finish, affront—open insult, peruse—read, expedite—hasten, inquire—ask, remark—say, valiant—brave

Formal words are long and of foreign origin (derived ultimately from Greek or Latin roots, usually); colloquial (= informal) words are short, native words.

'Informal' (or colloquial) words are used in contexts less ceremonial or institutionalized than the ones mentioned above, e.g., conversation, personal letters, familiar speech and writing. The language here shows a simpler grammatical structure, a greater use of idioms. It is everyday, ordinary language. The distinction between formal and informal language matches the distinction between dressing for a special occasion and being in everyday clothes.

The words here are usually short and of native stock, i.e., Anglo-Saxon. (For a list of specimen words, see under *formal*, above.) Here is an American political science professor talking to a columnist: *I don't think Bush will do as well as he did four years ago. I think his stock is down a little. I'm not gonna kid you* (*NYT*, 6 February 2004).

(i) Slang

Slang has more than one meaning. The meaning relevant for us is: '...highly informal usage that is outside of conversational or standard usage and consists of both coined words and phrases and of new and extended meanings attached to established terms. Slang develops from the attempt to find fresh and vigorous and colourful, pungent or humorous, expressions, and generally either passes into disuse or comes to have a more formal status' (*Webster*, 1984).

Common words like *mob, bike* were at one time 'slang'; *acid* was slang for a particular drug; also *pot*. Now these words are listed as informal or colloquial in standard dictionaries. There are dictionaries of slang, the pioneering work being Eric Partridge's *Dictionary of Slang and Unconventional English*. As the lifespan of slang is very short, new slang words are constantly being produced, resulting in newer dictionaries of slang or revisions of old ones (like Eric Partridge's).

Since slang is *very* informal, it has no place even in informal writing—until it gets established as a regular word in the language.

(ii) Archaic and/or poetic

These may be words or particular senses of words. They are not in current use; restricted to certain specialized contexts like legal or religious use. Many of them can be found in the poetry of an earlier period. Some examples: *perchance* (perhaps), *ere* (before), *whilom* (at one time), *anon* (soon, shortly), *prithee, pray* (please), *methinks* (it seems to me), *whence* (from what place), *yclept* (called by the name), *alack* (an expression of regret or surprise), *whenas* (when), *albeit* (though), *anent* (concerning; still in use in the Scottish Parliament), *oft* (often), *save* (*except* but, all *save* him), *to wit* (that is to say).

Archaic words are listed in dictionaries mainly because they are found in literary and poetical works of earlier times. But with the tremendous growth of vocabulary in the last few decades, there is less and less room for archaic words in dictionaries. Many of the archaic words listed in the COD (1990) cannot be found in the NODE (1998).

Some archaic words may be found in modern writing used jocularly or in a humorous context. Older users of English in India continue to use some of them as though they are still current. I have received several letters from readers who, mildly disagreeing with something I had written in my column ask: *But prithee* (or *pray*) *dear Professor, how do you explain...? Albeit, save, to wit, whence* are other archaic words encountered in IE.

The terms *poetic/literary* are used of words restricted in their use to these fields. Some of them are now archaic, as this famous little poem shows: *Whenas in silks my Julia goes / Then, then, methinks, how sweetly flows / The liquefaction of her clothes* (Robert Herrick, 1591–1674). But there are also hundreds of words which are not archaic but purely literary: *eve* (evening), *morn* (morning), *visage* (face), *begone* (go away), *darkling* (growing darkness), to mention a few.

Literary words, like archaic words, are not for use in ordinary speech or writing. But they may be found in humorous writing.

3. The context of use refers to the specific context in which a word (or one of its senses) is used. *Bleak* has the meaning '(of a situation or future prospect) not hopeful or encouraging, unlikely to have a favourable outcome' (NODE), e.g., *He paints a bleak picture of a company that has lost its way.* But suppose you say (as a reporter did in a newspaper): *Bleak chances of an earthquake in Karnataka*, you can see how odd, ridiculous it sounds.

4. Collocational properties

Some words go with certain other words, e.g., *illegal immigrant, illicit liquor*; not *illicit immigrant, illegal liquor*. This kind of restriction on 'what goes with what' is a *collocational* restriction. It is the failure to be aware of this that makes many of us say: *I take coffee in the morning.* See COLLOCATIONS.

5. Field (subject) labels

These labels (law, medicine, physics, etc.) indicate the field of knowledge and activity in which the word (or some of its senses) so marked is generally used. Many are strictly restricted to their special areas and have no use in ordinary language: *axon* (anatomy), *thermite* (metallurgy), *alpha particle* (physics). Others have their counterparts in ordinary language: *leprose* (Biology, meaning 'scaly, furry'), *analgesic* (medicine, 'relieving pain'), *codicil* (law, 'an amending or explanatory note'). Still others have passed into general use with their technical meanings 'modified' or 'weakened'. Such are *arithmetic and geometrc progression* (mathematics), *quantum jump* (physics), *dilemma* (logic), *moron* (psychology). The technical sense and the 'weakened' sense are usually listed separately in a good dictionary.

In some cases, the technical terms may be familiar to the general user (the non-specialist), for special reasons. Churchgoers are likely to be familiar with terms like *nave, transept;* soccer fans will know the meaning of *offside* (a technical term in soccer and hockey). A good dictionary will include many technical terms from different fields of knowledge and activity. Selection depends on how the general public is likely to come into contact with the field, activity. (As against *transept* and *offside*, indicated above, no general dictionary will list *bound* and *free* as used in mathematics and logic.

Technical terms are, in general, to be avoided in ordinary language. Where a technical term has an ordinary language equivalent, the latter has to be used. See JARGON.

6. There are some other usage labels which may be briefly noted. *Taboo* (words which are prohibited by social customs and conventions from being used in polite society; chiefly words relating to sexual and excretory functions); *jocular* (words/senses for humorous or playful usage); *derogatory* (uses that are intentionally disparaging); *offensive* (words that cause offence, whether intended or not). On these last two, see POLITICAL CORRECTNESS. A comprehensive dictionary like the OED will also list many words that are *obsolete.* They were in use at one time but now, for long, they have not been in use. They are dead, e.g., the italicized words in these lines of verse: A *mickle* town and tall/ and a *wakeman* on the wall.

Dead words have a way of coming back to life: *balsom* which was not in use for 600 years is now again in use (an aromatic resinous substance used as a base for certain fragrances and medical preparations). This does not mean that you are free to use obsolete words. Leave it to more experienced word-doctors to revive them, if they can.

'doctorate'

A *doctorate* is the highest academic degree. The holder of such a degree is a *Doctor.* In IE *doctorate* is often used to refer to a person with a Ph.D. I have heard several headmasters say: *There are doctorates on my staff.*

Christian priests, even when they hold a doctor's degree (usually in Divinity) are addressed as *Father*. Their rank in the Church hierarchy forms part of their name: *Cardinal Spellman, Bishop Berkley.*

The title *Doctor* (abbreviated to *Dr*) becomes part of the person's name: *Dr Vinay Chandra*. When the title is given, the degree is omitted *Dr Vinay Chandra* (not: *Dr Vinay Chandra, Ph.D.*).

double inversion

How is the inversion in the following to be accounted for? *How credible, do you think, is the report of Israeli and American commandos preparing to guard Pakistani nuclear weapons in the event of...?* (AIR) Here we have two instances of inversion under question: (1) *How credible is the report...*and (2) *Do you think....* The second is almost parenthetical. The first one may be viewed as a question on the statement: *The report is X credible* (where X is a degree adverb which is being questioned). How did the second question arise?

Sentences with subordinate clauses show different patterns of behaviour in respect of questions. In a sentence like: *I know he is very clever,* we can question the main clause: *Do you know (that) he is very clever?* We can question the subordinate clause: *I know how clever he is.* We can question both: *Do you know how clever he is?* But we cannot have *How clever do you know he is?*

With the verb *say* in the main clause: *They say (that) they climbed that peak,* we can have: *Do they say that they climbed that peak?* (question on the main clause). We cannot question just the sub-clause. We cannot have: *They say which peak they climbed.* But we can question both: *Do they say which peak they climbed?* And we can also have: *Which peak do they say they climbed?* As should be clear by now, the possibilities depend on the main clause verb.

Now to go back to the sentence we started with. Assume an underlying structure like *I think the report is X credible.* Questioning the main clause we get *Do you think the report is X credible?* Now questioning the sub-clause we get *How credible do you think is the report?* (Commas separating *do you think* are optional.) Notice that the possibilities are different here (from what we saw earlier). We cannot question the sub-clause alone. Even when both are questioned, word order has to change. We cannot have *Do you think how credible the report is?*

Clearly there is more to be explained here, but I will not go further into the matter.

double passive

The culprits of the Gujarat carnage were never proposed to be caught. This makes sense (or seems to) but is not grammatical.

There are two passive phrases in the sentence: '*were never proposed*', '*to be caught*'. Supposing we remove one of the passives, i.e., turn it into the active. [*The authorities*] *did not propose the culprits to be caught.* You see that *culprits* cannot function as the object of *proposed*. If the sentence has to mean anything we should have: *The authorities did not propose* (or *never proposed*) *that the culprits (should) be caught.*

The point has not received much attention in usage manuals after Fowler. But Fowler (1926) thought (and rightly so) that the double passive (when not permissible) was a monstrosity. His very first example illustrates this: *The point is sought to be evaded.* Remove one of the passives and you get the absurd *(They) sought the point to be evaded.* Was there something like *a-point-to-be-evaded* which they sought?

Fowler goes on to point out that in legal and quasi-legal language, the construction has some justification. But not in literary English.

But even in ordinary English, there are cases where a double passive is fine. *The minister ordered the man to be transferred.* This can be changed to *The man was ordered (by the minister) to be transferred.* This is fine because in *The minister ordered the man*...the noun *man* can function as the object of *ordered.* But the verbs which admit the double passive are so few that it is best to avoid the construction. This structure can get to be hopelessly muddled. *His orders were attempted to be carried out* (R.L. Trask, *Mind the Gaffe*, Penguin, 2001). Surely, the clumsy sentence *Was any action decided to be taken?* can be sensibly rephrased as *Was it intended to take any action?* Or (quite simply) *Was any action taken?*

To go back to the sentence we began with: The sentence is much better this way: *It was never proposed to catch the culprits of the Gujarat carnage.* (Passive only in the main clause).

'do you know swimming?'
(gerund as object)

Do you know swimming? / Do you know driving? These are commonly asked questions among us and everyone knows perfectly well what they mean. But they are not Standard English forms. The correct questions are: *Do you know how to swim? Do you know how to drive?*

And yet it is not as though *swimming* and *driving* cannot be used as nouns.

Swimming is a good exercise. Driving through the mountains is an experience. Why then are the forms *Do you know swimming/driving* ruled out?

Words like *swimming, driving, dancing, reading* refer to the acts indicated by the corresponding verbs. So while we can predicate something (i.e., say something about them, e.g. *Reading is fun/I like reading,* a knowledge about them can only mean 'how to do...' *I know how to read/to dance/to swim.* Cf also: *I went skiing/I know how to ski.*

Faced with sentences like: **I know diving/Driving gives me a thrill,* one may be misled into thinking that these forms in *-ing* (they are called gerunds) can be used as subjects but not as objects. It is not so. They can be used as objects, too, provided the sentence does not mean *how to* but says something about these activities. *I like swimming/dancing/reading* (But not: *I know swimming/dancing,* etc.).

due/by/because

Some care is needed to use these words correctly. As usual, dictionaries define each word in terms of the other, though in actual usage they appear in different contexts. Here is a graduate student writing about the body and certain yogic exercises. '*...helps to gain weight due to stimulating the parasympathetic nervous system, whereas...helps to maintain body weight due to stimulating the sympathetic nervous system.*'

Why does the body gain weight? Because the parasympathetic nervous system is stimulated. So the stimulation is the means by which the body gains weight. Clearly the word needed here is not *due to* but *by;* *...helps to gain body weight by stimulating....* In the second part of the sentence, too, the preposition needed is *by.*

The distinction between *means/agency* and *cause* is a subtle but a real one. *By* indicates the means; agency, the process responsible for something to happen. *By heating water we get steam./By lowering taxes you stimulate the economy./Machines are driven by steam, water power, electricity, etc. Due to* refers to the cause of some result. *Due to the continuous downpour, power lines got disrupted. Due to excess pressure, the boiler burst.* We can also use *because of* here. *Because of the continuous downpour....*

e

economic/economical

The adjective *economic* is used of what concerns the economy of a country—trade, commerce, industry, financial management, etc. or the subject economics: *the economic situation in the country; Economic Advisor to the Government; economic theory*. *Economical* (adjective) means 'being careful in the spending of money and resources: *an economical plan for slum clearance; an economical scheme for providing drinking water*.

There are some contexts where *economy* is used in this sense: *economy class* (in air travel); *economy size* (in toothpaste). What is incorrect is to use *economic* in this sense: *No one thought that learning was so economic but we made it happen*. (From a computer school flier.) This mistaken use is widespread and is found in English-speaking countries also.

elegant variation

A police report may read: *There were 30 cases of robbery; 5 incidents of kidnapping; 15 instances of housebreaking; 80 occurrences of eve-teasing*.

Here we have what has been called 'elegant variation'. Why should robberies be *cases*, kidnapping *incidents*, housebreaking *instances*, and eve-teasing *occurrences*? What is the difference between an *instance* and an *occurrence*? Or between *incidents* and *instances*? If there were some murders also, what would they be called?

Fowler (1926) who was the first to notice this fault of style has some interesting examples which are classics of their kind. *The Bohemian Diet will be the second parliament to elect women deputies, for Sweden already has lady deputies. / Mr John Redmond has just now a path to tread even more thorny than that which Mr Asquith has to walk*. Fowler asks: 'What has Bohemia done that its female deputies should be mere women? Can Mr Asquith really have taught himself to walk without treading?'

The point is that this sort of variation is totally unnecessary and even misleading. In the police report given above, one might begin to wonder whether the choice of of the words (*incident, instance, occurrence*, and *case*) was somehow dependent on the gravity of the crime.

There is a rule of style that words should not be repeated in the same line or at some nearby interval, say, twenty or thirty words. This 'rule', if it is a rule, is a caution against unsightly, awkward repetition. It is no different from saying that you should not repeat a name again in a short span. *Suresh went home from school. Suresh had some snacks and went out again to play*. This is bad as any schoolboy knows. *Suresh* must be replaced by *he*. The rule against repetition is not as simple as this but it is not very different. Certainly it sounds pretty bad to say that *there were thirty cases of robbery; five cases of kidnapping; fifteen cases of housebreaking;*

and eighty cases of eve-teasing. The solution is not to replace *case* by words like *instance and incident*. The solution is to change the structure of the sentence. *Criminal incidents last month: robbery: fifty; kidnapping: five; housebreaking: fifteen; eve-teasing: eighty.*

We have now avoided both monotonous repetition and mindless variation. No general guidance can be given on how to avoid awkward repetition in any given case. There are different strategies. The careful writer will have to work out these for himself. What this means is: Good writing is not something mechanical; it calls for constant thinking.

How ridiculous elegant variation can be is seen in this extraordinary sentence. *Rarely does the 'Little Summer' [in England] linger beyond November but at times its stay has been prolonged until quite late in the year's penultimate month*. The writer must have been mad to think that *the year's penultimate month* is a good substitute for *November*. If he didn't want to repeat *November* he could have said: *Rarely does the 'Little Summer' linger until November but at times it has been known to extend far into that month.*

Here is another stylist perpetrating an atrocity. *They spend a few weeks more in their winter home than in their summer habitat*. Are they humans or animals?

The point I am making till now is: Where there is no change in meaning, either repeat the word or, if you think it sounds awkward, change the structure and omit the word altogether. *Edwards and Dick Gephardt are plausible fly boys; and Bob Graham might have been at one time* (*Time*, 19 May 2003). Sometimes you can get over the problem by using a pronoun or some other means of reference (see *that month* above).

The situation can also be saved by carefully chosen synonyms. *That he was an eccentric seemed beyond doubt; that he had touched a chord among the masses was equally apparent; that he was a potent political force soon became clear* (Tharoor, *Nehru—The Invention of India*, 2003, p. 28).

With proper names repeated reference can be successfully made by using well-known sobriquets, or self-explanatory descriptive phrases. *Today Mother Teresa announced that she is so moved by the plight of the Romanian children she is going to do something about it. The Noble Peace Prize winner will open a mission in Bucharest to care for the children* (quoted in Burchfield). *The USSR's progress in such diverse areas as agriculture and literacy...made a deeply positive impression on the Indian nationalist. Jawaharlal's first book was, therefore, a paean in praise of the Soviet Union* (Tharoor, p. 57). Here the order is reversed. The identifying phrase comes first.

Where a word has to be repeated in a different sense, there is no question of changing it or omitting it. Just keep it. *I am serious in describing the situation as serious.* Nothing to complain here. The two occurrences of *serious* have different meanings. *Allow me to point out that the points you have raised have been taken note of.* Repetition is also justified in the context of a 'correction'. *The question is not whether.... The question is...*; and emphasis: *The economy is on the brink of collapse; the health care system is on the brink of collapse; the schools are literally collapsing* (*Time*, 19 May 2003). This kind of repetition is actually a rhetorical device. Meaningful and really elegant variation can be achieved by shifting focus. Tony Blair, writing about the Iraq war said: *[Iraq] is a battle we have to fight, a struggle we have to win* (as reported in *San Jose Mercury News*, 12 April 2004).

else

The international edition of the *Indian Express* has some choice expressions which make it readable but not for the right reasons. The management is unlikely to be happy about this.

On Page 6 of the 2 May 2003 issue we read: *The* Indian Express *North American Edition covers India like no one does.* Isn't there something wrong here? Shouldn't *it* be: *like no one else?*

If you are thinking of a set, *else* marks off *x*, a member of the set, from every other member of the set; x is like nobody else in the set. But without this *else*, *x* is not marked off or separated from the rest of the set. *The* Indian Express...*covers India like nobody else* makes sense. (It covers India better than any other paper.) But to say that *The* Indian Express covers *India like no one does* means that it covers India better than everybody, i.e., better than all the papers. But this includes the *Indian Express* also. So the *Indian Express* covers India better than the *Indian Express.* Cf *Rohit is taller than anybody else in the class.*/*Rohit is taller than everybody in the class.*

endow/bestow

The two words have some aspects of meaning in common but if one made a study of their distribution, it would be found that they have distinct contexts of use. In respect of mental abilities and talents (inherited from ancestors or given by nature), the word is *endow,* usually in the passive. *He was endowed with an outstanding memory for detail and an ability to grasp the key issues in a situation.* If an active construction were required, the subject would be *Nature/Providence.* (*Nature/Providence had endowed him with...*). The noun *endowment* is usually used in the plural followed by the preposition *with: Not everyone is born with such endowments as you* (ALD).

As against this, *bestow* would be generally found in contexts where someone gives something to a person. *His grandfather had bestowed a fortune (up)on him. The King/Queen/State had bestowed many high honours on him.* Note the preposition. It is *on*.

Having said this, it must be admitted that, especially in literature, *bestow* might be found in contexts where we might expect *endow. Nature had bestowed on him a profusion of abilities.* But the distinction suggested above is what is generally found today.

This apart, *endow* has another meaning irrelevant for present purposes: to provide a person or an institution with a permanent income by depositing money or assets in the name of the person/institution; *to endow* (support, pay for) *a chair* (= a professorship) *at a university; an endowment scholarship.* In the field of insurance, there is *an endowment policy.*

end preposition

From the days of Dryden onwards, there has been a view that a sentence in English should not end with a preposition. Dryden himself went through his prefaces removing all the end prepositions he had left in the first edition.

Apparently Dryden took his cue from Latin where a preposition has to precede the noun it governs and so cannot be left stranded at the end of a sentence/clause. But this is not so in English. Shakespeare, for example, has: *Who do you speak to?* (*As You Like It*). And grammarians from Robert Lowth on have pointed out that the end preposition is quite natural in English. *This is an idiom, which our language is strongly given to* (Robert Lowth, *Short Introduction to English Grammar,* 1775). But Lowth goes on to say: '...the placing of a preposition before the relative, is more graceful, as well as more perspicuous; and agrees much better with the solemn and elevated style'. Such advice, repeated by generations of schoolmasters, tended to enforce the view that in serious writing, a preposition should not be left hanging at the end.

Fowler gives several examples of awkward, if not bad, sentences, all trying to avoid an end preposition. Here is one: *The War Office does not care, the Disposal Board is indifferent and there is no one on whom to fix the blame or to hang.* Compare this with: *No one to fix the blame on or to hang.* One can get into worse situations trying to avoid putting a preposition at the end. Reacting to one such sentence (in a memo submitted to him), Churchill made this marginal comment: *This is the sort of sentence up with which I will not put.* (Cf *This is the sort of sentence which I will not put up with*). Churchill was in effect showing how ridiculous it can be trying to avoid an end preposition. Avoiding an end preposition may result in an absurdity. What about not avoiding them? Here is a constructed example (quoted in Burchfield, 1998):

> Sick child: *I want to be read to.*
> Nurse: *What book do you want to be read out of?*
> Sick child: Robinson Crusoe.
> (Nurse goes out and returns with *The Swiss Family Robinson.*)
> Sick child: *What did you bring me that book to be read to out of for?*

Let us now see when (i.e., under what circumstances) a preposition can be naturally left stranded: (a) in relative clauses where the relative word governed by the preposition can be omitted. *He is not a man on whom you can rely. He is not a man who you can rely on.* = *He is not a man you can rely on.* (b) In *wh-* questions when the preposition governs the word questioned: *We shall talk about what? What shall we talk about?* (c) In passives *We have sent for the doctor.* = *The doctor has been sent for.*

With the exception of exclamatives (*What a hopeless state you are in!*) These are about all the cases where a preposition can be left at the end of a sentence/clause. (Burchfield also cites some cases involving infinitives, e.g., *He still had quite enough work to live on*, but these can be analysed as falling under case (a) Of the three cases mentioned above, in the first two there is a choice between having the preposition at the end of the sentence or before the noun it governs. But in informal usage, the preposition is always left at the end, more so in questions (case b). In the third case (passive), there is no option. The preposition has to appear at the end.

The choice between ending a sentence/clause with a preposition or not doing so (where the possibility exists) is one of style. Quite often the construction with the end preposition is more forceful than the alternative construction. Surely it is better to say: *People worth talking to*, instead of: *People with whom it is worthwhile to talk* (example from Fowler).

We cannot do better than close with this observation of Kingsley Amis (1998): 'It is natural and harmless in English to use a preposition to end a sentence with.'

enlighten/enlightenment

You enlighten a person on some topic or point when you give him/her relevant information to understand it. *He gave a lucid, enlightening lecture on globalization. Can you enlighten me on the intricacies of this balance sheet?*

Enlightenment refers primarily to the state of mind when a person has realized the 'truth'. *Buddha found enlightenment at Gaya.* Used in other contexts it can be sarcastic. *Thank you for the enlightenment you have provided on the working of our company.*

Enlightened is used attributively, i.e., as modifying a noun. *Enlightened public opinion* is opinion that is well-informed and free from prejudice or partisan feelings. Similarly *enlightened attitudes, ideas; an enlightened approach to family planning.*

Notice the three distinct meanings we have been explicating: (1) to shed light on, inform, explain (*enlighten*), (2) spiritual or religious awakening (*enlightenment*) and (3) rational, unbiased attitudes, opinions, etc. (*enlightened*).

ensure/assure

The formulations available in the market cannot be ensured to be safe unless they are evaluated scientifically.

The point is about the word *ensure*. A manufacturer may say: *We have taken pains to ensure* (= to make sure) *that the products are safe*. But can someone, say, a drug inspector use this word?

The drug inspector himself is not making the product. So he cannot *ensure* that it is safe. What he can do is to *assure* you that it is safe (after testing it) or to inspire confidence in you for you to assume that it is safe. In no case can he *ensure* that it is safe.

With *assume* the sentence could read: *It cannot be assumed that the product is safe unless....* With *assure* the sentence could be: *You cannot be assured that the product is safe unless....*

If an impersonal construction is needed: *The safety of the products cannot be assured unless....*

euphemism

Physically challenged—this is the current expression to refer to people with physical disabilities. *Blind, deaf, lame...*terms like these are felt to be offensive. *Visually impaired* is a more polite term than *blind*. A common expression for people with physical 'defects' (that is a bad word) or shortcomings was *disabled*. But even this term is now felt to be somewhat harsh and crude. *Physically challenged* is the correct term now.

A long time ago Fowler fulminated against expressions of this type. '...those who used to be known as backward and troublesome are now *maladjusted*; insanity is now *mental disorder*; lunatic asylums are *mental hospitals....*' Yes. These expressions are to be condemned if it is right to call a spade a spade, always. But it is not so. There is no point in embarrassing (and even humiliating) people for what they are (and for no fault of theirs). *Physically* (or *mentally*) *challenged* would be the best (and least offensive) way of describing such people.

Fowler is on firmer ground when he protests against euphemisms (that's the word for expressions of this type) employed merely to bolster one's sense of self-importance: *prison officers* (gaolers), *rodent operatives* (rat catchers) *street orderlies* (refuse collectors) are of this type. In our own country, peons are now *class four officials*; English coaching classes are *Institutes for the Development of Personality and Communicative Skills*; the persons who operate these sweat shops are *Directors*; used car (itself an euphemism for second-hand cars) salesmen are *Automobile Consultants*; managers of chit funds (who usually decamp with the cash once a sizeable amount has been collected!) are *Finance Directors*. Tailors are *Gentlemen's outfitters*; barbers, *Hair Dressers*, and door-to-door salesmen, *Direct Marketing Personnel*. In the examples considered above we have passed on from euphemism to upscalism. Euphemism substitutes a better sounding expression for one which has negative associations (*visually impaired* for *blind*); with upscalism we have a high sounding expression for something quite modest (*gentlemen's outfitter* for *tailor*). The vanity evident in such expressions should be roundly condemned. We join Fowler in booing such hollow pomposities.

A third category of euphemistic expressions has to do with the so-called 'taboo' words: words relating to natural body functions, activities and certain body parts—sex, sex organs, excretion, etc. While Victorian prudery dished up a number of these (*powder room* for *toilet* is still in use in the USA), current novelists have, with a vengeance, taken the stand that there is nothing which cannot be put into print and described in great detail. They call *shit shit*. Our own Arundhati Roy has the knack of talking about these things not only without reservation but hilariously as well.

But in polite society these words continue to be replaced by euphemisms. I see little point in protesting against them. As long as we feel the need to cover the body with clothes, euphemisms will continue to be used in this field.

Our innate sense of the dignity of human life compels us to be euphemistic when speaking about the dead in public.

A fourth (and final?) category of these expressions is polite substitutes to cover up facts which would (or should) normally provoke anger and outrage. Economists don't speak of people starving and dying like dogs on the street. They talk of people *below the poverty line*. Military bosses don't speak of the dead and the wounded. They speak of *casualties*. The Bosnian murderers did not kill the Serbs. They were engaged in *ethnic cleansing*.

Corporations don't talk of lay-offs. It is *'an ongoing effort to align resources with long term business strategies.'* (ADOBE spokesman as reported in the *San Jose Mercury News*, 14 November 2003).

We have now identified four principal motivations for the use of euphemistic expressions: (1) to avoid giving hurt to others, (2) to avoid embarrassment in polite society, (3) to inflate one's sense of self-importance and (4) to cover up reprehensible misdeeds and unpleasant situations. Needless to say, only in the first two cases is there some justification for not calling a spade a spade.

exceptional generic phrases

In 'man's best friend', *man* is used in a 'generic' sense, i.e., referring to mankind in general and not to any particular individual. But this usage with *man* is exceptional. The only other word in the language which can be used in this way is (not surprisingly) *woman*. *Woman's alleged inferiority to man. Boy meets girl* is an idiom; so is *Diamond cut diamond*. I ignore here words like *mankind* and *humankind*.

With names of animals, the generic sense is possible in three different constructions: *The dog is man's best friend. / Dogs are lovable animals. / A dog will never forsake his master.* But there is no way you can get the generic sense with the singular form *dog*, with no article. There is, of course, the expression *Dog does not eat dog* from which the later version *dog eat dog* has been formed. But this is not a productive usage. See ARTICLES.

'exert efforts'

The word *effect* can be used in a countable or an uncountable sense. In the uncountable sense, it suggests an application of strength, energy. *A waste* of time and effort. / He moved that heavy furniture without much effort. / You should put some more effort into your work.

In the countable sense (attempt to do something), it can appear in the plural form. *All our efforts proved fruitless. / I made every effort to change her mind.*

But even in the countable sense, *effort* cannot be preceded by a numeral. You cannot say: *I made two efforts to get that job done.* If a numerical sense is intended, the word needed is *attempt*: *I made two attempts.* It follows that you cannot also say: *I made an extra effort.*

Note finally that the verb which goes with *effort* in this sense is *make*: *to make an effort.* Other verbs with more specific meanings are also possible: *to redouble/intensify one's efforts,* etc. This is a matter of collocation (see COLLOCATIONS).

It should now be clear that a phrase like *'an individual's willingness to exert extra efforts'* (a citation) is inadmissible. The intended sense here is: the first one. So no plural form is possible. And the verb needed is *put in* (*put in more effort*).

expose/exposition

This is a noun and there is no problem with it. *Chinmayanandaji's exposition of the Geeta was always illuminating.*

The problem arises when one tries to use the word as a verb. Not many are aware that *expose* (v) is not the equivalent of *exposition* (n). *To expose* has several meanings illustrated in such phrases as *to expose oneself to danger/cold; to expose a film to sunlight. To expose oneself* has the more specific meaning of 'showing one's sexual organs to a stranger in a public place', an offence under the law. As applied to persons (usually public figures), their activities and principles, *to expose* means 'to reveal the truth about them, to unmask them'.

The reader can now see for himself how odd this statement (from the blurb of a book on Sri Aurobindo) sounds. *'This book seeks to expose the principles of [his] teaching'* (*The Teaching of Sri Aurobindo,* Dipti Publications, 1999).

The word required in contexts like this is *expound*. To *expound* means 'to explain, make clear; *to make an exposition of.*

expressing futurity

English has no future tense, i.e., there is no form of the English verb to express the future as there is a form to express the past. *Went* is the form of *go* to express the past. What is the form to express the future? None.

This does not mean that English has no way of expressing futurity. Indeed there are several ways of doing so.

1. With *shall, will*

With first person subjects, the future is expressed by *shall*; with second and third persons by using *will*.

We shall be back by evening. / *I shall send the book to you in a day or two.* / *Don't worry. You will be fine in a few days.* / *Rajesh will be here on Monday.*

In negative sentences: *I shan't (shall not) be late.* / *Go ahead as planned. He won't mind it.*

In questions, *shall* (with first person subjects) asks of the *will* of the hearer. *Shall I keep the door open? Shall we go trekking in Kabini?*

As noted earlier, here, too, *will* is used with second and third person subjects. *Will you come to the meeting?*

With third person subjects, however, although what is asked is the *will* of the subject, the question is addressed to the hearer. *Will she respond if I write to her?* / *Will he remember to mail the letter?*

2. With the present tense

(a) The simple present is normally used in connection with a schedule of activities in the future, and in timetables.

We leave for Delhi on the 20th, stay there for a couple of days, and then go to Haridwar. The Rajdhani Express leaves Bangalore City station at 10 a.m. on alternate days.

(b) It is also used in subordinate adverbial clauses of time. *His brother and sister will be at the airport to receive him when Rajesh arrives next Monday from New York* (not: *when Rajesh will arrive*).

3. With the present progressive

Isolated events in the future already fixed (expressing an intention) and near future events are generally expressed with the present progressive. *I'm taking the children to the zoo next Saturday.* / *Suresh is coming for dinner tomorrow.* / *Rachel is leaving for Chennai next week.*

4. By using *going to*

To talk about informal plans. The emphasis is on the decision made. *I'm going to see him tomorrow.* The construction is also found with non-personal subjects. There is a suggestion of imminence or certainty in these cases. *Looks like it's going to rain. It's going to take a long time for the economy to turn around.*

5. With the infinitive after a form of BE: (1) *We are to be married next week.* / *We are to meet at Shalini's.* (2) *Lights are to be switched off by 10 p.m.*

(3) *The worst is yet to come.* As with the other constructions discussed above (2 and 3), this, too, conveys more than just futurity: (1) expresses a mutual arrangement, (2) a command, and (3) destiny (= something beyond our control).

expressing interval

Two points in space and time can be indicated by *at: at London and New Delhi; at 8 a.m. and 10 p.m.* The notion of 'interval' requires the use of *between: between London and New Delhi; between 8 a.m. and 10 p.m.* The sense of 'continuity', of something happening continuously in an interval, requires *from: It rained from 8 a.m. to 10 p.m.* The sense of 'open possibility', i.e., of an action taking place any time in the interval is expressed by using *any time: any time between 8 a.m. and 10 p.m.*

Consider now this advertisement for the KFC (Kentucky Fried Chicken) restaurant, Bangalore: *Head for KFC any time between 11 a.m. to 11 p.m.*

As we have seen, the notion of interval is given by *between: between 11 a.m. and 11 p.m.* The sense of 'open possibility' is given by 'any time': *any time between 11 a.m. and 11 p.m.* So what is *to* doing? It is not just redundant but incorrect. If *to* is to be retained, the copy should read: *Head for KFC. Open from 11 a.m. to 11 p.m.* But *any time between 11 a.m. and 11 p.m.* is better.

expressing simultaneity

A very common mistake with us is the use of *till* in place of *as long as.* Here is a recent example: '...the post second World War history is proof of the fact that till Russia reigned we had more peace in the world than the post-1990 period' (from a recent book on management, Vikas, 2002).

The word *till* is correctly used in cases like the following: (1) The main clause event begins after the event indicated in the *till*-phrase has happened. *Don't go till I come;* (2) or begins earlier and ends when the event indicated in the *till-* phrase begins. *He gambled till dawn. / Keep your eyes closed till I say open.* The expression with *till*, therefore, either marks the beginning or the end of the event indicated in the main clause. In the second case, it gives an indication of the duration of the main clause event.

Now here is the important point: there is no case where the main clause event and the event in the *till*-phrase run simultaneously or concurrently. To indicate this simultaneity we have to use *while* (*She danced while I sang*). This is open ended. It doesn't specifically indicate when the main clause event ended. To get this idea we have to use *as long* as: *As long as he was a judge, he kept himself away from all social events. As long as there is repression, there will be tension and violent upheavals in society.*

There are two ways of looking at events which are running simultaneously: (a) We can view them as going on concurrently; or (b) we can frame one event as continuing till the other ends. (1) *As long as there is repression, there will be tension and upheavals in society (simultaneity).* (2) *There will be tension and upheaval in society till repression ends.*

Now to go back to the citation we started with: There are two events here: Russian supremacy and world peace. The two events ran simultaneously: *As long as there was Russian supremacy, there was world peace.* Or we can say: *There was world peace till the breakdown of Russian supremacy.* Before we close let's see how one falls into the trap of using *till* wrongly (as in the sentence discussed).

In *He gambled till dawn/6 o'clock*, the *till* phrase necessarily marks the duration of gambling, its end. But in *Till Russia reigned we had more peace*, the *till* phrase gives us no indication of whether it was till the Russian reign began or ended. With either of the words (*began, ended*), the meaning would have been clear (though, in the context, the word needed is *ended*). While clock time is quite specific, time given in respect of events is not always so. If we don't realize this, we feel that we can say *till Russians reigned* in the same way as we can say *till 1996*.

f

'fearing'

'Then why is he fearing Rule 184?', a prominent MP said, as reported in *Deccan Herald*, 19 April 2002.

Fear (v) cannot be used in this way. You can say: *Why does he fear Rule 184?* Or (better): *Why is he afraid of Rule 184?* But not: *Why is he fearing Rule 184?*.

This is exactly as with such verbs as *know, own, love, hate*, etc. which cannot be used in the progressive form. *I am loving you./You must be knowing him.* These are stative verbs, i.e., verbs which imply more a relation than an action. *He is building a house.* But: *He owns a house* (not *He is owning a house*).

The progressive form with stative verbs is quite common in IE. Here is a citation involving *know. Senior officials in the Seismological Department of the country's top institution in atomic research told PTI that they were not knowing about the explosions planned for today (Deccan Herald, 12 May 1996).*

The restriction on the -*ing* form with these verbs applies only when they occur in main clauses. They can appear in the -*ing* form in a subordinate clause. *Owning a large house, he looks down on others. / Hating his boss, he quit his job. / Fearing a public scandal, he went into hiding.*

figures of speech

A *figure of speech* may be broadly defined as any intentional use of language which departs from normal, ordinary usage. The point is made clear best by a few examples. The *iron curtain* of the cold war days was not really a curtain made of iron. When somebody is *in hot water*, he may actually be taking a cold water shower.

Figures of speech are often spoken of as 'ornaments' added on 'to beautify' discourse. This is a mistaken view and completely misses the point about them. They are devices which enhance the expressive power of language. It is for this reason that they are found in such large measure even in ordinary usage. They are not confined to higher forms of discourse like poetry and poetic drama. When we speak of the *foot* of a hill or the *mouth* of a cave, we are using a figure of speech, a metaphor. These expressions have been so long in use that one might not realize, at first, that they are indeed departures from ordinary usage. The hill has no foot nor the cave a mouth. Without the use of hundreds of such 'dead' metaphors, it would have been extremely difficult to communicate our thoughts.

Figures of speech are best studied in terms of the levels at which they operate. From this point they can be divided into two groups: figures of structure and figures of composition.

Figures of structure are concerned with the manipulation of structure at all levels—sound, spelling, syntax; alliteration, for example, is a figure at the level of sound.

Figures of composition do not involve the manipulation of grammatical structure. They are concerned with concepts and the organization of ideas. They can be divided into: *figures of reference* (e.g., METAPHOR) and *figures of statement* (e.g., HYPERBOLE).

Of the *figures of statement*, some are concerned with the way a direct statement can be made more pointed and effective (figures of statement—1); others are concerned with how a statement can be made in various indirect ways (figures of statement—2). They can be called, if so desired, *figures of indirection*.

figures of speech: reference—1

Figures of references help us to refer to objects and things in a graphic way. They are: simile, metaphor, metonymy, synecdoche, personification, and apostrophe.

Similes and metaphors are very close to each other. In a simile, A is spoken of as being similar to B in some respect(s) and the comparison is made explicit by 'like' or 'as'. In *Her eyes* (A) *sparkle like diamonds* (B), the word *like* makes the comparison explicit. The eyes are not identified with diamonds; they are only compared to diamonds.

Over the centuries, people have been comparing things and objects and a host of similes have come up. Among these are: *as cool as a cucumber, as hard as nails, as sly as a fox, as green as grass, as obstinate as a mule, as busy as a bee, as clear as a bell, as hot as hell, as safe as houses* (for a fuller list, see CLICHE) .... In a non-native situation like ours, there is an impression that it is a sign of mastery over the language to use such expressions. But this view is mistaken. These comparisons have now become stale by overuse. They have become cliches. A good writer is well advised to avoid them.

George Orwell who, like many others before him, condemned stale phrases and imagery, has a fresh simile to enforce his point. Speaking of the lazy writer who doesn't think for himself he says: '[His words] like cavalry horses answering the bugle, group themselves automatically into the dreary pattern' (*Collected Essays*, Vol. 4, p. 137).

In a metaphor, the explicit comparison of a simile is missing: *All the world's a stage, the slings and arrows of outrageous fortune, a sea of troubles* (Shakespeare).

Metaphor has always been regarded as the most significant of the 'tropes' (= figures of speech). The great Roman rhetorician Quintilian praised it for achieving 'the supremely difficult task of providing a name for everything'. How true when you look at words like: *mouse, windows, menu, toolbar* (to take some contemporary examples)! But a metaphor need not always be a name. Its main point is that it offers a new way of looking at things, enhancing our understanding of them. It is for this reason that the language of poetry is highly metaphorical. The expressive power of poetry comes mainly from its images, its metaphors. Prose, too, becomes more expressive to the extent that it employs striking metaphors. Here is an example from a recent biographical study. *Both Charles and Diana allowed friends to lob hand grenades of gossip* (J. Mulvaney, *Diana and Jackie*). One should ponder over this observation of Aristotle: 'Midway between the unintelligible and the commonplace, it is the metaphor which produces most knowledge.'

A keen observation, the ability to see similarities between totally disparate things and, finally, a facility in the use of words are indispensable if one has to come up with an interesting new metaphor or simile. P.G. Wodehouse had a rare facility in this as in other aspects of writing. *Jeeves coughed one soft, low, gentle cough like a sheep with a blade of grass stuck in its throat* (*The Inimitable Jeeves*, Chapter 13); *a laugh like a squadron of cavalry charging over a tin bridge* (*Carry on Jeeves: The Rummy affair of Old Billy*). Describing the heat wave that swept over France in 2003, a writer says: *The heat choked the city [Paris] like a wool scarf pulled tight over its pretty mouth* (*Time*, 25 August 2003). And speaking of books, Kafka said: *A book must be an ice axe to break the seas frozen inside our soul.* Readers will appreciate this from a recent novel by an Indian writer, *The core of the mango stones lay in blood red oil like dead and mutilated soldiers in a battlefield of yogurt and rice* (Amulya Malladi, *The Mango Season*). A little ingenuity can bring even a cliched metaphor into life: *Google allows searchers to find digital needles in haystacks of data* (*New York Times*, 13 August 2003).

Very few of us can come up with new and striking metaphors. We get along merrily with stale and cliched metaphors (as we do with similes): *to play ducks and drakes* (with one's fortune), *to burn the midnight oil, to pour oil on troubled waters, to fish in troubled waters, to take up the cudgel....* And because we really don't think while using them, we commit such absurdities as *to inject the poison of communal virus into the secular fabric of our society.* What is the point in injecting a poison into a fabric? And how is a virus a poison? *The Economist* points out to this masterpiece from its own pages: *Bulgaria is on its knees. A long simmering economic crisis has erupted, gripping the country in a fierce and unrelenting embrace* (*The Economist Style Guide*, p. 45). These are examples of mixed metaphors. Avoid them. (The classic example here is: *The sacred cows have all come to roost.* By the end of the sentence, the cows have become birds.)

Even greater care should be exercised in avoiding incongruous, misleading metaphors. *The Bangalore-Mysore Expressway yet to get off the ground? The booming economy shows signs of cooling down./The rising tide of mediocrity must be nipped in the bud./Suspended official in a pickle.* Gowers (1956) has, perhaps, the most remarkable examples of this kind: *Population squeezed flat by inflation; a virgin field pregnant with possibilities* (announcement by a researcher); and, the most famous of all, a *worldwide bottleneck.*

Mention was made earlier of the dead and invisible metaphors of ordinary language. Besides these there are other metaphors which are not so completely assimilated into the general vocabulary of the language but are no longer felt as living metaphors: *a roadblock* (to progress), *a U-turn* (in policy), *a stepping stone* (to success), *iron resolution*, etc. No harm in using them.

figures of speech: reference—2

We frequently hear of somebody being elevated from *the bar* to *the bench*. The meaning is that a person practising at the bar (a lawyer, an advocate) has been made a judge. The use of 'the bar' to represent advocates collectively (cf *the Bar Association*) or *the bench* to refer to the judges is a figure of speech, a METONYMY. Similarly *the Crown*, in England now, refers to Her Majesty the Queen; *top brass* everywhere refers to the military higher-ups. In all these cases, we see a person (or persons) being referred to by something closely connected with him/them. Some more examples: *The White House is adamant on the issue* (the President of the USA); *Raj Bhavan has declined to make any comment* (the Governor, in India); *The House has been adjourned* (the Lok Sabha or the Rajya Sabha, or even a State Assembly in India); *the Saffron Brigade* (BJP activists; Mussolini's men were known as *the Black Shirts*; English troops during the American War of Independence were *the Red Coats*).

Metonymy works by association (unlike simile and metaphor which work by comparison). The association may take other forms than the one illustrated above: *no bread to eat* (no food; a specimen used to refer to a class); *denim is very popular these days* (material for the finished product); *the cup that cheers* (a reference to tea); *the bottle* (meaning liquor; *to hit the bottle* is to take to drinking). In the last two cases we have the container used to refer to the contained. In *The pen is mightier than the sword* we have an instrument used to stand for the effects it produces. Cf Maugham's statement: *Many rush to the pen as one would rush to the bottle.* The name of an author may be used to stand for his works:

Wodehouse is laughter at its best. The saying *Even Homer nods* reminds us that even very great writers can be, occasionally, dull.

In SYNECDOCHE, a closely related figure, either a part is used to refer to the whole: *the best brains are at the job* (persons), or vice versa: *India beat Pakistan by six wickets* (Indian XI); *The ship sank. All the hands were lost* (the crew); *India is a developing country but it has many mouths to feed. Everyone wants a roof over his head*.

There are two more figures of speech: PERSONIFICATION and APOSTROPHE. In personification, non-persons (ideas, objects) are spoken of as persons. Examples abound in literature, especially poetry and poetic drama. *Death lays his icy hand on kings. / Danger knows full well that Caesar is more dangerous than he* (Shakespeare, *Julius Caesar*). Animals are usually personified in fables.

Apostrophe is 'an exclamatory passage addressed to a particular person (frequently dead or absent) or thing (*Shorter Oxford Dictionary*).' This again is frequently found in poetry: *O Death, where is thy sting? O grave where is thy victory?* (I Corinthians, 15:55). *O mighty Caesar! Dost thou lie so low? / Are all thy conquests, glories, triumphs, spoils / Sunk to this little measure?* (*Julius Caesar*, 3.1.112–14). *Stern Daughter of the voice of God! Duty...* (Wordsworth). In many cases (as in the above examples), apostrophe goes with personification.

Personification and apostrophe are, as noted above, chiefly found in poetry (and also in impassioned prose). Metonymy and synecdoche are more in use in ordinary language, metonymy perhaps to a larger extent: *to address the chair, to invite the press, to make money on the turf* (horse racing), *to play to the gallery* (to appeal to the tastes and sentiments of the crowd)....

Quite often an expression which can be interpreted as a metonymy or a synecdoche has that meaning only in that restricted context, not outside of it. *Tongue* has the meaning *language* in the phrase *mother tongue*. But you cannot say of a dictionary that it is a *tongue container*. Ever more ridiculous will be the result unless these figures are used with a sense of discretion and decorum. *The hand that rocked the cradle has kicked the bucket*.

It is easy enough to personify; but without a sense fo decorum and propriety one may end up in such absurdities as: *Inoculation, Thou heavenly maid* (an eighteenth century poet). And while using personification, make sure that you are consistent. Don't write a sentence like: *India may be a poor country but it can be justly proud of her ancient civilization.*

figures of speech: statement—1

Questioned repeatedly on the WMDs (weapons of mass destruction), in the days and weeks after the Iraq war, Donald Rumsfeld, the Defence Secretary was fond of saying: 'Absence of evidence is not evidence of absence.' And Tony Blair, the British Prime Minister, told his party at its Brighton meeting: 'We expect certain things to happen but the things that happen may not be the things we expected.' These are smart replies. As you can see, they are not just ordinary sentences. They embody a figure of speech, EPANADOS.

This figure parallels (in a way) at the sentence level, what is known as a palindrome at the word level—where the letters can be read backwards or forwards giving the same words. A famous palindrome (attributed to Napoleon) is this: *Able was I ere I saw Elba.* Try reading it backwards. Of course, neither Rumsfeld nor Blair was the first to use this figure. As always, everything can be found in Shakespeare. In *Measure for Measure* he has this profound sentence: *Greater knowledge would speak with deeper love, and deeper love with greater knowledge.* Think over this in the context of someone you don't like.

Here are some more examples: *Fair is foul and foul is fair* (*Macbeth*, 1.1.12). *The Sabbath was made for man and not man for the Sabbath* (Mark 2:27). *We pay taxes when we earn money. We don't earn money to pay taxes* (Kay S. Wye).

Figures of statement (like epanados) are not concerned with the manipulation of grammatical categories or structure. They are concerned with how statements are made.

The simplest figure here involves the repetition of some word or phrase. *Vanity of vanities, saith the preacher, vanity of vanities, all is vanity* (Ecclesiastics 1;1). *Reputation, reputation, reputation! Oh! I have lost my reputation* (*Othello*, 2. 3. 264). *O villain villain, smiling, damned villain* (*Hamlet*, 1.5.106). The figure is REPITITIO.

The repeated phrase may be the opening phrase of a sentence: *This royal throne of kings, this sceptred isle, this blessed spot, this earth, this realm, this England* (*Richard* II 2.1.40). It need not be the subject but whatever appears at the beginning of a sentence. *Blessed are the poor in spirit for theirs is the kingdom of heaven. Blessed are they that mourn for they shall be comforted. Blessed are the meek for they shall inherit the earth* (Matthew, 2.1.40). The figure of speech here is ANAPHORA.

The repeated phrase may be one at the end. *I'll have my bond! Speak not against my bond! I have sworn an oath that I will have my bond (The Merchant of Venice,* 3.3.45). This is EPISTROPHE.

A clause, word may begin and end with the same word: *Common sense is not so common. The deep calling to the deep. The business of America is business.* The figure here is EPANALEPSIS.

The phrase / clause that appears at the end of one sentence may begin the next clause / sentence: *Everything that can be said, can be said clearly.* A whole sequence of clauses, sentences can be constructed in this way, especially in poetry. Thus in Eliot, *All our knowledge brings us nearer to our ignorance / All our ignorance brings us nearer to death. / But nearness to death no nearer to God.* Shakespeare in *As You Like It* (5.2.37) has this amusing sequence: *No sooner met but they looked; no sooner looked but they loved; no sooner loved but they sighed; no sooner sighed but they asked one another the reason; no sooner they knew the reason but they sought the remedy.* This is ANANDIPLOSIS.

The technical names are not important. What is important is to see how much more there is to effective writing than mere grammatical sentences. The devices described are not found just in poetry. They are found in prose also; even in ordinary language as I have tried to show in my examples above.

figures of speech: statement—2

Continuing with the figures discussed in *figures of statement—1*, a striking use of the language is seen in the well-known saying, a modern proverb: *The tougher they come, the harder they fall.* The meaning, roughly, is: 'no matter who opposes us, we will bring them down'. This is a case of repetition where a certain grammatical form (here, the comparative degree) is repeated further down in the sentence. Another (a constructed) example is: *The older he grew, the lonelier he became.* And if you want a topical one (regarding politicians, who else?), here it is: *The more they promise, the less they deliver.* The figure is ISOCOLON.

In the examples above we repeated a grammatical form. We can also repeat a word or phrase in a different grammatical form. This naturally changes the meaning of the word. *Love is an irresistible desire to be irresistibly loved* (Robert Frost). The philosopher Nietzsche made this profound statement: *Man should sooner have void for his purpose than be void of purpose.* And Francis Bacon shrewdly remarked: *Man wants not only to be loved but to be lovely.* The figure is POLYPTOTON.

Or, a word may be just repeated, as it is, but in a different sense. *Let the dead bury their dead* (Matthew 3:22). Benjamin Franklin, the American statesman, is credited with this sentence: *We must all hang together, or assuredly we shall all hang separately.* The most famous line of this type in Britain is: *The King is dead. Long live the King* (= monarchy). This is ANTANCLASIS.

Shylock (*Merchant of Venice*) used repetition (isocolon) to great effect in his declamation in the court: *If you prick us, do we not bleed? If you tickle us, do we not laugh? If you poison us, do we not die? If you wrong us, shall we not revenge?* (*The Merchant of Venice*, 3.1.55–7.)

Rather than merely repeat, in whatever way, a writer may choose to clarify and make precise a previous phrase, statement. When this is done in the same sentence, the effect can be memorable. Dr Johnson was a great master of this construction. Here is an example: *A model of encomiastic prose, exact without pomp and minute without exaggeration.* Shakespeare in *Love's Labours Lost* has: *Your reasons at dinner have been sharp and sententious; pleasant without scurrility; witty without affectation; audacious without impunity; learned without opinion; strange without heresy* (5.1.2). And if you think that this type of writing is no longer current, here is the *Time* magazine writing about Queen Elizabeth II, *Royal without arrogance, glorious without extravagance, gracious without familiarity* (*Time*, 1952, quoted in its December 2002 issue). This is another form of isocolon.

The remaining figures of speech (statement) are: ANTITHESIS, CLIMAX, EUPHEMISM, HYPERBOLE, IRONY, LITOTES, OXYMORON, PARADOX, PARENTHESIS, PATHETIC FALLACY, and PUN. See them in their dictionary places.

These are figures of indirection: a statement is made in an indirect way. When an Englishman says: 'Not bad; not bad at all', he actually means *very good*. This is an example of litotes. *Darkness visible* is an indirect way of saying how dark it was. The figure here is oxymoron.

In a sense all figures involve 'indirection'. But the figures indicated above show that indirectness not just in a phrase or word; the whole expression, the sentence, is an indirect way of saying something.

figures of speech: structure—1

1. Spelling. The general term for figures involving the manipulation of spelling is: METAPLASMUS. The writer intentionally manipulates the spelling of a word to achieve a certain effect. When Shakespeare writes: *I call spirits from the vasty deep*, he is misspelling *vast*. The addition of *-y* has the effect of enhancing our feeling of the depth of the ocean. The misspelling ('modified' spelling may be a better word) may be for the sake of metre: *Thou thy worldly task hast done / Home art gone and tak'n thy wages* (taken). Cleopatra's talk about *the knot intrinsicate* of life is, perhaps, meant to suggest 'intrinsic + intricate'.

James Joyce's *Finnegans Wake* revels in the rhetorical manipulation of spelling. The hero *sinduces* his daughter into an act of incest (sin + induce). At a lower level, it is not uncommon to find *shop* spelt *shoppee* (*Ye Olde Shoppee = The Old Shop*) in some big cities to give a hint of the charm of earlier days. In the US, many stores announce a President's Day *Sale-A-Bration*.

2. At the level of sound we have ALLITERATION, ASSONANCE, ONOMATOPOEIA. Alliteration is 'the occurrence of the same letter or sound at the beginning of adjacent or closely connected words' (COD). *Apt alliteration's artful aid* is a frequently quoted example. Another line that readily comes to mind is *Full fathom five thy father lies* (Shakespeare, *The Tempest*). In everyday speech we have such alliterative phrases as: *cool and collected, loud and long, kith and kin, a cute kitten, part and parcel*, etc.

Assonance is 'the resemblance of sound between two syllables in nearby words' (COD). There may be two or more accented vowels of the same sound, e.g., *sonnet, porridge*; or identical consonants with different vowels, e.g., *cold, killed*.

Onomatopoeia is a 'sequence of words whose sound suggests what it describes' (Burchfield's edition of Fowler): *Myriads of rivulets hurrying thro' the lawn / The moan of doves in immemorial elms, / And the murmur of innumerable bees* (Tennyson). In his *Essay on Criticism*, Pope has some memorable lines: *When Ajax strives some rock's vast weight to throw / The line, too, labours and the words move slow. / Not so when swift Camilla scours the plains / Flies o'er th' unbending corn and skims along the main.*

figures of speech: structure—2

At the level of grammatical structure any intended deviation from normal structure must be considered a rhetorical device. *I came, I saw, I conquered*

(Julius Caesar). The absence of the conjunction *and* adds force to the statement. Caesar is suggesting how easy it was for him to conquer. The figure here is ASYNDETON. *Is this the region, this the soil, the clime...this the seat/That we must change for heav'n* (Milton, *Paradise Lost*, 1. 242–4). Here is an everyday example: *He entered the room, turned on the light, opened the window, looked at the ground below, and jumped.* The absence of conjunctions suggests how quickly the actions followed one another.

There is also the case where more conjunctions are used than (strictly) necessary. When Yeats writes: *When you are old and grey and full of sleep...* we have the figure POLYSYNDETON. The Bible is full of this construction: *And I will bring you out from the people, and will gather you out of the countries wherin you are scattered, with a mighty hand, and with a stretched out arm, and with fury poured out. And I will bring you into the witness of the people, and there will I plead with you face to face* (Ezekiel, 20:34–5).

Omission can take many forms. In grammar this is treated under ELLIPSIS (which is also a term in Rhetoric). Ellipsis is generally possible (and legitimate) when what is omitted can be recovered from some other part of the sentence, e.g., *Everybody's job is nobody's (job).* 'Can you copy this figure?' *I'm afraid I can't.* Often the omitted portion can be understood from the physical situation—as in Caeser's famous cry: *Et, tu, Brute* (You also, Brutus!) or as in this passage from Hobbes: *No arts, no letters, no society; and which is worst of all, continual fear and danger of violent death; and the life of man, solitary, poor, nasty, brutish, and short.*

A particularly interesting case of omission is that of the verb. Several cases can be distinguished.

1. Where a single verb is used with two nouns and is understood in different senses: *Here thou great Anna whom three realms obey/Dost sometimes counsel take and sometimes tea* (Pope, *The Rape of the Lock*, Canto 3, 7–8). *He caught the night flight and a bad cold.*

2. Where the verb cannot be understood in the case of the second noun: A suitable verb in the same semantic field has to be supplied by the reader *With weeping eyes and heart* (grieving).

3. Where the verb agrees grammatically with only one of the nouns: *He works his work, I mine* (Tennyson). The second clause requires the plural form of the verb (*work*).

These cases distinguished and illustrated above have been a source of much confusion in the literature. Fowler (1926) called case (1) SYLLEPSIS.

The remaining two cases he called ZEUGMA. Gowers in his revision of Fowler (1965) kept to the distinction. But the COD combined (I) and 3) and called it syllepsis. So syllepsis, which for Fowler, was always grammatical, would now sometimes be ungrammatical.

There is no need to continue further with the variations in the definitions of these two terms. Suffice it to say that for Burchfield, case (3) is just ungrammatical. 'Classical students continue to observe the distinction between the terms syllepsis and zeugma, but in practice, syllepsis is no longer applied to any English rhetorical device of the present day. The ancient distinctions have lost their usefulness in the late twentieth century.'

So only cases (1) and (2) remain. They are instances of zeugma. Rather than just two terms, a verb (with its object) can be made to govern more than two terms or clauses. *Histories make men wise; poets witty; morals grave; logic and rhetoric able to contend.* This is PROZEUGMA. There are other varieties with their own names. We shall not go into all that.

A second class of figures at the structural level has to do with *substitution*. The simplest case is where one part of speech is substituted for another. It is not uncommon for nouns to be used as verbs. So we may see nothing special or strange in: *He lords it over his subordinates.* But in: *Lord Angelo dukes it well* (Shakespeare, *Measure for Measure*) we notice it. And in this from Rabelias: *I am going in search of the great perhaps.* Although pronouns routinely stand for nouns, a substitution can take our breath away: *The fair, the chaste, and unexpressive she* (Shakespeare, *As You Like it*, 3.2.10). A very famous line from the American poet, Cummings, is this: *He sang his didn't, he danced his did* (did = achivements; didn't = failures). If you are curious to know the name of this figure, it is ANTHIMERIA.

Substitution of a prepositional phrase for an adjective + noun is common in the Bible: *the kingdom of glory* (for: *the glorious kingdom*). *A perfect bond* becomes *a bond of perfection* (Coleridge); *a strong tower* becomes *a tower of strength* (Shakespeare). This figure is called ANTIPTOSIS.

Sometimes the substitution (it may be one adjective for another) appears so incompatible as to be incomprehensible. Thus in Milton's *blind mouths* (Lycidas). Milton is attacking the clergy who are there only to grab (*mouths*) but cannot guide or lead (*blind*). One more example: *A man that seeks revenge keeps his own wounds green* (Bacon). This kind of substitution is CATACHRESIS.

Catachresis is also defined more broadly as 'a misuse of words', e.g., use of *infer* for *imply*, *militate* for *mitigate*, etc. This definition is too wide. We should distinguish deliberate 'misuse' (*blind mouths*, Lycidas, 99) from misuses born of ignorance.

We shall note two more deliberate 'misuses' before closing this section. Asked for his opinion on how mangoes should be, the Urdu poet Ghalib is reported to have said: 'They should be sweet and abundant'. Here we have two incongruous adjectives brought together making for a memorable phrase.

An even more remarkable use of the incongruous was achieved by George Clerihew (he gave his name to a type of verse.) Speaking of King George the Third, he said: *George the Third/Should never have occurred./It is a wonder/How nature could suffer such a blunder.* Occur is used of events like birth and death, and more generally of events and activities. But the occurrence of a man leaves us open-mouthed.

At a higher level of structure, subordination may be replaced by coordination. *Thine is the gloriously powerful kingdom* becomes *Thine is the kingdom, the power, and the glory* (Matthew 6.12). *I am the way, the truth and the life* (= *I am the true way of life*). The figure of speech here is HENDYADIS. In ordinary usage, too, we have: *nice and warm* (for *nicely warm*), *try and do better* (for *try to do better*).

We reach the ultimate when there is a general breakdown of grammatical structure. This is ANACOLUTHON: 'A sentence or construction which lacks grammatical sequence' (COD). Fowler (1926) makes the point clear: 'A sentence in which there is wrongly substituted for completion of a construction something that presupposes a different beginning', e.g., *Can I not make you understand that if you don't get reconciled to your father what is to happen to you?* The word *that* signals a statement. But we end up with a question. This type of construction may be seen in emotive speech; elsewhere it is simply ungrammatical. (Indian English has a curious structure which begins as a question, turns into what looks like a statement and ends up as a question: *He asked that why she came.*)

figures of speech structure—3

Expressing his anger and disgust at a sentence where a writer had clumsily tried to avoid ending a sentence with a preposition, Churchill made this marginal comment: 'This is the sort of English up with which I will not put.'

Here we see an unusual word order. It would normally read: '... English which I will not put up with'. But this would violate the so-called rule of 'No preposition at the end'. Churchill's point was to show how absurd the rule was. If you try to follow the rule, you end up with: *up with which I will not put.*

Less dramatic (and for that reason hardly noticed) departures from normal word order are quite common in daily speech: *This I must see./ Here comes the bus./Out you go* (to a cat). Some journalists, too, are much given to this type of inversion (adverbial preposing). *In searching the web, Google has found riches./In the US Elation wrestles with Anxiety./In the Arab world, shock and dismay over Hussain's fall* (*The New York Times*, 13 April 2003).

In literature, this is a very common practice. Here is Shakespeare (*Measure for Measure*): *Some rise by sin, and some by virtue fall* (*Measure for Measure*, 2.1.38; cf *fall by virtue*). In *Othello*, the hero says: *that whiter skin of hers than snow* (of Desdemona, whose skin is whiter than snow). Cf also Browning's title: *Wanting is—what?*

Such deviations from the usual word order is a figure of speech. The general name for this figure is HYPERBATON.

There is a particular type of displacement (where adjectives are concerned) which is specially interesting. Adjectives generally precede the nouns they qualify. (There are some exceptions: *Secretary-General; Plenipotentiary Extraordinary; Lords Spiritual; Lords Temporal; heir apparent* and a few more. These are fixed expressions.) But they can be made to appear after their nouns for rhetorical effect. This is a common device in Milton. His poem, 'Lycidas', ends with these lines: *At last he rose, and twitched his mantle blue:/Tomorrow to fresh woods and pastures new.* Shakespeare in his delightful play, *As You Like It*, has a whole bunch of these inverted phrases. I give a partial list: *the retort courteous, the quip modest, the reply churlish,...the lie direct* (5.4.94). T.S. Eliot has these profound lines: *Time present and time past/Are both perhaps present in time future,/And time future contained in time past* (*Burnt Norton*, 1–3). This is ANASTROPHE.

There is also the case where an adjective is placed before a noun with which it usually does not go. When you say: *I had a restless night*, it was not the night which was restless. When Thomas Gray ('Elegy

Written in a Country Churchyard') writes: *The ploughman homeward plods his weary way*, it is not the way that is weary. These are cases of the well-known figure of speech, transferred epithet. (The epithet, i.e., adjective, is transferred to a noun to which it really doesn't belong.) The classical name of this figure is: HYPALLAGE. A modern instance of this figure is *red eye flight* (USA, night flight).

In the two earlier pieces on Figures of Structure we looked at Figures of Substitution and Ellipsis. With this account of the Figures of Re-ordering (or Re-arrangement), we complete our sketch of Figures of Structure.

'for last some time'

...*the NAV of the unit [U.S.-64] is hovering around Rs 6.50 for last some time.* (*Business Times*, 19 January 2002).

In the context of a present tense (in this case a present progressive), the phrase *for some time* necessarily carries with it a sense of 'past'. (With a future tense in the clause, the same phrase would imply *some time* in the future: *The NAV will be depressingly low for some time*.) The addition of *last* here, is not only unnecessary but ungrammatical. If *last* is used, it should be preceded by *the*, and some specified time extent should be mentioned: *For the last six months/for the last four weeks*. In the absence of any such specific time expression, the phrase can only be: *for some time*.

'forfeit'

If the entrepreneurs fail to implement their plans within a stipulated time then the government would forfeit the land (News report).

This is a very common misuse of the word *forfeit* in Indian English. *Forfeit* is a legal term which the COD defines in this way: 'Property or a right or privilege lost as a legal penalty'. Such being the case, if the entrepreneurs who have been given land at a concessional rate do not implement the plans (for which the land was given) who will lose the land?—the government or the entrepreneurs?

In the case of a mortgage, if the mortgager (= the debtor) defaults on his payments, the mortgagee (the creditor) *can foreclose on the mortgage*, i.e., stop a mortgage from being redeemable. You lose whatever instalments you had paid; and the property is taken over by the creditor.

g

gay

Everybody knows the meaning of *gay* now (a homosexual male; the female in this context is *a lesbian*). But this is a recent, very recent development in the history of this word. For centuries, the word *gay* meant 'filled with, expressing, inclined to, joy and lively feeling; merry, light-hearted, cheerful' (as Wyld puts it). It is in this sense that Wordsworth uses it in his poem 'The Daffodils', which every schoolboy, at one time, knew: *A poet could not but be gay/In such a jocund company.* Nicholas Rowe (1674–1718) asks, *Is this that haughty, gallant, gay Lothario?* (*The Fair Penitent*). And Milton, describing Delilah (*Samson Agonistes*, Line 700) asks: *Who is this, what thing of sea or land?/Female of sex it seems,/That so bedecked and ornate and gay,/Comes this way sailing.*

But all this has changed since about 1960. 'The centuries-old...senses of *gay* meaning either 'carefree'or 'bright and showy' have more or less dropped out of natural use.' (NODE)

gerund or infinitive?

Looking forward to meeting you soon./I expect to meet you shortly.

Why *meeting* in one case and *meet* in another?

Meeting is what is called a GERUND; *meet* (more correctly *to meet*) an INFINITIVE. A verb in the *-ing* form may be a PRESENT PARTICIPLE; e.g. *I'll be coming home late in the evening* or it may be a gerund as in the sentence we began with).

The present participle is preceded by a form of BE: *is raining, was sleeping, am working*. It generally indicates an action going on at the time of speaking (or at some other time). It is part of what is called the continuous or progressive tense.

The gerund is more a noun than a verb. (It is sometimes called a verbal noun.) It can show number inflection: *lootings, burning*; be preceded by an article: *A shooting took place here last night*; be the subject or object in a sentence: *Swimming is an exhilarating exercise/I hate shopping.*

The infinitive, on the other hand, is a verb. It is usually preceded by *to. It is good to walk./I love to trek in the mountains./we plan to go on a holiday this summer.* It can also appear with certain verbs without *to: Can you help me wash the clothes?* With the MODAL AUXILIARIES (*shall, will, may, can* etc. a verb can only appear in the infinitive form: *We will meet again soon./I shall talk to her later*. (The infinitive with *to* is called the *to infinitive*; the infinitive without *to*, the *bare* (or *plain*) *infinitive*.)

Now for some comments on the distribution of these two categories.

The gerund (and not the infinitive) is found in the following cases.

1. In prepositional phrases:

Without saying a word, he walked out of the room.

As for writing letters, most people don't have the time for it.

There is no point in noting small details.

With a view to curbing inflation, interest rates have been cut.

2. As the object of a number of verbs, among which are: *avoid, deny, detest, enjoy, finish, stop*; also after such verbal groups as: *give up. it's no good, can't help, put off, don't mind, do you mind*, and some others.

He denied sending her the letter.

I have given up smoking.

I can't help thinking that you were rash.

It's no use crying over spilt milk.

Do you mind keeping this window open?

Have you finished typing the letter?

3. Either the gerund or the infinitive may be used after: *begin, continue, fear, intend, propose, hate, love; prefer, try*, among others.

It began raining/to rain.

I hate going (to go) through these accounts.

We propose going over (to go over) these figures again.

I tried calling (to call) his number again.

4. With *remember* and *forget* there is a change in meaning depending on whether a gerund or infinitive follows. *Remember to post the letter* (future reference). *I remember visiting them some years ago* (past reference)

Subtle differences of meaning may be observed as between the use of the gerund or the infinitive with some other verbs also: *try, begin, start, cease*. With verbs like *hate, like, dislike, prefer*, the gerund is preferred in general statements while the infinitive has reference to a particular occasion. *I like swimming but today I'd like to just bask in the sun*. But these are not hard and fast distinctions, though careful speakers and writers observe them. But the usages indicated at (1) and (2) above are more important. Failure to observe them would result in ungrammatical writing. With the vast majority of verbs (other than those mentioned at (2) and (3) above, only the infinitive with *to* is found.

'give a drop'

The man who protests: *'I don't touch a drop'* is in fact saying that he is a teetotaller. He doesn't drink; not one drop. The sense of *drop* found in: *I usually have my whisky with just a drop of soda* (= a little soda) is extended to mean 'liquor'. These are standard usages. *Drop* is also found in phrases suggesting motion: *She usually drops the kids off at school on her way to work.*/*Drop by whenever you are in this area* (= visit us).

This particular sense has been extended in Indian English to mean 'to give a lift' by using *drop* as a noun *I will give you a drop* (= 'I will take you to where you are going'). It is understood that the distance is not too far. 'Hi, where are you going?' 'To the post office.' Come in, (or, 'Jump in, as the case may be) I'll give you a *drop*.'

I am sure readers will vouch to have heard this expression used in this way, especially in its Kannada–English bilingual form: *ondu drop koduthiira?* (Will you give me a *drop*?)

'give stress'

The verb *give* can be used with a number of nouns when the structure *give* + noun has the same meaning as a verb corresponding to the noun: *give a shout = shout; give a kiss = kiss; give a kick = kick; give a shrug = shrug; give permission = permit.*

But *stress* (as a noun) is used with the verbs *lay, put* in the structure *lay/put stress on something. The Deputy PM laid stress on conduct* (= emphasized the importance of conduct). You can neither *give stress to conduct* (as a paper reported) nor *give stress on conduct.* There is another sense of *stress:* pressure/strain, mental, physical, or both. *Kids are under great stress during exam time.* Even here you can't say: *Exams give kids great stress.*

grammar and communication—1

It may sound paradoxical but it is true that in early life we begin the study of a subject without asking what the subject is about. Children begin adding and subtracting without ever asking what arithmetic is. This is perfectly natural and justified. You cannot answer the question: What is arithmetic? without a good deal of acquaintance with numbers. You cannot say what physics is without first doing several courses in physics.

The same is true of grammar. But in this case, the situation is complicated by the fact that few, if any, pursue the study of grammar for any length of time. For most people, it is no more than a distant (and distasteful) memory of some definitions (A sentence is a group of words which makes complete meaning...) and incomprehensible rules (The subject and verb must agree in number, person, and gender...). No wonder, very few have any idea of what grammar is, while they do have some idea of what arithmetic and physics are. But, surprisingly, even scholarly attempts at defining grammar sometimes give a skewed picture of it.

The *Advanced Learner's Dictionary* defines grammar as: 'rules for forming words and combining them into sentences'. Since the common man is rarely given to forming words, 'rules for combining words into sentences' would be an appropriate definition of grammar for most people. Certainly, in a language like English, word order is most important: *The book on the table* is correct but not *book the table is the on.* Also, while you can say *Tell me how it is done* you cannot say *Explain me how it is done.* It has to be: *Explain to me how it is done.*

This notion of order and sequence of elements in a sentence came to be particularly emphasized in the 1950s and 1960s by American linguists. The emphasis was all on structure. This in turn gave rise to the structural approach to language teaching. 'Pattern practice' became the order of the day.

But language is not just so many patterns or structures. There is structure all right, but we use it to convey meanings. Language is basically an instrument for communicating our thoughts and feelings.

Emphasis shifted in the 1970s to the so-called communicative approach to language teaching. A significant book of this time was *A Communicative Grammar of English* (Geoffrey Leech and Jan Svartvik, 1975).

Leech and Svartvik have such sections as 'Partition: part and whole'. There is an explanatory comment followed by these phrases: *the whole cake, a slice of cake, half (of) the cake* (p. 44). Under 'Warnings, promises and threats', they have: *Mind your head./Look out!/Be careful (of your clothes)./I warn you it's going to be foggy....* Under 'Promise' we find: *I'll let you know tomorrow./I promise (you) I'll be quick./You won't lose money, I promise you* (p. 150).

But this is not grammar. In what sense can the grammar of English be said to be concerned with the different ways of uttering a warning or making a promise? Can any grammatical structure be identified as concerned with the making of promises? Is there, for example, a modal auxiliary with the meaning of *to make a promise*? The sort of example sentences cited above are what one would expect in a phrase book.

Grammar is certainly more than structure. It is also concerned with meanings. But not the sort of meanings given above.

How structure and grammatical meanings combine to make possible communication and the role of grammar in communication will be examined in the next part of this article. Meanwhile note there is no 'communicative grammar' of English (or indeed of any language).

grammar and communication—2

An impala can leap three metres into the air and seven metres across. You can look up in the dictionary the meanings of these words: *impala, leap, metre, three, seven.* But putting these meanings together you still will not have accounted for these facts: that the statement is true not of just one impala but of all impalas; that this is not some ancient, antiquated fact but is true even today; that the animal in question is not extinct but is very much found even today. On the other hand the sentence: *The dodo is extinct* informs us that not just one bird but the entire species called *dodo* is no longer found on earth.

These are some simple examples to show how grammar contributes to the 'total' meaning of a sentence. Lexical meanings (= the meanings of the words: *impala, dodo, leap,* etc.) cannot, by themselves, convey what we want to say. It is the grammatical meanings, in conjunction with the lexical meanings, that help express our thoughts. For example, in the first sentence, it is the 'article' *a* which, in conjunction with the present tense of the verb, tells us that the statement is made about all impalas and not just one of them; the present tense seen in *can* tells us that what is asserted in the sentence (more strictly, proposition) holds good now, as it will in the future, and did so in the past.

I can swim and *can I swim?* Both contain the same number of words; in fact, the same words. Yet the first sentence is understood as making a statement, or assertion, while the second is understood as asking for permission. The two different ways in which these two identical sets of words are understood is wholly a matter of grammar. (In speech there is an additional dimension, intonation. We will ignore it here.) It is the word order—statement word order as against question word order— which decides the interpretation in both the cases.

Examples like this can be easily multiplied to show how much grammar contributes to the expression of meaning (and to the understanding of them). 'Content' words (e.g., *impala, dodo, leap, extinct, swim*) are set in appropriate grammatical frames. These frames not only ensure the acceptable order—or sequence of words in the language (more generally 'well-formedness'); they also contribute certain essential meanings without which there could be no propositions—statements or questions or whatever.

Each speech community has its own view of the world embodied in the grammatical system of its language. This 'world-view', as we may call it, is seen best, in English, in the number system, the article system, the tense–modal system, to mention the more prominent ones. The Englishman's world-view is not the same as, say, the Indian's. We have nothing in our languages which parallels the English article system. Sanskrit has a three-way number system (singular, dual, plural) while English has only a two-way number system (singular, plural). And English has far fewer tenses than Sanskrit.

The contribution of grammar to communication, then, is a very specific and specialized one. It provides the frames which make possible the propositions of the language, incorporating the world-view of the speakers of that language.

But all this is only at the sentence level. Grammar, as generally understood, is only concerned with sentences. It is a 'sentence grammar'.

But 'communication' goes beyond sentences; it develops into discourse. And discourse is governed by its own principles which are no part of grammar. Style and rhetoric also have an important role to play in the organization of discourse. The social conventions of language use—'good morning', 'good evening', 'thank you', etc. form another dimension of 'language-in-use'.

The role of grammar, then, in the communication act, is limited but fundamental. It organizes the vocabulary of a language into the basic units of communication (phrase/clause) encoding the world-view of the speakers of the language. And, as a carrier of information, it has built-in safeguards against loss of information.

grammar and communication—3

In the phrase *two boy*, the idea of plurality is already given by the word *two*. Why should we say *two boys*? Why indicate again plurality in the noun?

Again: *He writes* has the notion of 'singularity' conveyed twice: in the subject *he* (a third person singular pronoun) and the verb form: *writes*—the *-s* ending marking it as singular.

These are but two instances of the redundancy factor in English. Redundancy makes sure that information is not easily lost. Information is repeated elsewhere in the phrase / sentence to ensure that it is recovered.

In the sentence: *John hurt himself*—the form *self* makes clear that the person hurt is John. But this is repeated in the pronoun: *him*.

The special form *am* (*I am a teacher*) ensures the listener gets to know that the person is talking about himself; that the subject of the sentence is *I*.

Going further into the structure of English, we see that there is a great deal of *predictability* about it. This means that we know what type of item is coming next. An article, for example, must be followed by a noun: *a...*, *an...*, *the...*. The blanks here may be followed by one or more adjectives, or even a verbal group, but the 'head' of the phrase must be a noun: *a man, a young, handsome man; a young hard-working man*. With the demonstratives, too, the next item has to be, ultimately, a noun: *this toy, this wonderful toy, this wonderful, expensive, beautiful, not-easily-found toy*. The same is true of possessives: *my book; my recent, highly successful book....*

These two aspects of English—and more generally of all languages—redundancy and predictability are the necessary adjuncts of an information system. They ensure that loss of information is minimal and (if lost) recoverable.

Consider the sentence: *Lying under a heap of dust for years, the Secretary finally found the records of the Club*. The subject of *lying* has been left out. We tend to understand it as *the Secretary*. But this cannot be so. Hence this is a bad construction (often referred to as 'the dangling participle construction'). The structure does not allow us to understand the omitted subject of *lying* as being *the records of the Club*. In short, it is incorrect, wrong, to omit the subject of *lying* here. The condition of recoverability of deleted items does not permit it.

Consider now an example of a different type to illustrate the condition of recoverability on deletion. In the structure: *the man who you met at the theatre,* the relative pronoun, *who* can be dropped. You get: *the man you met at the theatre*. This is fine. No information has been lost. The dropped relative pronoun was standing for *man* (the object of *met: you met the man*). And when we drop it, nothing is lost. The word *man* is there as the antecedent of the relative clause. But in *the man whose father you met at the theatre,* you cannot drop *whose father*. Because the information contained in this phrase is not recoverable from any part of the structure after deletion.

There is naturally more to be said on these matters but we shall stop here. Redundancy, predictability, and the condition on recoverability of deleted items—these are some of the features which ensure that language operates as an effective communicative system. And these are among the basic principles of grammar.

It is time that learners and teachers thought of grammar as an information coding device and not just as a set of rules for writing sentences.

See also CLEFT, PSEUDO-CLEFT, PASSIVE.

h

hedonism/epicurean

Hedonism is the philosophical doctrine which states that the pursuit of happiness (as defined in terms of pleasure) is the sole and proper goal of human life. Aristippus of Cyrene is credited with the popularization of this view around the fourth century BC. His followers the cyrenaics claimed that the art of living consists in maximizing the enjoyment of each moment through the pleasure of the senses.

Epicurus (341–270 BC) advocated a more refined view emphasizing the superiority of mental over physical pleasures. He also urged moderation and cautioned against excessive self-indulgence, for example, drinking too much.

In common usage, *hedonism* now means the pursuit of pleasure, especially of the senses. An *epicurean* is one who takes delight in food and drinks. If you describe someone as *an epicurean*, you are paying him a compliment. But if you call someone *a hedonist*, you are, in fact, criticizing him.

'highly impossible'

A very common expression among us but not in Standard English. In Standard English you will find *highly desirable/probable/amusing*. To bring out the sense of *highly impossible*, you will have to say *just not possible*. Similarly one hears *highly unlikely*. It is better to say *very unlikely*. These are matters of COLLOCATIONS.

'hundred per cent success'

...the state VHP president G. Pulla Reddy and General Secretary Muralidhar Rao claimed that the bundh (organized in connection with the Godhra incident) was 100 per cent success.

Success is used here as a noun. So it must be preceded by, in this case, the indefinite article *a: a hundred per cent success* (= a complete success). Without the article, the adjective form would be needed: *the bundh was 100 per cent successful.*

The IE expression derives, I think, from the way *success* is used in our regional languages.

hyperbole

When you say: *A thousand apologies*, you don't really mean 999 + 1 apologies. You are using an exaggerated expression to indicate the depth of your feelings. You are using a figure of speech, the HYPERBOLE: 'A figure of speech consisting in exaggerated or extravagant statement, used to express strong feeling or produce strong impression and meant not to be taken seriously' (*The New Shorter Oxford English Dictionary,* 5th edn, 2002). Strongly opposing some outrageous proposal, you may say: *Over my dead body.* Thus a conservative father, shocked at his son's decision to marry a girl outside his community and religion, may shout: *Over my dead body.* Politicians are much given to this form of speech. They will fight for their motherland *till the last drop of their blood.* And, in a border dispute, *not one inch of territory will be given.*

But when a lawyer says to his client: '*We will fight this case to your last penny*', he is making a factual statement. No hyperbole here!

Literature, especially poetry and poetic drama, is full of hyperboles. Thus, in Shakespeare's *Hamlet*, Laertes, brother of Ophelia, jumps into her grave and says: 'Now pile your dust upon the quick and the dead/ That of the flat a mountain you have made/To overtop old Pelion or the skyish head of old Olympus'. (5.1.272–6; Pelion and Olympus are mountains in Greece.)

To this Hamlet replies: 'Who is he whose grief/Bears such an emphasis? Whose phrase of sorrow/Conjures the wandering stars, and makes them stand/Like wonder-wounded hearers? This is I/Hamlet the Dane.... I loved Ophelia. Forty thousand brothers/Could not with all their quantity of love/Make up my sum...' (5.1.276–80; ibid., 291–3).

Hyperboles are the very life and spirit of real estate marketing—at least in the West—when it comes to upper-bracket homes. A house which sold for close to US $ 2 million (in Redwood City, California) was advertised in this way: *Meandering garden paths invite contemplative wanderers to discover the richly varied foliage and sylvan moods of the bucolic setting, and to pause upon the enchanting hand-crafted stone bridge that arches over a seasonal brook.* Here is another prose-poem on a housing development: *In the midst of a Redwood grove inspiration comes naturally. As homebuilders we invited gifted architects, land planners, and landscape architects to open themselves to an environment that we have sought to complement for nearly a decade. The result— a rare collection of homes. This is Woods Grove, an enclave without fences. An offering of estate residences, richly crafted and individually sited, to embrace their majestic setting. Landscapes designed around an irreplaceable palette of noble trees and native plants. Yet this is only the beginning of the story. Explore and see where it leads. Beyond fences. Beyond conformity. Above the commonplace. Seek the extraordinary and find yourself at Woods Grove.* (Extracts from *San Jose Mercury News*, 7 July 2003)

The 'overstatements' of journalists (as Kingsley Amis calls them) are also hyperboles. A minor dissension becomes a *revolt*; there is *panic* in the PM's camp. In India politicians never simply *criticize*; they *lash* or *flay*. But things being what they are in the country, statements like *Pandemonium in both Houses*; *PM flayed*; *Mamta lashes at the BJP* are quite often not hyperboles but factual statements.

A hyperbole may be just a mannerism (as in journalistic writing); a ploy to entice (as in some types of advertisements); or a rhetorical flourish (as in political speeches). In these cases they are mostly vacuous; at best they may hold our attention briefly and, perhaps, excite some curiosity. But there are genuine contexts of use for hyperboles. They are, like metaphors, indispensable tools for expressing the inexpressible. No wonder many metaphors are also hyperboles: '*a Titan among men*' is a metaphor; it is also a hyperbole.

i

if-, a restriction on

Here is a restriction on *if-* clauses not usually noticed: *Even if they may look fanciful or absurd....*

The remark occurs in a passage on 'brainstorming'. You should not dismiss somebody's suggestion offhand even if it appears fanciful or absurd. As you can see, the sentence comes out well without *may*. With *may* it sounds odd. It is not as though the modal *may* cannot appear in an *if-* clause. It can. Consider: *If I may say so....* This is an apologetic opening where the speaker is going to say something which may not be quite palatable (!) to the hearer. The meaning of *may* here is 'permission'. *If I am permitted to say so*.... But in *Even if they may look fanciful*, the meaning of *may* is *possibly*. But this meaning is already there in *if*. It is for this reason that the phrase sounds odd. A case of tautology not immediately obvious; 'indirect tautology' if I may so label it.

if- clauses

Consider this (authentic) sentence: *If life were the greatest of teachers, then you are its most gifted student.*

The use of the plural verb (*were*) with a singular subject (*life*) is a special construction in English to denote the non-fact, i.e., an unrealized state of affairs. *If I were the President of India*.... / *If I were Margaret Thatcher*.... Given these impossible conditions, the suggested consequences, whatever they are, would not, naturally, follow. The consequences will remain unrealized. *If I were a bird, I would fly to the Himalayas.*

But there is no doubt that life *is* the greatest of teachers. What the writer wants to say is: *If it is true, as it necessarily is, that life is the greatest of teachers...then*....

Such being the case, the use of *were* (justified in non-fact cases) is here totally unjustified. The *if-* clause should read: *If life is the greatest of teachers, you are its most gifted student.* The first part is indisputable; so the conclusion, it is suggested, is equally indisputable.

Semantically an *if-* clause can be related to its main clause in a number of ways. One common case is where the *if-* clause states a condition under which the main clause will be true. (1) *If you heat water, it will boil.* Another case is where the *if-* clause states a non-fact. The main clause activity is, therefore, not actualized. (2) *If I were a bird, I would fly to the Himalayas.* A third case is where the main clause can only be false and this, in turn, falsifies the *if-* clause. (3) *If Hitler was a strategist, then Napoleon was a plumber.* (4) A fourth case is where the *if-* clause expresses an undisputed truth and the main clause, therefore, is also taken (or suggested) to be true. *If life is the greatest of teachers, then*....

The fourth case considered above is possible only when both clauses are, in fact, true or the *if-* clause is obviously true and the main clause not necessarily false but could be true. In such a situation, the structure is one way of emphasizing the truth of the main clause. There is no doubt that life is the greatest of teachers. This gives weight to the presumption that you are its most gifted student.

To summarize the analysis so far. Sentences with an *if-* clause are of four different types. Denoting the *if-* clause by A and the main clause by B, we have: (1) A realized, B true. *If you drop the glass, it will break.* (2) A not realizable, therefore, B remains unrealized. *If I were a bird....* (3) A false, because B is false. *If Hitler was a strategist, Napoleon was a plumber.* (4) A true, therefore, B is true. *If life is the greatest of teachers, then....*

Cases (2) and (3) are clearly distinct. What about (1) and (4)? In (1) we have the relation of condition and consequence. In (2) we have supposition–conclusion. It is a type of clever argument often used to persuade, browbeat, etc. *If life is for living, then all talk about austerity is nonsense. if it is true that experience comes with age, you must listen to elders.* Obviously *if-* clauses can be potent instruments of persuasion.

Notice, finally, that in only one case (case 2) we have *were*. In all other cases we have normal agreement.

if: in case

These two are not synonyms. There are contexts where either of them can be used: *Pull the hood over your head if/in case it rains* (mother to her child). But in *Take an umbrella in case it rains*, we cannot have *if*.

Clearly, where an action is contingent on something else happening (as in the first example), either expression is possible; cf also: *Take a cab if/in case it rains.* But where an action is done in anticipation of some other event, only *if* is possible (the second example); cf also: *Keep the room ready in case she comes tomorrow.*

These distinctions apart, note the IE tautological phrase *if in case; Take the umbrella if in case it rains.*

if/whether

Writing about a resort which is seeking an 'ISO like' certification, a reporter (*The Times of India*, 4 June 2002) says: 'If a certification comes or not, implementing eco-friendly measures are more important.'

If and *whether* are often substitutable. *Do you know if/whether he is married?/I could not say if/whether she was laughing or crying.* Here we have indirect yes/no questions (i.e., questions which can be answered with a Yes or No). Cf *Is he married? Is she laughing or crying?* The verbs introducing these questions are *ask, know, wonder*, etc.

But there are some restrictions. In the following cases only *whether* is possible: (1) After a preposition: *We had a heated debate about whether our forces should cross the LoC in Kashmir./It depends on whether Musharraf keeps his word or not.* (2) When there is a following infinitive: *He can't decide whether to take up a job or study further.* (Not: *if to take up a job....*) (3) When the indirect question is fronted: *Whether I'll have time to go there, I'm not sure at the moment.* (4) When the alternative question is itself the subject or the complement: *Whether I can stay with my brother is another question./ The question is whether you can depend on him.*

Now what about the sentence we began with? Does it fall under any of the cases outlined above?

Clearly the intended meaning is: *Regardless of whether a certificate comes or not.*

If we had *regardless*, it would be necessarily followed by the preposition *of* and then we would have no choice but to use *whether* (case 1 above). In the context of the alternatives (*comes or not*) being explicitly mentioned, *regardless* can be dropped. Then the preposition, too, would go. We would be left with: *Whether the certification comes or not....* So this is the correct construction.

illumine/illuminated

Is the Mysore Palace *illumined* or *illuminated* during Dussera?

Both words have the same Latin origin, meaning 'to light up, brighten'. But in current English, the word usually preferred when a place is lit up by lights is *illuminated*. *Illuminations* (plural) refers to the colourful lights used to make a place bright and beautiful: *the Brindavan Garden illuminations*. In the figurative sense of 'making clear, throwing light on some obscure/difficult point', the word in use is *illuminating*: *an illuminating commentary*. *Illumine* (v) is used in this sense only. *We pray to the Universal Spirit to illumine the mind.*

impersonal 'one'

One is generally used as an indefinite pronoun referring to people in general: *One is bound to lose in the end* (COD). *One should always do one's duty.* In these cases, the speaker is also naturally included but the emphasis is on 'people in general'. This is the impersonal *one*.

There is another use of *one* where it is no more than a substitute for the speaker; i.e., a substitute for *I. He asked me to review his new novel. Of course, one did not like to refuse* (Zandvoort). This use of *one* was condemned by Fowler as 'a mere misuse of the impersonal *one*'. How pretentious this use can sound can be gauged by these examples: *One is rather busy just now./One is glad to have seen you.* The usage has not found approval even today. This is what the COD has to say: *often regarded as an affectation*. In the light of these observations, the reader can judge for himself the tone of these sentences from a review. *Honestly one did not know that she had authored another ten books since one had harshly commented on* Starry Nights *in a syndicated column some years ago and decided never to touch a De again. But one must confess that the temptation to know her better literally forced oneself to try once again*. I hold no brief for Shobha De but the reviewer's assumed air of superiority borders on the ridiculous.

The use of *one* in this sense is best avoided. As for the use of *one* in the sense of 'people in general, including the speaker', the use is most often found in general statements. *One must do one's duty*. It is formal. In common, informal use, the pronoun *you* is generally used. Cf *One can do what one likes here./You can do what you like here. What can one do in such cases?/What can you do in such cases?* The word *man* is also found in this usage. *What can a man do in such cases?*

In the impersonal use, British English usually has *one* as the coreferential pronoun. *One doesn't know what one should do*. In American English, *he/her* and related forms are found in this construction. *One doesn't know what one must do. One must allow himself some rest from time to time*. If a tag question appears, *one* can be referred to by *you* also. *One can't be too careful, can one?/Can you?*

Here as in so many other matters, IE follows (without knowing it) American usage. The use of *he, her*, etc. to refer back to *one* (introduced earlier) is quite common. Strict schoolmasters—if there are any such today—continue to correct such 'lapses'.

'inmates'

The word is standardly used of persons kept in a hospital, prison, or lunatic asylum. *The inmates escaped after beating up the wardens*. But in IE, the word has acquired an extended sense. One routinely hears of *the inmates of the hostel, of the house*, etc. Perhaps we use the word *inmate* in these cases because no equally short substitute is available. The word *residents* (in the case of a hostel) is sometimes found in an effort to avoid *inmates*. Another word would be *members*.

introductory 'there'

How many boys are in the class? How much water is in the tank? Questions like these can be heard in many classrooms. The correct forms are: *How many boys are there in the class? How much water is there in the tank?*

To see why this is so, look at the corresponding statements. *There are x-many boys in the class. There is x-much water in the tank.* (I use *x-many* to indicate a possible number; *x-much* is used to indicate some possible quantity/amount.) These structures already contain *there*. In questions, *how many boys/how much water* appear in initial position.

This triggers inversion. That is, the subject word *there* and the verb change places. So we get: *How many boys are there in the class?/How much water is there in the tank?*

There in these structures is called the *introductory there*, to be distinguished from the *adverbial there*. Both can be found in the same sentence. *There is a lizard over there on the wall.*

Why does *there* appear in these sentences?

Sentences indicating location (*X is in the garden*), existence (*X is/was*), and containing a form of BE (*is, are*, etc.) cannot begin with 'indefinite' subjects. 'Indefinite' is a technical term meaning 'not introduced or mentioned before'. So we can't have *A lizard is on the wall*. We have to move a *lizard* to a position after *is: -a lizard on the wall*. The subject position is now empty. It has to be filled. (This is a requirement of English, though not of all languages.) For this purpose, English uses the empty word *there*. And so we get: *There is a lizard on the wall.*

This account explains why we can't say *Twenty boys are in the class.* We have to say *There are twenty boys in the class.*

This restriction on indefinite subjects is found only with 'existential' and 'locational' sentences with BE and a couple of other verbs. Hence we can say *An old man lived in a forest* since there is no form of BE here. Where the sense is not of existence or location, indefinite subjects can freely occur. *A kangaroo jumped into the room./An owl peeped through the window.* And even in the sense of existence/location, definite subjects can appear without *there*. *The doctor is in the other room./The library is further down the street.* See also: *there* in IE.

Irish bull?

The climate in the centre of Australia is so terrible that the inhabitants have to live elsewhere. What was that again? The inhabitants live elsewhere? Then how are they inhabitants? This is an example of a form of utterance called the *Irish bull*. It seems to make sense. Then on closer reading, you notice there is an absurd contradiction. Nevertheless, the overall impression remains that a point has been made.

The foreman of a jury gave the verdict: *We find the man who stole the horse not guilty.* And Sam Goldwyn, the legendary head of MGM is reported to have said, *A verbal agreement is not worth the paper it is written on.* The baseball player Yogi Berra was much given to this way of talking. He once remarked of a restaurant: *That restaurant is so crowded, nobody goes there anymore.*

Are the speakers aware of the contradictions in what they say? Possibly not. And for that reason they are held up to ridicule. But the fact remains that many of these statements, ridiculous as they seem, do make sense. They are interpretable.

If nobody goes to the restaurant anymore, how is it crowded? Obviously it is still crowded. But you and people who you know don't go there anymore. This way the sentence makes sense. Not all cases of Irish bulls can be explained in this way. But the apparent contradiction can, usually, be resolved. In the foreman's verdict, *the man who stole the horse* should be interpreted as: *the man who allegedly stole the horse.* As for Sam Goldwyn's statement, the contradiction becomes clear when we understand verbal as oral. How can an oral agreement be on paper? Now how to resolve the contradiction? The phrase 'the paper on which it is written' should be interpreted as something of no value, as indeed it is. The paper is worthless. Then we can see how useless an oral agreement is. Even greater ingenuity is needed to resolve the contradiction in the sentence on Australia.

To understand better how an Irish bull works (or at least the class of Irish bulls now being considered), let us compare it with the figure of speech, the oxymoron. An oxymoron and an Irish bull both involve a contradiction. *Wedded maid, a modern classic,* these are oxymorons. The interpretation of such phrases assumes that both the opposites are true. Mary is a maid but she is also a mother. The book is a modern one; it has all the aesthetic and literary qualities of a classic. But in an Irish bull, the contradiction is used to emphasize a point. 'The climate in Central Australia is terrible.' This is emphasized by the self-contradictory statement: *The inhabitants live elsewhere.*

Seeing how these statements work, one can perhaps use the Irish bull—now understood as a rhetorical device—to make a point. Here is an example: *She intrigues me. She reminds me of someone I have forgotten.* Not all so-called Irish bulls work this way. Some of them are just contradictory or incongruous statements begging the question. *'I am glad I hate onions because if I liked onions, I'd eat them, and I can't stand onions.'*

Webster's *New World Dictionary* (1986) from which the last citation is taken defines Irish bull in this way: *a ludicrously illogical or incongruous mistake in statement.* And the OED says: *an expression containing a manifest contradiction in terms or involving a ludicrous inconsistency unperceived by the speaker.* But in a subset of Irish bulls, the ones we have examined, it is possible to discern a structure and meaning and set up Irish bull as a rhetorical device.

Irishman may be given naturally to this way of talking but it should be possible for others, too, to come out with 'bulls' exploiting contradiction. And so it is. The famous Groucho Marx said: 'Please accept my resignation. I don't want to belong to any club that will have me as a member.' And Woody Allen, the actor: 'The food there is terrible and the portions small.' And Marx again: 'Excuse me for not answering your letter sooner,' but I have been so busy not answering letters that I couldn't get around to not answering yours in time.' 'Wagner's music is better than it sounds' (Mark Twain).

Indeed as a Dublin University professor put it, characteristically: 'An Irish bull is always pregnant.'

irony

Irony as a figure of speech should be distinguished from the way the word is used in ordinary language. In ordinary language, it is used to refer to 'a state of affairs or an event that seems deliberately contrary to what one expects and is often amusing as a result' (NODE). *It is one of the ironies of history that had Jawaharlal Nehru been a brighter achiever in his youth, he might never have attained the political heights he did in adulthood* (Tharoor, 2003, p. 17).

As a figure, irony involves the use of language that normally signifies the opposite of that expressed by the words. Supposing an adoring father says of his 10-year-old son: 'He is a boy wonder, the hope of humanity'. You may say: 'Well, you seem to have a great sense of modesty'—that would be ironic. A famous literary example would be Antony's frequent reference to Brutus as *'an honourable man'* in his funeral oration over the murdered Caesar.

Dramatic irony is a term in literary criticism. It refers to a 'technique originally used in Greek tragedy, by which the full significance of a character's words or actions are clear to the audience or reader although unknown to the character' (NODE). Thus in Sophocles' *Oedipus Rex*, the king asks repeatedly, in anguish, who the vile villain is whose actions have brought a great calamity on his kingdom, not knowing that the villain is himself (Scene 1). The audience, to whom the story is known beforehand watches with great commiseration as the poor king, unaware of the heinous crimes he has committed in ignorance, goes about trying to find the villain and slowly learns the horrible truth.

'it costed me'

A very common mistake in the use of verbs is seen in the form *costed*. Many are under the impression that the past form of *cost* is *costed*. *Nice furniture.—Yes. It costed me a cool fifty thousand.* You can't blame the man who says *costed*. That, in fact, follows the pattern in which most verbs form the past tense: *walk-walked, talk-talked, jump-jumped....* Incidentally, verbs which form their past tense in this way are called 'weak' verbs. They form the past form by adding *d, ed,* or *t* to the present form. But the past form of *cost* is *cost*.

Other verbs whose past forms are the same as their present are: *hurt, let, cast, shut, split, spread, cut, thrust*. Surprisingly nobody says *cutted*. But I have been assured of the existence of *thrusted*. A senior executive of a firm in Bangalore told me that he was quite used to people in his organization saying 'What can I do? It has been thrusted upon me.'

The verb *have* when used as an auxiliary (= helping verb) must be followed by a past participle form. *I have seen him* (not *I have saw him*). *I have written to him* (not *I have wrote to him*). The 'weak' verbs listed above show no change. Their past participle form, too, is the same as their present tense form. *I have cut the rope./I have split the wood./I have put away my winter clothes.*

With other verbs, their past participle forms must be learned. Failure to do so results in a sentence like: *...women's organizations, media...have constantly raised the issue of violence against women and have strived to create public awareness....*

Here we have two instances of *have* + verb: *have raised, have strived*. The first one is correct. The past participle of *raise* is the same as its past tense form, i.e., *raised*. But the past participle of *strive* is *striven*. (The past tense form is *strove*.) The term *strived* is doubly incorrect. There is no form like *strived*. What we need here is the past participle form *striven*. *...women's organizations...have striven to create public awareness....*

Usually three forms of each verb are listed: the 'stem' or 'base' form (also called the 'dictionary' form because that is how verbs are listed in the dictionary), the past tense form and the past participle form. There is one more form, the present participle form. But this creates no problems. It is the form which ends in *-ing* and is the same for all verbs: *reading, writing, cutting, putting*.... (When speaking about a verb, the convention is to write it with *to: to speak, to write*: 'What is the past tense of the verb *to speak*?' More recently the convention of writing in capital letters has been adopted. 'What is the past form of SPEAK?')

Failure to use the past participle form of the verb with HAVE is not limited to the one example cited. *I have wrote* is also common. More generally the past participle seems to present some difficulty to non-native speakers as seen in the famous phrase *'English as she is spoke.'* There is no HAVE here. But the sentence is in the passive. So the verbal group must contain a form of BE followed by the past participle of the verb SPEAK: *'English as she is spoken.'* Incidentally the phrase is the title of a Portugese-English conversation guide published in the eighteenth century.

In the colonial days, the natives working in English households had developed their own brand of English, Butler English. One distinguishing feature of this English was the formation of the past participle by adding *done. I done tell* ('I have told'), *done come* ('actually arrived').

j

jargon

Jargon has been defined variously. In one definition, it is the technical language of the sciences and, more generally, of serious, scholarly writing (philosophy, literary criticism, art, etc.). It is in the light of this definition that we will examine jargon in the context of good writing.

Clearly the various branches of knowledge have to develop their own special vocabulary: concepts have to be identified, analysed, named; and their interaction with other concepts analysed in appropriate terms. In the process, a large number of precisely defined terms will emerge—the technical vocabulary of the subject. When someone reads: *The Receptor: The distal end of a dendrite or sensory structure associated with the distal end of a neuron; it responds to a stimulus by initiating a localized depolarization that, if it is of threshold value, initiates a nerve impulse in a sensory neuron.* (Tottora, et al., *Laboratory Exercises in Anatomy and Physiology*, p. 246); or 'An off-line Turing machine is a multiple TM whose input tape is read-only' (J.E. Hopcroft and J.D. Ullman, *Introduction to Automata Theory*), he won't understand anything unless he has some aquaintance with physiology or automata theory. No one in his senses can (or will) pick fault with this kind of writing as being 'unintelligible'.

It is when we come to the social sciences—economics, sociology, education for example—that we become restive and begin to wonder why the author doesn't write in a more comprehensible way (if that is the case).

Fowler quotes this passage as an illustration of writers suffering from the disease of 'abstractitis': *Whereas the micro-economic neo-classical theory of distribution was based on a postulate of rationality suited to their static analysis and institutional assumptions, we are no longer justified in accepting this basis and are set the problem of discovering the value premises suited to the expectational analysis and the institutional nature of modern business....*

If this is from a popular book on economics, we can protest that this is just so much gibberish. But if it is from a technical publication, we have no one but ourselves to blame for trying to read it. *Microeconomics, neoclassical theory of distribution, state analysis, institutional assumptions* are technical terms perfectly justified in their proper context. Economics has come a long way from the days of Adam Smith and *The Wealth of Nations*.

Burchfield (1998) quotes with approval John Searle bemoaning the rise of such terms as *ethnicity, hegemony, empowerment, post-structuralism,* and *deconstruction*. I see little point in condemning these terms. Studies in the humanities and social sciences are moving from a pre-theoretical to a theoretical stage. Inevitably there is a burgeoning of complex ideas and technical terms. It is when familiar concepts—all too familiar to everyone—are clothed in mystifying terminology that one cannot but protest. The family and society are not esoteric entities like dendrites or abstract concepts like a Turing machine. So one expects a discussion on the family life to be reasonably intelligible. But when we read: *The home then is the specific zone of functional potency that grows about a live parenthood; a zone at the periphery of which is an active interfacial membrane or surface furthering exchange—from within outwards and from without inwards—a mutualizing membrane between the family and the society in which it lives* (quoted in Fowler, 1965), this is surely the 'scientific approach' gone mad—by flaunting a battery of pseudo-technical terms for quite simple concepts. *The specific zone of functional potency that grows about a live parenthood* can only mean (if it means anything at all) 'parents and their children'. The classic example of this misplaced analytic precision is Dr Johnson's definition of 'network' in his dictionary: *Anything reticulated or decussated at equal distances, with interstices between the intersections.*

Other areas where the pseudo-scientific approach has resulted in pompous vacuity are business management and education. The BM jargon is particularly hilarious. I give a couple of quotations from *The Dilbert Principle* by Scott Adams.

A Mission Statement: We will produce the highest quality products, using empowered team dynamics in a new Total Quality Paradigm until we become the industry leader.

'The Business Service Leadership Team will enhance the organization in order to continue on the journey toward a Market Facing Organization (MFO) model. To that end we are consolidating the Object Management for Business Services into a cross strata team'.

The Dilbert Principle is a satirical book on modern business management. Even so it gives a fairly clear idea of Bizspeak. Here is a high official of the Directorate-General of Tourism, Government of India, writing in the publication, *Travellers India* '... We plan to create a synergy to project a unified image of India.' *Synergy, commitment, competitive edge, philosophy, framework, empowerment*...are the common counters of this lingo. One authority who harps on *actualizing practices* urges managers *to promote into management those people who have people first values and translate your people first values into actions everyday.* Another talks about *adult time structuring index* (*Deccan Herald*, 31 December 2003). This piece of jargon can be matched with *a structured negotiating stance* (*The Indian Express*, 15 March 2004).

The politico-economic scene at the international level is a fertile ground for much obfuscatory writing. See some citations under PERIPHRASIS. Here I will content myself with just two specimens (both from the same paper—*News Asia* 14–20 January 2004). *The volatility of the global economy and its unpredictable economic stresses have evidently affected the poor disproportionately.../ The government should pursue interactive and participatory methods of political engagement in domestic context for bringing more and more people and groups on board for the dialogue.*

There is no need, I think, to belabour the point further with specimens of educational jargon. But I must cite a *new* development in this area—initialisms, especially as used in ELT (English Language Teaching). I once sat through a seminar on teacher training and noted this extraordinary sentence: *If a TT from the RIE who wanted to study ELT came to the...and opted to specialize in ESP as against, say, EAP or EGP, what sort of ET should we devise for him?* (TT = Teacher Trainee; RIE = Regional Institute of English; ELT = English Language Teaching; ESP = English for Special Purposes; EAP = English for Academic Purposes; ET = Entrance Test).

It is well to recall Fowler's observations on such matters made a long time ago. These writers seem to suffer a feeling 'that the lack of any abstruseness in their subject demands a compensatory abstruseness in their language.'

Now for the intrusion of jargon into the ordinary language (OL) of daily life. *Decimate* is a term from the military. It originally meant 'to execute one man in ten as a punishment among mutinous troops'. In popular language it does not have this meaning, of course. It came in for criticism but now the word means (in addition to its original sense) 'to destroy or kill a large part of'. This is generally what happens when technical words enter popular usage. *Arithmetic progression* and *geometric progression* have a precise meaning in mathematics. But when you read: *Agricultural production is increasing in arithmetic progression while population growth is rising in geometric progression*—all that is meant is that the increase in agricultural production is nothing compared to the growth in population. Similarly terms from other disciplines: *moron, psychopath* (from psychology); *allergic* (from medicine); *chain reaction* (from physics) have entered OL with their sharp, technical meanings smoothened and rounded off.

I see no reason why these usages should be condemned. They are what one would expect in a lively, growing language. Ordinary language (OL) not only borrows words from other languages; it borrows words from the specialized registers of the same language.

What is condemnable is the use of 'strongly' technical words in OL. By strongly technical words I mean technical words which will not be 'smoothened' and 'rounded off' as OL words. *Envelope* is a technical word in mathematics but it is in use now in OL in the phrase *to push the envelope* ('to extend the limits of what is possible'). But you cannot speak to your friend about *embolism;* you should be talking about a blood clot. Such usages are rare but I know of a college principal who was flabbergasted to receive a leave note from a lecturer that he wanted a day's casual leave as he was in a *febrile state* (= feverish).

More pervasive is the use of 'analytical language', full of abstractions—periphrasis involving scientific/pseudo-scientific terms—

in daily usage. I have heard an executive tell his 10-year old son that he *should budget his time* and prioritize *his activities*. I should not be surprised if he should tell him, at a later date, that he should *make advance provision for future contingencies of a destabilizing nature* (= save for a rainy day).

jealousy and envy

Jealous and *envious* are usually glossed in terms of each other. But the forms *jealous, envy* can have different meanings. While you can say *I envy your new car*, you cannot say *I am jealous of your new car*. And while you can say *They jealously guard their rights*, you cannot say *They enviously guard their rights*.

Jealous (adj.) means (in the relevant sense): 'watchful, eager to protect, afraid of losing but unwilling to lose'. Thus: *a jealous husband / lover*. Envy (v) means (again in the relevant sense): 'admiring something but unhappy that you don't have it'.

There is nothing pejorative about *They jealously protect their rights*; nor is there anything to be ashamed of in: *I envy your talent as a singer*. It is just a handsome compliment.

Then how do these words acquire the negative import usually associated with them?

It depends on *your* reaction to another's success or possession. If you are unhappy and angry about it, you are *jealous and envious* in the negative sense.

'join duty'

An Indianism. The Standard English phrase is: *to take up duties*. In Standard English, you join the armed forces / a club.

It would be of interest to know how IE got this phrase. We not only *join duty;* we have a *joining report*. Perhaps someone has an appointment order issued in the 1930s. I would like to know how it is worded.

Many of the official expressions we use are what the British taught us. So how did we get the phrase—*to join duty?*

I

language of the marriage market

A look at the matrimonial columns of an English daily gives interesting clues to the ways IE is developing in this area of usage.

Everyone knows about *cultured/educated, eminent/orthodox families*. (The boy usually comes from some such family and the parents are looking for a girl from a similar family.)

An innovative phrase in this context is a *status family*. ...*match for status family*... *Brahmin boy*. An IAS officer calls upon *parents of v. beautiful, well-educated girl from status family* to send *kundli* (= horoscope) and photo'.

In the usual cases of *cultured/educated/orthodox family*, the phrases are equivalent to 'the family is educated/cultured/orthodox'. That is, the words *cultured/educated/orthodox* can appear in the predicate position after *is*. But *status* is not like one of these words. There is no construction: *the family is status*. So *status family* is not possible.

There is the phrase a *status symbol* meaning 'something indicating status or high position'. But this cannot be the meaning of *status family*. The intended meaning is: 'a family of some status'. But there is no way that we can legitimately get this meaning from a *status family*.

A man of wealth = 'a wealthy man'; *a woman of sense* = 'a sensible woman'; *a man of eminence* = 'an eminent man'. But there is no corresponding adjective for *status*.

Another interesting phrase is a *convented girl*: *Fair, beautiful 24/25 year, tall, slim, convented, tech. quali.* [technically qualified]...*non-Kashyap girl of status family for handsome Sr. Er. PSU boy...* (= Senior Engineer in a Public Sector Undertaking).

A *convent* (cf *monastery*) is a place where women of a Christian religious order live together. There was the practice (at an earlier age) of sending a woman to a convent—to live the life of a spinster. *Convented* (v., non-existent) cannot be taken in this sense.

Obviously what is intended now is: 'one who has been educated in a convent school'. The verb, in this sense too, is non-existent. (In the sense of living in a convent, we have the verb *cloistered*—'monastic life of seclusion').

English has *homely* in the sense of: 'simple, plain; unpretentious (of people or their features), not attractive in appearance, ugly (COD, 8th edn). But in IE, it has acquired quite a different meaning. It is used to mean 'home loving'. A *homely girl* is one who is attached to the home; as against one who is keen on making a career for herself. *Suitable match for a handsome Bhumihar boy.... Girl should be fair, educated, and homely.*

I wish the boy good luck. It is becoming more and more difficult to get 'homely' girls.

You can be good at athletics, gymnastics.... But academics? Apparently this, too, is possible. *Bhumihar Vats parents seek alliance for their son...girl should be slim, beautiful with good academics.*

English has *academic* in the sense of 'a member of a university teaching staff, a scholarly person.' The plural can only refer to such persons. But the advertiser is thinking of the girl's scholastic record. She must have a distinguished record at school and college.

In a matrimonial ad. where every word has to be paid for, brevity is all important. Even so, a *professional match* may leave one stumped. A *professional match* is not a match arranged/organized by a professional group of matchmakers. It is a specification about the spouse required. He/she must be a professional. *Kumadri Brahmin, well placed MBA. Status family professional match required.*

I will end with an ad. where the reader can work out for himself what *sober* is supposed to mean. *For best marriage proposals, of handsome, educated, industrialist boys/pretty, sober girls....*

The primary meaning of *sober* is 'not drunk'. (All citations are from *The Sunday Times of India*, New Delhi, 11 January 2000.)

'legacy is prevalent?'

A publicity release of the Karnataka Information speaks of Gandhiji's love for the development of the rural masses, Nehru's passion for science and technology, Dr Ambedkar's commitment for [*sic*] social justice and adds: *This legacy is prevalent in Karnataka.* (*Deccan Herald*, 15 August 2001, p. 10).

Prevalent is generally used in respect of customs, beliefs, and (yes!) diseases as in: *Polyandry is still prevalent among some Polynesian tribes./ The belief in ghosts and spirits is widely prevalent even among educated people./ Yellow fever is prevalent in certain regions of Africa.* The meaning is, 'it exists, is found'.

Legacy is an inheritance. It may be a piece of property, jewellery (*The diamond brooch was a legacy from a distant aunt*) or anything passed on from a predecessor or an earlier age. *Our railways and postal system are a legacy of the British rule in India./Many feel that the Kashmir problem is a legacy of Nehru's diplomacy.*

In the examples given above, *legacy* has not been used as a subject. Suppose we use it as a subject. What is the verb (or class of verbs) that goes with it? Specifically, can we say; 'Legacy is prevalent?'

We should distinguish between *legacy* and the specifics or content of a *legacy*. The specifics of a *legacy*, e.g., the colonial mentality (part of the *legacy* of the British rule) may be said to be still prevalent/to exist/to be widespread. Similarly, belief in witches and witchcraft (a *legacy* of the Middle Ages) still persists (or is prevalent) in parts of Europe. But *legacy* itself can only be alive or dead or forgotten. *Forgetting their priceless legacy, many Indians are trying to make a living abroad. Gandhiji's legacy, like the Buddha's, is now dead in India.*

It can now be seen that the release of the Karnataka Information should have read: *These ideals still guide us in Karnataka.* Or: *This legacy is still very much alive in Karnataka.*

lest

A somewhat infrequent word in current English is the word *lest*. The word means something like; 'for fear that, in order that...no'. *She is using headphones lest she disturb anyone. He has sought protection lest he be attacked.* Notice the phrases: *lest he be attacked/lest she disturb anyone.* It is not *lest he was attacked* or *lest she disturbs anyone.*

One would suppose that according to the rules of agreement, the singular subjects *he/she* would be followed by the singular verbs *was/disturbs*.

This construction, where there is no subject-verb agreement, is an example of what is known as the 'subjunctive' in English. The use of the subjunctive is quite rare in current English (except in such formulaic expressions as *God save the Queen*, etc.). But one of the contexts where it necessarily occurs is after the word *lest*.

In the examples discussed, there is no finite verb (*be, disturb* are not finite). But we have a finite verb in cases like: *He ran away* lest he should *be seen./She was afraid* lest he might *return* (ALD). How is this possible?

The only finite forms possible are those which express not a fact but a possibility. Hence *should* can occur after *lest*; also *might*.

In the light of this discussion, it will be seen that the following sentence (an authentic one) is inadmissible: *Judicial intervention is necessary for a country like India where [sic] majority are ignorant about laws, lest our Constitution will be in jeopardy.* It should have read: *lest our Constitution be in jeopardy.* Here is another citation: *The time had come for the two neighbouring countries to work together for progress and development, lest the two countries lagged further behind the global race to prosperity.* Rather than use the near-archaic term *lest*, one could very well use the paraphrase *so that...not: Judicial intervention is necessary so that our constitution will not break down.*

litotes

This is defined by the COD as the expression of an affirmative by the negative of its contrary, e.g., *I shan't be sorry* for: *I shall be glad.*

Litotes is the opposite of hyperbole. While hyperbole makes its point by an overstatement, litotes makes its point by an understatement. It is a way of indicating a positive value by negating a term suggesting a low value, e.g., *a no mean scholar* (a great scholar); *a no mean batsman* (a great batsman). *The leaders of the Labour party have been denouncing the communists in no uncertain terms* (Orwell, *Collected Essays*, p. 185).

The negative particle in litotes is usually *no. Not* generally has just a negative meaning; *He is not Tendulkar* can be said in a situation where your friend mistakenly thinks that X is Tendulkar. But *Dravid is no Tendulkar* means that there is no way you can compare D with T as a batsman.

locality/local

She still reads books regularly from our locality library. Here we see a confusion between *local* and *locality. Local* is the adjective meaning 'belonging to a particular place or district'. Thus we have: *the local doctor/grocer/shopkeeper*, etc. Hence also *the local library.*

Locality (n) refers to the position of a thing or object; its location, also, 'a neighbourhood', the place where one lives or where something happens. *After Togadia's visit, the whole locality was in a feverish state.*

'logged with water'

Of the many types of compounds in English, compounds whose first element is a noun and the second element a verb are particularly interesting. These are compounds of the type *housekeeping, daybreak, bloodshed*, etc. It is usually possible to paraphrase them as in *the shedding of blood, keeping the house* (i.e. managing household affairs), etc.

But such paraphrases are not always available. *Jam-packed* does not mean 'packed with jam'; *self-defeating* is not 'defeating the self'. But the fact that a paraphrase is available in many cases misleads one into believing that a paraphrase is available in every case.

Waterlogged means 'saturated with, or full of, water'. *The recent rains have left many roads and areas waterlogged.* It derives from *waterlog* ('make a ship unmanageable by flooding'). But you can't say *logged with water*. The following sentence (an authentic one) is inadmissible: *Every time it rains, the entire area is logged with water. Log* as a verb has several meanings but none where it means 'fill with'.

m

make it clear

The point about this construction becomes clear when we examine a sentence like: *He made it clear that the proposal was not acceptable to him.* We understand the object of *made* to be: *that the proposal was not acceptable to him.* But if this clausal object remains after *made*, it will be quite difficult to process the sentence: *He made that the proposal was not acceptable to him clear.* To facilitate easy processing, the clause is shifted to the end of the sentence. It is *extraposed,* to use the technical term. Then the empty object position is filled by the dummy object *it.* This *it* refers to the extraposed clause.

Supposing the object had been a noun phrase (and not a clause). It would then stay in its original position. *He made the point clear* (not *He made it clear the point.* Or *He made clear the point*).

Consider now the case where the clause has its own head, a noun phrase: *the point that the proposal was not acceptable to him.* The original sentence will now read: *He made the point clear that the proposal was not acceptable to him.* The noun phrase head will stay after *made* but the clause which depends on the head will be extraposed. Note also: you cannot have: **He made it clear the point that the proposal was not acceptable to him.*

In this construction, then, *make* takes an object and an 'object complement' (= the adjective *clear*). If the object is a simple noun phrase, it will stay after *make* (*He made the point clear*). If the object is a clause, it will be shifted to the end and the now empty object position filled by *it.* If the object is a noun phrase with a clause following it, the noun phrase will stay after *make.* The clause will be shifted to the end (= exraposed). It is only in one case, where the object is just a clause, that *make* is followed by *it* and we get *make it clear.*

Consider now a last case where *make clear* appears without *it. That he would not oppose the move was made clear by his silence.* This is a passive construction. In the active version we would have *His silence made it clear that he would not oppose the move.*

So it is only when the object clause is shifted to the right that *it* appears. When it is shifted to the left (under *passivization*), no *it* appears between *make* and *clear.*

In a few cases, the verb + adjective forms so close a unit as to become inseparable. In such cases, we don't find *it.* This is so, for example, with *think* and the adjectives *fit, right, proper. After ten years of devoted service he thought fit to dismiss her without a pension* (Zandvoort).

'make the first impression'?

Some years ago, *The Times of India* carried an advertisement for Raymond suitings. There was a picture of a well-dressed man; a brief sentence, split into four fragments, made up the copy. 'You don't get a second chance to make the first impression' (*The Times of India*, 25 October 2002).

Almost three years earlier in one of my pieces ('Copy that clicks', *Deccan Herald*, 19 September 1999) I had talked about some striking pieces of ad. writing, beginning with the one I had seen on some New York buses: *If it is in fashion, it is in Vogue* (This ad. actually reads: *Before it's in fashion, it's in Vogue*).

Continuing, I had suggested: *No second chance for a first impression.* This could be, I had said, an advertisement for a piece of fine suiting or even a toothpaste (the accompanying picture could show a person with a glamorous smile and a dazzling set of teeth).

I couldn't then imagine that one day the copy I then wrote would actually turn up, slightly modified, advertising a piece of fine suiting!

I would like to believe that this was just a coincidence and not plagiarism; that the copywriter for the agency had hit upon the same words by a stroke of serendipity.

But do you 'make the first impression'? You might make a good/bad/favourable/unfavourable impression. But how do you 'make the first impression'? You should take every precaution to see that the first impression people have of you is a favourable one. If you fail in the first attempt, there is no way that you can get the first chance again. It is gone for good.

It is for this reason that I wrote: *No second chance for a first impression.* The copy is terser and makes sense.

Make can go with 'impression' when there is a preceding adjective (as already noted): *make a good impression.* It can also be used without any adjective: *He made an impression.* This is understood as a 'favourable, good impression'. But *He made the first impression* makes little sense.

miles and kilometres

The metric system is the order of the day—except in America. The Americans are quite unwilling to give up the old 'foot-pound' system. The story is told of a shopkeeper who decided (under pressure) to announce that he was going 'metric'. He wanted to have a signboard put up to that effect. The painter asked him 'how big do you want the board to be?' The shopkeeper said: 'Well, about two feet long and twelve inches wide' (*The New York Times* gave this story to show why America would never go metric).

How about us? Distances are now generally given in kilometres; liquids are dispensed in litres, and the currency, too, is in terms of 100 units. Although we still have the rupee, it is no longer sixteen *annas* but a hundred *paise*. Even old-timers have given up saying 'eight annas' and 'four annas'. It is 'fifty paise' and 'twenty-five paise'.

But if you look at the language, the old forms continue: *mooru kaasiguu prayojanavilla* (Kannada: not worth even three *kaasu*—the old minimal unit when a rupee was worth 192 of them—utterly useless). I can cite many more sayings, proverbial and otherwise, where the old forms are still retained. I'm sure readers will find parallels in their own languages. This is so in English, too. We still speak of 'mileage' (in connnection with cars and scooters) when it is all kilometres now. Manufacturers, I think, speak of 'so many kilometres per litre'. The question would be: How many kilometres per litre? But people do ask, I think, *How's the mileage*? In any case, the suffix -*age* cannot be added to kilometre.

This apart, *mile* survives in the expression: *A miss is good as a mile*. Distances are marked on highways on a stone and this is a *milestone*. It is unlikely that this will ever become a *kilometrestone*. In the figurative sense, too, it is simply ridiculous to say that C.V. Raman's work marks a *kilometrestone* in the study of optics. The famous line 'I have miles to go before I sleep' (Robert Frost) is likely to last as long as the English language is there. The phrases *miles better* ('You had a severe headache this morning. How are you feeling now?' 'Miles better'.); *beat them by miles* (*we are always beating our opponents in cricket by miles before the match begins*) will never be replaced by 'kilometre'.

In the literal sense, too (in addition to the phrases listed earlier), *miles* survives (and will survive!). In a context like 'We have been walking for miles. Don't you think it is time to stop and rest?' I can't imagine how anybody can use *kilometre*.

The point has a more practical angle. Teachers in lower classes are warned, it appears, not to use the word *mile* since it is now *kilometre*. If it is meant to cover all contexts, I can only say: 'God save the children.'

In spite of millimetre, centimetre, and metre, we continue to use the phrases: *inch by inch* (*We made our way up the cliff inch by inch*); *give somebody an inch and he will take a mile*; *yardstick* (= standard used for comparison. *We tend to bring in China as a yardstick to measure our progress in any field*).

It is not just in this area but in other areas, too, concepts discarded for scientific (or other) reasons continue to live in the language and people continue to use them. The age of chivalry and duels is gone but we still speak of *throwing in the gauntlet* (= challenging). Even those who scoff at astrology will say: 'Well, his stars are on the ascendant.'

The fact that some terms have been replaced by other terms (for scientific or other reasons) does not mean that such terms will die and disappear from the language. For this reason, teachers should not put children under a handicap by not teaching those terms.

missing heads

Here is an interesting linguistic phenomenon. To distinguish gardens from places where animals are kept, the expression *zoological gardens* came into use. But subsequently, the modifier *zoological* took on an independent existence. It became a noun: *zoo*. *Coffee* with the caffeine taken out was *decaffeinated coffee*. But now it has become just *decaf*.

Not surprisingly this is not a recent phenomenon. Theatres were there long before the motion picture came on the scene. So we got *cinema theatre*. But then this got shortened to *cinema*.

Safire, who discusses this question briefly (*Watching My Language*, 1997, p. 150) cites a number of other such expressions sent to him by a correspondent. Here are some of them: *oral exams—orals; final exams—finals; glossy photos—glossies; bell-bottom trousers—bellbottoms; daily newspapers—dailies*.

Indeed this is a very productive way of forming new nouns. Safire's correspondent could have easily noted (along with *dailies*) such other nouns as *weeklies, monthlies*, and *annuals*. When it comes to travel by train we have in our country (possibly elsewhere, too) *passenger, mail*, and *express—* all understood as nouns, although they really stand for *passenger train, mail train*, and *express train*. Some people travel by *AC*. Sometimes this is further distinguished as *First AC, Second AC*. Similarly *Two-tier* and *Three-tier*.

My Lord

There is a move to do away with the practice of addressing High Court judges as 'My Lord'. The custom, established from the days of the British rule in India, is viewed as a vestige of colonialism, best done away with.

My Lord

The title *Lord* is part of the feudal privileges enjoyed by members of the British aristocracy like marquises, earls, viscounts, and barons. These are persons who are entitled to sit in the House of Lords by virtue of their birth. They are the 'peers of the realm'; others (they are also Lords) may be elevated to sit in the House of Lords for their life—'life peers'.

Besides these two classes of Lords, there are others whose designation carries the title *Lord: Lord Mayor, Lord Provost, Lord Steward, Lord High Commissioner, Lord President of the Council,* etc.

A member of the House of Lords (whether a peer of the realm or a life peer) is referred to as 'Lord': *Lord Russell, Lord Swraj Paul.* Menials and socially inferior persons may address them as 'My Lord'. But a gentleman meeting a member of the aristocracy socially, on a basis of equality, does not do so.

However, a Bishop is always addressed as 'My Lord'; also judges of the High Court when on the Bench.

When referring to the members of the aristocracy, it is customary to use the form 'Lord X', rather than, say, 'Viscount X'.

Now to come back to the point we started with. We are a republic and not a monarchy. All are equal and, in principle, no one can claim any social superiority over others, least of all by virtue of birth. It is another matter that Britain, the oldest democracy in the world, has a hereditary aristocracy.

Having said all this, one must still admit that there is a point in holding on to tradition, especially when it is harmless, inflicts no injustice on others, and adds to the dignity of an activity. Addressing a High Court judge when in court as *My Lord* does not mean that he is a Lord in the temporal or spiritual sense (as in Britain) or that he is being equated with Lord Rama or Lord Krishna. It is a polite convention and should not create bitterness in anyone or rouse anyone's passion.

If one should object to such forms of address on egalitarian grounds, what about such conventions as 'the Honourable member' (of a House of Representatives) or the 'Honourable Minister' (or Chief Minister)—when the member/the Chief Minister may be a dacoit-turned-politician!

The same remarks apply to the practice of an attender accompanying a judge with a mace in hand. It is a symbol of authority. A mace is placed on the table in front of the Speaker of the House of Commons as a symbol of the authority of the House. On ceremonial occasions, a silver mace is carried before the vice-chancellor of a university. These are customs which have been invested with some meaning and there is no point in protesting against them. Shorn of traditional symbols, all ceremonial activities become drab and pointless.

'Your Honour' is a polite form of address when speaking to a circuit judge (UK) or a mayor (US). Perhaps the usage has got extended as a form of address to judges in general (in our country). In any case, it is 'Your Honour' and not 'My Honour'—although it is 'My Lord' and not 'Your Lord'. If *your* has to be used, it is 'Your Lordship'. The situation is somewhat parallel to *My King* vs *Your Highness*. In the third person, the forms are: His Lordship, His Honour, His Highness.

n

neither–nor

Is the following sentence correct?

When thousands of people were made refugees in their own land, neither did the... Home Minister descend from New Delhi, nor did he make any attempt at assuaging the problems faced by the hapless (Sunday Spotlight, DH, 14 July 2002).

The sentence involves the use of the correlative *neither-nor*. The grammar of this pair is a bit tricky. To begin with, note that the sentence is ungrammatical; *neither* does not trigger inversion even when it is in the initial position of its clause. The sentence should read: *The Home Minister neither descended from New Delhi, nor did he make any attempt to....* (The preferred order is for *neither* to follow the subject in this case. See below.)

Neither-nor are used in a negative context. But it is not required that they be always used as a pair. They can be used singly, as non-correlatives. *The Home Minister did not descend from ND, nor did he make any attempt to...*(nor here can be replaced by *neither* but *nor* is usually preferred).

Nor always triggers inversion in its clause if the subject is present. *Rajesh does not like Maths, nor does he want to do computers.* But if the subject is not present, naturally there is no inversion: *Rajesh neither likes Maths nor wants to do computers.*

Now for some points about *neither*. Although the sentence cited has *neither*, its use is not obligatory here. The sentence could have read: *The Home Minister did not descend from ND nor/neither did he attempt to assuage....* *Neither* would be required (1) if a negative predication is made on two conjoined subjects: *Neither the Home Minister nor the PM acted in time;* (2) a conjoined negative predication is made on a single subject: *The HM neither descended from ND, nor made an attempt to....* Observe the absence of an explicit subject after *nor*.

'no least doubt'

From a reader citing a superior court judgement. Is this correct?

The superlative form should be preceded by: *the best solution, the best course,* etc. So it should be *the least doubt.*

Now how do you negate this?

No can appear in noun phrases: *No less a man than/No two persons are the same/No clear reply was given,* etc.

But *no* cannot occur when there is an article: *Not a hand was raised* (*No a hand was raised* is impossible). So it has to be *Not the least doubt.*

Further: the sentence *I have not the least doubt* can be understood in two ways. *I have (not the least doubt); I have not (the least doubt).* This is because *not* is a sentence negative; it can also negate certain noun phrases.

non-sexist language

An off-shoot of the feminist movement is the concern (among those who are sympathetic to that movement) to do away with all expressions in the language which, in their view, show a male bias. Several publications have appeared making recommendations in the matter, *The Non-Sexist Word Finder: A Dictionary of Gender-free Usage* (R. Maggio, 1988) being, perhaps, the most thorough-going one.

Proponents of a gender-free language have focused their attention on
1. gender-marked occupational terms:
    actor-actress, poet-poetess...
2. words containing the element *man*
    chairman, postman, policeman...
3. referring pronouns: *he, his...*
4. Miscellaneous contexts highlighting one gender over the other
5. quotations and sayings containing gender-specific references.

1. This is the least controversial area. Everyone will agree that it is pointless to speak of a person as an *authoress* or *poetess* where sex is wholly irrelevant. There is no point in identifying a person as a *lady doctor.* Why a *male nurse* and not just a *nurse*? (On this see below.) We don't have sex-marked words for *teacher, architect, pilot, carpenter* and a host of others terms indicating a trade or a profession. Then why a *poetess*?

But even here problems remain. Shall we do away with the word *heroine*? This apart, the adoption of *Ms* as the preferred title before a woman's name is a welcome move. When *Mr* will do for men (married or single) why should woman use the forms *Miss, Mrs*?

2. *Chairman* has drawn a lot of flak. How can you address a woman in the chair as *chairman*? *Chairperson* was in fashion for sometime; then, *Chair*. Many felt uneasy at this. It strongly suggested a piece of furniture. So quite a few have gone back to *chairman*. *Madam Chairman* is not felt to be either ridiculous or awkward. But determined liberators would have *coordinator of a committee/department* (as the case may be) or *head* (of a department).

But a host of other words with *man*—*mailman, postman, policeman, fireman, watchman, businessman,* etc. have had acceptable alternatives suggested: *mail person/carrier, (police) officer, firefighter, guard/security, business executive....* The *common man* is *ordinary people; mankind* is *human kind. Manhole, manhandle, manslaughter* are more difficult to handle. It is difficult to see why every word with *man* has to be changed even when the word confers no special status on men as such.

3. English has no gender-free third person singular noun. Traditionally *he/his* have been used as referring pronouns; e.g. *when a judge gives his judgement.* This, it is held, conditions the mind to accepting that a woman cannot be a judge. If you use the passive, the problem doesn't arise: *when a judgement is given.* Another strategy is to use the plural: *When students have turned in their papers* (Not: *When a student has turned in his paper*), or (and this is a bit awkward) to use both *he/she* (and related forms): *When a student has a doubt he/she should be encouraged to seek clarification.* A magazine on Mother and Child refers to the baby as *she* in one paragraph and *he* in another.

Indefinite pronouns (with the exception of *some* and a few others) have singular reference only. If you begin a sentence with *each, every, any* (and the compound forms *everyone, anyone,* etc) you will have to refer to them with *he/she.* If you want to avoid this awkward expression, cast the sentence in the plural. *They all staked their claims* (instead of *Each staked his claim*). If you use *one,* continue with *one. One does not know what one should do.*

It should be clear by now that there is a point in favouring non-sexist language and in many cases it can be achieved without much awkwardness. But to insist on a wholesale and thorough jettisoning of all 'sexist' expressions would be to take an extreme step; the resulting expressions can be quite awkward, unwieldy or comical (*maintenance hole,* for example, for *manhole*).

4. Why should it be *boys and girls* and not *girls and boys*? Why *men and women* and not *women and men*? *Pradhan has two sons and three daughters.* Why not: *Pradhan has three daughters and two sons?*

Proponents of non-sexist language wish to see all suggestion of any 'male superiority' (as they see it) removed.

This can go to unbelievable lengths. *Founding Fathers*? Really. Why not *founders*? '*Einstein was the father of relativity theory*. Oh, why not *the founder of relativity theory*? (Since he can't be the mother, I suppose.)

It is not just any suggestion of male superiority that should be questioned. All hints of women being the 'weaker sex' should go. It is not just traditional adjectives as in *the fair sex, the gentle sex,* that should go. We shouldn't use any adjective or forms of reference that single out a particular sex. A girl is not a *tomboy*. She is *bold and adventurous*. Don't say that somebody is a *sissy*. Say, rather, that the person is *tender and caring*. Any singling out of women should go. *Five persons were injured in the accident, including two women.* No. *Five persons were injured in the accident.*

One can go on but one has to stop. The general idea should be clear.

5. When it comes to famous maxims and quotations we face a real problem. It is easy enough to translate: *One man's meat is another man's poison* into: *What is food for one man is poison for another; Man is a political animal* into: *The human being is a political animal.* And quotations which outrageously malign woman (*Frailty, thy name is woman*, etc) stand self-condemned. But hundreds of others, although they include the word *man* cannot be condemned as exhibiting a male bias; to change them would be to ruin them. What will you do with: *Man is the measure of all things / Man proposes, God disposes* or such eloquent pieces as: *What a piece of work is man!*...(Hamlet 2.2.) and the passage, in the same play where Hamlet rhapsodizes about a (presumed) lawyer's skull: *where be his quiddities now, his quillets, his cases his tenures, and his tricks*? (5.1.)

The hard-boiled ones would say: cut them out (See Maggio). But many will go on quoting these lines regardless of what some feminist may feel about it. Many women writers themselves, as Burchfield has noted, have blithely ignored the suggestions of their shrill feminist sisters and gone on merrily using the old, abhorrent sexist forms.

Beyond adopting *Ms* as the preferred title before a woman's name, not much seems to have been done by way of using a gender-free language in India. Jobs are advertised making perfectly clear whether a man or a woman is required for the job—as though sex determines what kind of a job a person can do. (But in our culture nurses may have to be distinguished as 'male' or 'female'.) None of the strategies outlined above for avoiding a male slant are adopted in the everyday use of English as a cursory reading of any newspaper or magazine will show.... But then the very structure of Indian languages has distinct masculine and feminine forms (in verbs even). So beyond asserting (or clamouring for) equality, feminism in India has had no impact on the use of English in the country.

non-standard/substandard

There seems to be some misunderstanding about the use of these expressions. Some people seem to feel that *substandard* is a pejorative expression. It is best to avoid it and use *non-standard* instead.

But the facts are slightly more complicated. Viewed in the context of, say, Standard British English, Indian English is a *non-standard* one. It hasn't yet achieved the legitimacy, authority of standard varieties of English other than British English, e.g., Australian English.

But within the context of British English (i.e., among the speakers of this variety of English), an expression like *ain't* would be viewed not as *non-standard* but *substandard*. In American English, too, it is generally felt to be substandard, though acceptable in certain contexts.

The two expressions, then, are not just alternatives, one preferable to the other.

'nothing but'

In Standard English, the expression is used as in: *Nothing but peace can save the world* (Only peace can save the world). *He is nothing but a common criminal. / Nothing but a miracle can save us now. / I want nothing but the best for my children. Nothing but the best will do.* (Examples from standard British dictionaries.)

As against these usages, we have in IE examples like: *the [sic] promotion is nothing but one of the rewards given to the employee by his / her organization. / An institution is nothing but a group of individuals of varied abilities, temperaments, skills, and knowledge coming together for a common goal.*

On comparing the two usages, you will find that in British English, *nothing but* is used in the sense of: (1) 'X and nothing else' and (2) 'just that and nothing else'. In both cases there is an emphatic assertion of a point which *could* be debatable. The IE usage introduces a *definition*. The British usage *He is nothing but a common criminal* is not a definition. It is an emphatic identification.

The absurdity of the IE usage will be clear by definitions like: *A triangle is nothing but a three-sided figure. / A caterpillar is nothing but a butterfly in its earlier stages.* There may be a suggestion here that what is being described is really very simple but to talk like this is nothing but nonsense.

'not to happen'

Care will be taken not to happen such things in the future (Saptagiri, September 2002).

This sounds strange. Why?

Supposing the editor had used some other verb, say, *allow, permit.* The sentence wouldn't sound so strange. *Care will be taken not to allow/ permit such things.*

Allow, permit are transitive verbs. They can be directly followed by their objects, in this case, *such things.* But *happen* is an intransitive verb. It cannot have an object. Such things can only be the subject of *happen. Care will be taken to see that such things will not happen.*

'not un-' phrase
(doubly negative phrases)

In his essay 'Politics and the English Language' (*The Collected Essays Journalism and Letters of George Orwell,* Vol. 4, henceforth *Collected Essays*) comes down heavily on the *not un-* phrase. This, in his view, is one of those structures which modern writers easily slide into without giving much thought to what they are saying. By way of illustration, he cites this sentence from Harold Laski: 'I am not, indeed, sure whether it is not true to say that the Milton who once seemed not unlike a seventeenth century Shelley had not become, out of an experience ever more bitter in each year, more alien [*sic*] to the founder of that Jesuit sect which nothing could induce him to tolerate.' (From an essay in Laski's *Freedom of Expression,* p. 128).

Orwell notes that Laski 'uses five negatives in fifty-three words. One of these is superfluous making nonsense of the whole passage, and in addition there is the slip *alien* (for akin), making further nonsense' (p. 134). He earnestly hopes that the *not un-* formation would be laughed out of existence even as *explore every avenue* and *leave no stone unturned* were killed by the jeers of a few journalists (p. 136). Orwell suggests memorizing the sentence *A not unlike dog was chasing a not unlike rabbit across a not ungreen field* as a reminder to writers never again to use the *not un-* phrase. Granted that the Laski passage is indeed laughable and (in the strict sense) nonsensical, does it follow that the *not un-* phrase should be 'got rid of'? Is it indefensible and meaningless?

Consider again the Laski sentence. The plethora of negatives (one of them superfluous) makes the sentence laughable. But look at the portion specifically referring to Milton: *Milton once seemed not unlike a seventeenth century Shelley*. What is ridiculous or wrong about it? Milton is not Shelley. But at one point in his life he came close to being (in his views and attitudes) like Shelley. How else can you express this other than by saying: *seemed not unlike...Shelley?*

Let's examine now the meanings expressed by the *not un-* phrase:

1. When used of persons, objects, the *not un-* phrase retains the identity of the entities being talked about, emphasizing at the same time their closeness to each other; their similarity. The meaning here may be summed up as 'identity in difference'. *Driving down the hill we came across a massive stone bull, not unlike the one at Mysore on the Chamundi Hills.*

2. When used of thoughts, actions, etc. the *not un-* phrase rejects the negative suggestion in the *un-* word and makes for a more emphatic statement. *The not unrealistic proposal of a 6 per cent growth in the economy....* The suggestion that the proposed growth is unrealistic is rejected. The meaning here may be described as 'affirming a point by denying its opposite'. Here is an example from Orwell himself: 'They (Secker & Warburg) are also anxious to reprint *Coming up for Air*...but not unnaturally, they are only willing to do all this if they can have a comprehensive contract giving them control of anything I write' (*Collected Essays*, Vol. 4, p. 308). He could have said: *They are willing to do all this. Naturally they want a comprehensive contract.* But now there is no rejection of a possible objection that it (a comprehensive contract) was *an unnatural demand*.

3. In social and personal contexts, the *not un-* phrase may be interpreted as a litotes. The OED has this citation: 'we say well and elegantly, not ungrateful, for very grateful'. The citation is dated 1671. But the idiom has not changed. Fowler (1926) attributes the 'success' of phrases of this type to 'a stubborn national dislike of putting things too strongly'. He gives two contemporary citations and translates *not infrequently* as 'often' and *will not be altogether unrelieved* as 'will be much relieved'.

4. In a *factual* context, the *not un-* phrase suggests an intermediate degree by denying the negation without asserting its opposite. *Sati is not unknown in parts of Rajasthan even today.* This can only mean that there are still some stray incidents of *sati* in Rajasthan. The meaning here, it will be

noted, is quite the opposite of what was noted in the social, personal contexts. To give another example: a researcher examining various texts for the occurrences of some linguistic feature, say, verb forms, may have examined only one text of travelogue (as against considerably more texts of other types). He can then say: 'Travelogue was not unrepresented in the study' (see H.V. George, *A Verb-form Frequency Count*, CIE). Here is another 'While not known here, it has not been possible to identify the author' (A. Silcock, *Verse and Worse*, London: Faber and Faber). 'In all these cases, the *not un-* phrase enables the writer to suggest an intermediate stage: between *represented—not represented; known—not known*'. Cf also: *Failure of recollection is common. Innocent misrecollection is not uncommon.* (Instruction to jurors in Calfornia; see PERIPHRASIS).

The *not un-* phrase falls into a broader category of phrases which may be labelled *Doubly Negative phrases*. They may occur not just as noun phrases (as in the examples above) but as adverbial phrases also; the particle *not* may be found in the verbal group, too, marking the sentence as negative; and the word negated may be any negative word—lexical or affixal. (See OPPOSITE WORDS). The *not un-* phrase we are examinig is a structural negation of an affixal negative word. But in all cases, the interpretation of these structures is on the lines sketched above.

Now follow some citations. *Personal responsibility could be avoided in the event one was late—a not infrequent occurrence in that part of the world* (Safire, *Watching my Language*, p. 269). *It wasn't unlike the fight for gays and lesbians today* (Time, 25 June 2004, p. 61).

Whitewater prosecution (or 'persecution' as Clinton called it, perhaps not inadvertently)... (Time, 28 June 2004, p. 27).

number in the noun phrase

The topic of number is presented in such a sketchy fashion in school grammars that quite a few are puzzled whether it is *a three-mile walk* or *a three-miles walk* (not to speak of *a three mile's walk*).

There are two aspects to be considered: one, the number of the head noun; (i.e. the noun which is the head of the phrase, e.g. in *my uncle's house*, the head is *house*. The other is the number of any nouns that modify a head noun, i.e., the number of the nouns in the attributive position. This second question is rarely discussed in school grammars.

Case 1. (a) The first noun indicates the sex of the person(s) referred to by the head noun: *lady doctors, girl guides, boy scouts*. Here plurality is shown on the head noun. (b) The modifying noun doesn't have this function: *men's clothes, women's dresses, boy's shoes.*

Case 2. Many nouns which normally can take a plural form appear in the singular in the attributive position: *a case for books,* but: *a bookcase; a brush for the teeth,* but: *a toothbrush.* Similarly *a dog show, a rose garden, an all-party meeting, a car park, a cycle stand, a bookshop, a stamp vendor.*

Case 3. The attributive noun is a noun indicating quantity, measure, amount. Preceded by a numeral higher than one it would normally appear in the plural (if in the head position). But in the attributive position, it is in the singular: *ten rupees* but *a ten-rupee note; four miles* but *a four-mile race.*

Case 4. Many nouns which otherwise would appear only in the plural form, appear in the singular in the attributive position: *a game of billiards* but *a billiard game/board; life in the barracks* but: *barrack life; spectacles* but *a spectacle-case.*

It should also be noted that some plurals of this type (invariable plurals) retain the plural form in the attributive position: *a savings bank; a goods train, an arms dealer, a clothes shop.* And others in this class may appear in the singular or plural: *trousers* but: *a trousers pocket* or *a trouser pocket; customs* (= duties) but *the custom-house, customs duties, a custom officer.*

Case 5. Nouns indicating number appear in the singular in the attributive position: *two dozen oranges; two hundred yards; five thousand rupees.* But *six foot two/six feet two* are both found. (On the use of words like *million,* see my *Current English,* OUP, 2001).

And now for a few words on the number of the head noun. Generally this is a straightforward matter, easily checked with a dictionary (*phenomenon*—singular or plural?) But the modifier in the NP may affect the number of the head. A case in point is this.

'I have more than one job offers', a software engineer, as reported in *India Today,* 11 May 2001. Is it job offers or job offer?

Supposing he had said: '*I have many job offers*', the sentence would have been unexceptionable. *More than one,* like *many,* conveys a sense of plurality. But *more than one job offers* is ungrammatical. Why?

On more than one occasion means 'on more occasions than one occasion'; *more than one student* means 'more students than one student'.

It is clear, then, that in the phrase *more than one,* there is an ellipsis after *more.* The full explicit phrase is *more Xs than one X.*

In the alternative, non-comparative phrase *many students*, there is no ellipsis after *many*. *Many* suggesting plurality requires that the noun it modifies should also be plural, e.g., *many students, many occasions*. But in the comparative phrase *more than one student*, the plural noun after *more* is omitted. The only noun seen is after *one*. This modifier, not suggesting a plurality, requires a singular noun after it: *more than one student*.

The same analysis holds good for the phrase *more than one job offer*. The plural noun required by *more* is omitted. The modifier *one* requires a singular noun.

The absurdity of the phrase discussed will stand out more clearly if we leave out *offer*. *I have more than one jobs*.

O

'office-goer'

An interesting Indianism is *office-goer*. *The lightning strike by bus drivers greatly inconvenienced office-goers*. The point to notice is that we do not speak of *factory-goers* or *bank-goers* or indeed of any other *goers*. Perhaps one has a feeling that people who go to factories actually do something. They are *factory-workers*.

And what about persons working in banks and other establishments? More often than not, it is a *bank employee* and not a *bank worker*. Possibly because *employee* sounds more dignified than *worker*. Notice that municipal workers have all become *municipal staff*.

Quite apart from whether any section of our society really takes work seriously, the fact remains that the public has a fixed impression that people going to offices do no more than go there. They are *office-goers*.

Office-goer, in the sense that we use it—of a person working in a government office—is not found in British English. An 'office-worker' is usually an employee in a business house.

one other/another

Both phrases are current and either may be used, depending on the context. *One other* is roughly equivalent to 'one more'. *There is one other point to be considered. We don't have the money to travel*. The suggestion is: We have considered so many points. There is one more (and by implication) the last one.

Another does not have this specific meaning. It simply means 'one more' (without being the last one); one additional, alternative point. *One reason for their poor performance is lack of training. Another, the poor wages.*

One another is used reciprocally, i.e., it refers to each member of a group in respect of each other. *They are a close-knit family. They love one another deeply.*

But *one another* in the sense of either 'one more' or 'one other alternative' does not exist. *One another classification* is not English.

opposite words

Words expressing opposites may be lexical opposites: *good–bad, beautiful–ugly, strong–weak.* Or the opposite meaning may be conveyed structurally. A common device is with the help of *not: true–not true.* The device is possible in all cases: *not good, not beautiful, not strong.* As should be evident even in these cases, the two sets of opposites do not mean the same thing: *'not beautiful* is not the same thing as *ugly.*

Another type of opposites is seen in *possible–impossible, perfect–imperfect, precise–imprecise.* This is closer to the structural negative seen earlier. Instead of the negative particle *not*, we have here the negative affix *-im.* Words in *-im* may express a meaning quite unrelated to what is expressed by the corresponding word without *-im.* Supposing you read a news item that a young man had been diagnosed as being pregnant. You would shout: *Impossible*, meaning *It can't be true.*

Negatives with *not* do not always yield an expression just the opposite of the one without *not.* There is clearly a difference in saying: *It is not possible/It is impossible.* The first one is just factual; the second one a bit emotional, emphatic. *You are not attentive* may be said on a particular occasion. But *You are inattentive* suggests a habitual trait.

More drastic differences are seen in *He is not concerned with it./He is unconcerned about it. He is not responsible for it./He is irresponsible.*

Is there any difference between *The claim was not allowed./The claim was disallowed?* Perhaps there is the suggestion of the claim being against some regulation in the second case. In the first case, the decision might have been quite arbitrary.

It should be clear by now that 'opposite words' are not always just opposites. The relation between lexical opposites is fairly straightforward. Not so in the case of other types of opposite words.

We have now distinguished and examined three types of negative words: lexical (*bad* as against *good*), structural (*not possible* as against *possible*), and affixal (*impossible* as against *possible*). There are further types: structural negation of an affixal negative and structural negation of a lexical negative. See NOT UN-PHRASE, DOUBLY NEGATIVE PHRASES.

oral/verbal

Some minor skirmishes have taken place in the world of usage over the words *oral* and *verbal*. Can *oral* and *verbal* be both used in the sense of 'spoken' as opposed to 'written'?

Examples are not wanting in standard writers where *verbal* is used in the sense of 'spoken'. Thus Henry Fielding writes: *The Captain returned a verbal answer to a long letter* (1755). *I would not consent to your being charged with a written answer, but perhaps you will take a verbal one* (Charles Dickens, 1859). This usage is attested from the sixteenth century onwards.

Etymologically, of course, the two words have different roots. *Verbal* comes from the Latin *verbum* (word) and oral from *os* (mouth). This has lead commentators from Hodgson (1881) onwards to insist on keeping the words separate.

But even by Fowler's time (1926), the usage had become so common that the Master felt the need to sound a note of warning and take a conservative stand. 'The supersession of oral is not yet so complete that those whose care for the niceties of language leads them to prefer it need fear a charge of pedantry.'

The fact is that both *oral* and *verbal* have many usages deriving from their root meanings and in these cases they are not interchangeable.

Thus: *oral sex, oral hygiene; verbal noun* (a gerund—it has the features of both a verb and a noun: *swimming is fun*), *a purely verbal distinction* (that is, one without any real substance); *verbal wit* (mainly depending on a play on words).

In a few cases—very few indeed!—the two are interchangeable: *an oral/verbal assurance; oral/verbal undertaking.*

And there are some cases in which *verbal* (in the sense 'spoken') is preferred: *a verbal agreement/contract,/a verbal exchange* (usually heated).

In all other cases where the meaning is 'spoken', the preferred word is oral. Thus *oral history/tradition, oral testimony, oral examination, a big oral report.*

When a contrast with *written* has to be emphasized, the word is *oral*. *I want a written guarantee, not an oral one.*

In American English, however, the roles are reversed. When a contrast with *written* has to be emphasized, the preferred word is *verbal*. 'The distinction now is between written and verbal, not between oral and written' (Safire, *Language Maven Strikes Again*)

Dictionaries, even usage-oriented ones, do not go into the subtleties of usage involved here. The use of *verbal* in the sense of 'spoken' is upheld as in *verbal agreement*. But the severe restrictions on the interchange of *oral* and *verbal* are not pointed out.

overlook/oversee

The use of *overlook* in the sense of *oversee* is a much debated point. The OED notes this as one of the meaning of the word and has this comment: 'Now rare or archaic' (There is a citation dated 1872. *To overlook the accounts of all the stewards*).

As for the meaning 'to fail to notice or observe; to pass over without notice (intentionally or unintentionally); to take no notice of, leave out of consideration, disregard, ignore', the OED says: 'the chief current sense'. Some citations: *The French found it prudent to overlook the insult* (1762); *He oversees all and overlooks none* (1872).

Robert Burchfield in his edition of *Fowler* (the third edition) gives 'to fail to notice, to condone' (an offence, etc.) as the first sense of *overlook*. As for the meaning 'to supervise', he notes that it is 'the primary sense of *oversee*.... It [i.e. *oversee*] is the normal word in this sense'.

Decades ago (1926), the doyen of all usage pundits, Fowler, had noted: '*overlook* though still used in the sense of inspect or supervise'...has as its chief current use the meaning of 'to look beyond and therefore fail to see, ignore, condone'. (He cites an amusing example of the ambiguity caused by using *overlook* in the sense of 'inspect': *Gentlemen are requested not to overlook the Ladies' Bathing Place*.)

In American usage, too, *overlook* is not recommended in place of *oversee*. *Webster's Dictionary of English Usage* (1989) says: '"to fail to notice" has long been established as the principal sense of *overlook*. The "supervise" sense now survives almost solely in the noun *overlooker*, a chief British synonym of *foreman*.'

Finally note that the tenth edition of the *Concise Oxford* (1999) gives the first meaning of *overlook* as: 'fail to notice, ignore or disregard'. The sense of 'supervise' is marked 'archaic', i.e., no longer current.

oxymoron, paradox

An oxymoron presents a concept as a conjunction of opposites. Broadly speaking, we can distinguish three groups of such expressions:

1. Some quality, state, is so intense or present to such a degree as to be described in terms of its opposite. Darkness and light are the two ends of a scale. Light makes things visible; darkness conceals them. But darkness can be so intense as to be visible; *darkness visible* (Milton); sorrow so deep as to be sweet; *sweet sorrow* (Shakespeare); similarly *proud humility* (Milton); *thunderous silence, bitter sweet.*

2. In another set of cases, something is lacking to such a degree as to reach or approach its opposite: *open secret* (no secret at all); *cold comfort* (no comfort at all); *random order.*

3. In a third set, the attributes mentioned are equally present: *virgin mother.* She has given birth to a child but she is still a virgin. A TA (Teaching Assistant in American universities) is a student and a teacher. Similarly a *modern classic, kind cruelty* (of a surgeon); *Icy Hot* (a medication); *sincere deceivers* (*The Economist,* 17–23 July 2004, describing Bush and Blair in the context of their stand on the Iraq war).

A paradox is closer to the third group of oxymorons. It is a statement which, at first, may seem absurd but, on deeper reflection, is seen to contain a profound truth. *In our beginning is our end*—yes, the very first breath we take brings us closer to our last breath, in a literal sense. *Time present is time past*: the ceaseless flow of Time makes the present instantaneously the past.

As used in logic and mathematics, a paradox is 'a statement or proposition, which despite sound reasoning from an acceptable premise, leads to a conclusion that is against sense, logically unacceptable or self-contradictory' (NODE). An example: If a barber in a village shaves all those who don't shave themselves, what about him? Does he shave himself or not?

See also IRISH BULL.

p

padding

Padding is a type of verbosity distinct from tautology, pleonasm, and periphrasis. In tautology, the same meaning is repeated in part or in whole; in pleonasm, it is expanded in terms of associated ideas; in periphrasis, it is presented in an analytical and roundabout way. But when a sentence is merely lengthened without affecting meaning in any way or in any of the ways just mentioned, we have to do with *padding*.

Padding may result from a variety of sources. Among these are: the use of certain constructions and compound prepositions; the mindless use of adjectives and adverbs as modifiers; the use of certain abstract words and adverbial and other phrases; and finally the use of certain discourse openers.

We will now take a brief look at each of these.

1. certain constructions

There are many constructions which can be replaced by briefer equivalent constructions. *They tried very hard but they could not get his wicket. Try as they might, they could not get his wicket.* / *While we were driving through the forest, we came across a herd of elephants. Driving through the forest we came across a herd of elephants.* These are matters of style.

But what are *acts of a hostile nature*? They are quite simply *hostile acts*. The longer version has no advantage over the shorter one. The longer version is merely a case of padding. It is with such constructions that we are concerned here.

(a) noun phrase expanded into a relative clause:
   unexpected events = events which are not expected
   a hopeless situation = a situation which is hopeless

(b) adverb replaced by a preposition phrase:
   hastily = in a hasty manner
   rashly = in a rash manner

(c) adverb replaced by a clause:
   doubtless = there is no doubt that
   fortunately = it was fortunate that

(d) subject noun/pronoun replaced by a clause:
   He worries too much about his health. = He is a man who worries
   The matter demands close study = It is a matter which demands

(e) predicate adjective expanded into a clause:
   His life is inspiring: His life is one which is inspiring
   He is dangerous = He is a man who is dangerous

These by no means exhaust the possibilities but they serve to illustrate the point.

2. compound prepositions

Compound prepositions are often condemned as inducing verbiage. This is far too sweeping. There are contexts where compound prepositions

are needed. *There is a tree in front of my house.* The simple preposition
before would be inappropriate here. A bank manager may write to a client:
*We have opened a recurring deposit of Rs 5000 a month according to your
instructions.* To replace the compound preposition here with: *as you
wished* would sound too familiar. In *Section 4 of these regulations should be
read in connection with Section 12, to get its full import, connection* has a
precise meaning. The *compound preposition* is justified. Then again it may
be a question of focus. *By way of introduction he made some casual remarks*
has a different focus from *He made some casual introductory remarks.*
Outside such special contexts, *compound prepositions* are just instruments
of padding sometimes resulting in periphrasis. The final preposition
requires a noun; depending on the choice of this noun, further verbiage
may result. *In the event of this development taking place...,* the choice of
development forces the following -*ing* phrase. Cf the alternative. *If this takes
place....* Even when the additional verbiage is not present, the compound
preposition is itself a word too many. It can be replaced by a simple
preposition / conjunction (with often minor changes; but see below) or
left out altogether.

Here is a list of compound prepositions (from Gowers, 1986). Shorter
substitutes are given in brackets.

as a consequence of (because of)
by means of (by, with, using)
by virtue of (by, under)
for the purpose of (to)
in accordance with (by, under)
in addition to (besides)
in as much as (since)
in association with (with)
in case of (if)
in excess of (more than, over)
in favour of (for)
in order to (to)
in the absence of (without)
in the course of (during)
in the event of (if)
in the nature of (like)
in the neighbourhood of (about)

in the vicinity of (near)
in view of (because)
on the grounds of (because of)
on the part of (by, among)
prior to (before)
subsequent to (after)
with a view to (to)
with the exception of (except)

Compound prepositions with no obvious paraphrase:

as regards
as to
in connection with
in regard to
in relation to
in respect of
in terms of
in the case of
in the context of
on the basis of
with respect to
relative to / with reference to
with regard to

And now for some illustrative citations, with suggested alternatives in brackets; compound prepositions in italics.

In such a situation what kind of accountability could have been there in the event of misuse of power by the elected representatives? (if the elected representatives misused power) (*The Hindu*, 3 February 2004). *US will continue to tolerate Pakistani transgressions for fear of a fundamentalist take over* (fearing a....) (*India Currents* February 2004, Vol. 17, No. 10.) *With regard to the Muslim community in India, we need to remember...*(about) (*News Asia.* 14–20 January 2004). *In order to understand India–Pakistan bilateral relations, one needs to look at shared meanings...*(to understand....) (*News Asia*, as above),*...a strategy of engaging the US on the basis of equality* (as equals) (*New Indian Express*, 13 March 2004). *The Sonia Gandhi led party, however, is clearly lagging behind...the BJP as far as taking the party message to the voters goes* (in taking the party....) (*Deccan Herald*, 17 March 2004). *In addition to some of those who released the charge sheet...leaders like...could* *have been also inducted* (Besides) (*Hindustan Times*, 17 March 2004)... *govt is misusing the taxpayer's money with reference to the India Shining ad. campaign* (on) (*The Times of India*, 23 February 2004).

3. adjectives and adverbs

Here we may recall the mindless use of certain adjectives noted under cliche': *active* consideration, *true/real* facts, *undue* delay, etc. The adjective in no way contributes to the meaning of the following noun.

Why should laughter be always *boisterous*, a grin *sheepish* and a scrutiny *close*? *Close scrutiny* is not only a cliche but a tautology as well. An examination may be cursory but a scrutiny by definition is a close examination, investigation. So what is the point in saying a *close scrutiny*? And why should a *turn* (or *twist*) of events be always *curious*?

There is no reason why these things should be the way they are except that we speak of them in that way by force of habit. The same is true of our use of certain adverbs: *definitely* harmful, *abundantly* clear, *downright* mistaken.... If something is harmful, it is harmful. Just that. Why *definitely harmful*? If something is *clear*, it is clear. Why *abundantly clear*? Can it be *sparsely clear*?

We cannot let nouns or adjectives go alone. Nouns must be backed by adjectives; adjectives propped up by adverbs. There is some mistaken notion of emphasis in all this.

Adjectives—unless they stand for qualities in the real world like *red, green, moist*, etc.—should be used to classify: a *financial crisis*, a *military disaster*, a *student unrest*. There is no harm in that. But you should be doubly careful when you use an adjective as an intensifier. Quite often your intensifying adjective will be pointless (as in a *grave crisis*). They are not everyday events where such strong adjectives are needed.

4. certain words/phrases that add nothing to the meaning. Cut them out or replace them by an alternative construction:

There are many cases of beggars having bank accounts. (*Many beggars have*)
In many cases, passengers had no photo identity. (Many passengers)
She has been admitted *on a provisional basis*. (*provisionally*)
Weather conditions next week. (*The weather next week*)
We have the worst options *at this point of time*. (*now*)

The word *fact* enters into a number of useful, idiomatic phrases: *in fact, in point of fact, as a matter of fact, the fact is*, etc. But *the fact that*...is an empty phrase and in combination with a compound preposition, there is more verbiage:

In spite of the fact that he had been warned.... (Though he had been)
May I *call your attention to the fact that*...(remind you)
I *was unaware of the fact that.* (did not know)
Owing to the fact that she was...(Since / Because)
The fact that he has not succeeded...(His failure)

Case has a real meaning in: *circumstances alter cases. / Two cases of death by malaria have been reported. / Have an umbrella in case it rains*.... But not in the examples we began with above. (See also ABSTRACT WORDS.)

5. Vacuous discourse initiators

Journalists (especially reporters) are fond of using phrases like *according to usually well-informed sources / knowledgeable circles / it is reliably learnt*. The reporter is making a guess (in some cases actually concocting a story) but he has to give it a certain degree of credibility. So these *unidentified, well-informed*, sources are brought in. Some go even further: *A high official in the Ministry / department said, on condition of anonymity*....

These expressions may be of some use for the reporter, but for the reader they are just so many empty phrases.

Another class of content-free expressions is exemplified by phrases like *It has been suggested / it can be said without fear of contradiction / it is well-known / I need hardly point out*.... In these cases, the writer is so timid he cannot make a direct statement himself. He needs to bolster up what he has to say by appealing to some non-existent authority.

Besides these two classes of empty phrases, there is a third one which may be called 'viewpoint' expression, for want of a better name. R.L Trask (*Mind the Gaffe: The Penguin Guide to Common Errors in English*) has compiled a list of 'omissible phrases' which seem to fall under this category. Here is his list: *all things considered / as a matter of fact / for all intents and purposes / for the most part / in a manner of speaking / in a very real sense / in the final analysis*. (Perhaps it is unwise to banish all such phrases. As with the abstract words *fact, case, etc.* noted earlier, some of them have their legitimate uses. Thus a writer, after a survey of various alternatives and possibilities regarding a proposal / suggestion may say: *All in all* (or *All things considered*) *the proposal merits implementation*. What is condemnable is the mindless use of these phrases without adequate contextual justification, as in this passage form Anthony Burgess (Burgess is mocking the use of cliches):

He was, however, on the whole, taking all things to consideration, by and large, not to put too fine a point on it, reasonably self-sufficient—quoted in Burchfield.

Where the writer does come out with something of his own (presented as such), he may still hum and haw with such expressions as: *in my humble (honest) opinion/the point I am trying to make is/what I mean to say is*. Some feel the need to assure us that whatever they are saying is *with all the emphasis at my command*.

These phrases add nothing to what you have to say. It is best to leave them out if you want to write prose that is lean, mean, effective.

Parallel to these opening vacuities, there is another set of empty formulaic phrases much preferred by officials. *I am to add, I am to further observe, I am to inform, I am to point out*.... In such ways, the official disclaims all personal responsibility for what he says (this for the benefit of the recipient) and also makes it clear that he is only carrying out orders (this for the benefit of his superiors). Lower officials cannot help adding: *This is for your kind information*.

Within the bureaucracy itself, the qualifications and reservations with which a proposal is made is strongly reminiscent of the multiplicity of nouns and verbs with which a legal document is drawn (to cover all contingencies). The official tries to buttress his position by all kinds of disclaimers, minimizing his own personal responsibility. He is playing safe. Here is a quote from Gowers (1951). The actual context there is different but it brings out the point well. 'In transmitting this matter to the council, the Minister feels that it may be of assistance to them to learn that, as at present advised, he is inclined to the view that, in existing circumstances, there is, prima facie, a case for....'

Padding may be the very heart and soul of bureaucratic writing. It may be part of 'official culture' and there may be little point in asking them to change. But it is well to remember what Churchill as Prime Minister wrote in a memorandum on 'Brevity' issued on 9 August 1940. He wrote:

'Let us have an end of such phrases as these:....' 'It is also of importance to bear in mind the following considerations...' or 'consideration should be given to the possibility of carrying into effect.' Most of these wordy phrases are mere padding, which can be left out altogether, or replaced by a single word. Let us not shrink from using the short expressive phrase even if it is conversational.

parallel structures

An interesting problem of structure arises in cases like this: *He was very fond of, almost addicted to, tea.* This is correct. *Fond, addicted*—each is followed by the correct preposition.

Now consider this. *He was aware and tried to make amends for his mistake.* *To make amends for* is correct. But *aware*? It should be *aware of*. To show that *his mistake* goes with both, the sentence should be punctuated in this way: *He was aware of, and tried to make amends for, his mistakes.*

The problem is more general and is not confined to prepositions alone. *He wanted to and dreamed of becoming an explorer.* Wrong. It should be: *He wanted to be, and dreamed of becoming, an explorer.*

Our forces are fully ready and capable of inflicting a defeat.... As it is, it would suggest that *ready* and *capable* are conjoined. Under that analysis, the sentence is incorrect. Since we have *capable of,* we are tempted to say *ready to.* We will then find the sentence becomes hopelessly ungrammatical. To save the situation we should take *ready* as an adjective qualifying *our forces* (cf *He is smart*). Then to achieve the parallelism required in conjoined phrases, we should say: *Our forces are ready and are capable of inflicting a defeat.*

Finally consider this. *We know that Atal Behari Vajpayee is an able, clean, and honest man—as good, if not the best, prime ministerial material we have had.* The meaning is perfectly clear. Still one may ask: How does the sentence read if the phrase *if not the best* is left out? The sentence doesn't read well. Obviously something is missing.

Supposing we had: *as good as any, if not the best, prime ministerial material we have had.* The sentence is now complete.

Moral: Make sure that no part of a sentence is left hanging in the air.

parenthesis

The COD defines this figure as follows: 'A word, clause, or sentence inserted as an explanation or afterthought into a passage which is grammatically complete without it, and usually marked off by brackets, or dashes or commas'.

The parenthetical statement might be one which could have come earlier: *Professor Amartya Sen—he was born in Kolkata—is a very distinguished economist*; the parenthetical statement might be one which could have come later: *Amartya Sen—he was subsequently to win the Nobel Prize in Economics—began teaching in a Kolkata college*; or the parenthetical statement might be a comment by the writer by way of an aside: *Amartya Sen—how little we know what the future holds—was born in Kolkata.*

The parenthetical device gives the writer the power to move his thoughts in time, shifting the past to the present or moving the future to the present or presenting the reader with his points of view by way of comments even as he is narrating. The statement in parenthesis is such that it does not justify a treatment in a separate paragraph (from the writer's point of view as he is narrating his story). But the fact is of some importance and cannot be left out. So it is put in parenthesis (See FIGURES OF INDIRECTION).

pathetic fallacy

Pathetic fallacy is the 'attribution of human feelings and responses to inanimate things, especially in art and literature' (COD); e.g., *a gloomy cave, smiling skies, angry waters.* Here is a passage about a river in Africa which, instead of joining the sea, finally disappears in sand: *The Kawango river begins life in Angola before flowing down the panhandle of Namibia.... Becoming bewildered and disoriented, the river wanders its way into northern Botswana...where it almost ties itself in knots as it crosses the sands of the Kalahari, eventually spilling out into the wide fan of the marshy delta'* (Paul Tingay, *Wildest Africa*, p. 167, Struik Publications (Pty) Ltd. 2000).

In the transferred epithet, the writer / speaker attributes his feelings to an inanimate object. In the case of pathetic fallacy, he sees human feelings and emotions in the things of nature. See FIGURES OF INDIRECTION.

perfect with 'since'

I haven't heard from him since Christmas. In sentences like this we see a perfect verbal group (*haven't heard*) followed by a *since-* phrase. The structure beginning with *since* is a temporal phrase giving the 'time of action'. Crudely put, the action of 'not-seeing-him' began since Christmas. The time-phrase can be a clause also. *I haven't heard from him since he left last Christmas.*

Now consider the sentence: *Ever since the great economic reforms have been set in motion...*(DH, 1 August 2001, p. 10). This is incorrect. It should be *Ever since the great economic reforms were set in motion....* The perfect is needed not in the *since-* phrase but in the main clause (as the writer's own sentence further down shows: *Ever since the great economic reforms have been set in motion, the Unit Trust of India, the Industrial Credit and*

Investment Corporation of India...have all entered into transactions.... The structure beginning with 'the Unit Trust of India' is the main clause).

Why does the writer use a perfect tense in both the clauses? One explanation would be to assume that the close association between *since* and the perfect tense has misled the writer into thinking that a perfect tense is needed in both the main clause and the *since*- clause. This explanation may hold good in some cases but not in the present one. I think we have to look for a different explanation.

Supposing we had: *Great economic reforms have been set in motion. The Unit Trust of India (and other financial institutions) have entered into transactions....* These sentences are correct.

The fact that a perfect tense occurs (correctly) in these sentences must have led the writer to believe that a perfect tense is needed even when the first tense is turned into a subordinate clause.

Does this mean that a perfect tense cannot occur in a subordinate clause? Of course not. *Although she has not spoken to him for months, he has not given up writing to her.* Further, the subordinate clause can even begin with *since* and yet have a perfect tense. *Since you haven't paid rent for over six months now, you are directed to vacate the premises immediately.*

What, then, is the restriction on the perfect tense in subordinate clauses?

It is this: The perfect tense cannot occur in a clause of time beginning with *since. He has never been the same since he returned from America* (Not *since he has returned from America*).

Why is this so? Why can't a perfect tense occur in a time-clause introduced by *since*?

A temporal clause/phrase introduced by *since* indicates a point of time in the past when a certain activity/event indicated in the main clause began. The function of the *since*- phrase is to indicate a point of time and no more. For this reason, it contains a verb in the simple past.

When the activity in terms of which time is indicated in the *since*-phrase is still going on, the verb may be in the past progressive: *Ever since he started teaching in the local college....* Or, there may be suitable lexical items to indicate the on-going nature of the activity: *Ever since the great economic reforms were set in motion....*

One final point: What is the difference between: (a) *Great economic reforms have been set in motion. The UTI and other financial institutions have entered into transactions....* (b) *Ever since the great economic reforms were introduced, the UTI and other financial institutions have entered into....?*

In (a) the two events are presented independently, as of equal importance. In (b) the focus is on the second event; the first event is subordinated to it and serves to provide a time frame.

periphrasis

Periphrasis is defined by the COD as 'a roundabout way of speaking, circumlocution'. It is a form of verbiage.

From Fowler (1926) onwards, two kinds of periphrases have been recognized. We may distinguish them as follows: (a) periphrasis arising from presenting an idea or concept in an analytical way, by breaking it up into its constituents, e.g., *I am of the opinion* (= I think); (b) periphrasis arising from the use of certain structures, structural words and phrases, e.g., *He is a man who...*(instead of *He...*).

We may, if we wish, label these as analytical (or lexical) periphrasis, and structural periphrasis. But a study of the facts will show that it is the former one, lexical periphrasis, which results in a 'roundabout way of speaking'. We will, therefore, restrict the term 'periphrasis' to the type of verbiage under (a). The one at (b) will be called PADDING.

The briefest (and still the best) example of analytical periphrasis is to refer to November as *the year's penultimate month*. Other classic cases are: *a relatively unstructured conversational interaction* (= an informal talk, Fowler, 1926); *The absence of intelligence is an indication of satisfactory development* (Gowers, 1951; periphrasis for *No news is good news*).

Mr Micawber (Charles Dickens, *David Copperfield*, 1850) can only speak periphrastically. Here is his way of saying 'you might lose your way in London'. 'Under the impression that your peregrinations in this metropolis have not as yet been extensive and that you might have some difficulty in penetrating the arcana of the Modern Babylon in the direction of the city Road....'

All the examples given above make use of learned Latin words. But that's not the point. The point is that they break up a concept into its constituent parts: a 'talk' is *a conversational exchange*; it is not designed and worked out in detail in advance; but it is not chaotic either. So, *relatively unstructured*.

The year's penultimate month precisely describes what November is. Sobriquets are also like this: they indirectly describe a person or object in terms of some prominent quality, trait, or characteristic feature. Thus: *the Iron Duke* (Wellington), *the Lady with the Lamp* (Florence Nightingale), *Emerald Island* (Ireland), *the Father of History* (Heredotus), *the Knight of the Rueful Countenance* (Don Quixote), *the Bard of Avon* (Shakespeare), etc.

The point about Latinate words may need a little clarification. When a concept is broken up into its constituents, the resulting abstractions are best expressed by words of Greek and Latin origin. *The company's finances* can be explicated as: *the financial position of the company. Dredging has stopped = A cessation of dredging operations has taken place.* Each noun introduced (while analysing a concept) will require a preposition to connect it with another noun: (*the financial position of the company*) or a predicate: *cessation has taken place.*

Circumlocution (lexical periphrasis) has always been a humorous device in literature (although for many in India it is Charles Dickens who is mostly associated with this type of writing). '*Sir, his definement suffers no perdition in you; though, I know to divide him inventorially*', says Hamlet of Laertes sarcasticallly, '*would dizzy the arithmetic of memory*' (*Hamlet*, 5.2). Leaving aside Fielding and others in England, we notice Voltaire (in *Candide*) describing Dr Pangloss as '*giving a lesson in experimental philosophy*' to the chambermaid behind a bush.

But today, polysyllabic humour is out of fashion. The man who says that he has to struggle with *a plethora of problems on the domestic front* is more likely to be laughed at (for talking like that) than anything else. Certain fields of discourse still entertain periphrastic writing: legal English, for example. *Failure of recollection is common. Innocent misrecollection is not uncommon.* (From the instructions that judges are required to give jurors in California.)

Periphrasis is also in evidence in our attempts to be 'politically correct'. *People below the poverty line* is the accepted phrase for the poor; *visually impaired/challenged* for the blind...(see EUPHEMISM). But outside these two areas, periphrasis is viewed as a feeble attempt at polysyllabic humour (if humour is intended) or a total lack of sense (if the aim is to impress). Generally speaking, speech and writing should be brief, precise, and clear. Periphrasis is a negation of all these virtues. It is well to keep in mind Alexander Pope's lines (*Essays in Criticism*, 309–10):

> Words are like leaves, and where they most abound
> Much fruit of sense beneath is rarely found.

But with us, periphrasis is still regarded as something worth cultivating. Even a casual observer cannot fail to hear such euphemisms as *to be in the family way*; such cliched idioms as *to make both ends meet*; such 'genteelisms' as *to arrange for a financial accommodation*; such introductory phrases as *to cut a long story short*; such sobriquets as *the Man of Steel* (Sardar Patel) or *the Father of the Nation* (Mahatma Gandhi). Here is a random selection from the print media. (As shown in the first quote, the sentence may include other faults of style like tautology and pleonasm.)

All said and done, the issue of pruning the bureaucracy would *continue to remain* (pleonasm) *an uphill task* (cliche) *as long as the political class has* no inclination to muster the requisite political will (periphrasis) and undertake effective girth control measures (pleonasm / periphrasis) *Deccan Herald*, 29 July 2003).

The tragedy of Indian aviation lies in the fact that we are having the worst of all options *at this point of time* (*Hindustan Times*, 14 January 2004). *That the two sides would continue bilateral discussions to work towards furthering the present spirit and achieving more concrete results is a development that makes for optimism* (*India Tribune*, 27 July 2004). *The present scenario in the country's sector is alarmingly dismal while floods are wreaking havoc in the Northeast and Eastern regions and drought is looming large in many parts of the Indian land mass....* (*The Hindu*, 27 July 2004).

picnic

In IE, 'to go on a picnic' is an accepted phrase; possibly a direct translation from the regional language.

But *picnic* means 'meal eaten out of doors, especially as part of a pleasant trip'. Thus there is a picnic hamper, lunch, etc. *We will go on the river and take a picnic with us.* (ALD). Also: *Shall we go for a picnic?*

pitfalls of negation
(neither–nor)
The octogenarian Chief Minister made it clear that he would neither be quitting active politics, let alone the Communist Party.

Neither is a correlative conjunction: *neither—nor*. It connects two negative statements. If the correspondent had written: ... *He would neither be quitting active politics nor the Communist Party*, the sentence would have been perfectly grammatical. But then the force of *let alone* would be missing. His quitting the Communist Party must have been presented by the Chief Minister (Mr Jyoti Basu) as an even more distant possibility;

in fact, one not to be entertained. To get this effect, the first clause should have begun with *not*:.... *He would not be quitting active politics, let alone the Communist Party.*

As this discussion should have made it clear, the conjunction joining two negative clauses need not necessarily be *neither–nor*. This correlative pair can be used only when nothing more is intended than to join two negative statements. *Neither Basu nor his deputy would say a word about the forthcoming Bengal Assembly elections.* Even here, if the conjoined statements are presented as independent statements, the correlative would not be used. *Mr Basu did not say a word about the forthcoming Assembly election. Neither did his deputy.* (One may also use the affirmative counterpart: *either–or. His deputy didn't say a word either.*

It is only when the first clause begins with *neither* that the second negative clause requires *nor*. If the first clause does not begin with *neither*, there is no question of using the correlative pair. Only *neither* appears.

This is an important point: in the second statement *neither* (or negative + *either*; see the example above) appears. Not *nor*.

The statement just made may appear to be contradicted by a sentence like: *She didn't phone that day, nor the next day.* What is the explanation?

Observe now that the subject of both the clauses is the same: *she*. But suppose we had different subjects. Then the sentence would be: *She didn't phone that day, neither did I.* (*Nor did I* would be ungrammatical.)

Nor by itself is the negative equivalent of *or*. *I don't know what she did that evening. Perhaps she read a novel or watched television.* / *She did not read any book, nor did she watch television.* This explains why when several alternatives (all negated) are presented with the same subject (or agent) *nor* appears. Otherwise (i.e., when the agents are different) *neither* appears.

'please accept....'
(possessive)

In his book, *In the Service of the Nation—Reminiscences,* General K.V. Krishna Rao states that on his appointment as Chief of Army Staff (COAS), he received a flood of congratulations, one of which read: 'Please accept my wife, and my congratulations' (as quoted in *India Today,* 22 October 2001, p. 95).

It is possible that there was *an apostrophe* and *s* on *wife* which, somehow, got left out during transmission. But I am very sceptical about this. The officer must have sent the congratulatory message just as it appears here.

The point becomes clear when we consider our own languages. In Kannada, for example, the message would read ...*nanna hendathi mathu nanna....sweekarisi*: Here *nanna* has the possessive case marker; but not *hendathi*. That word is in the nominative form. It can also be marked for the possessive case: *nanna hendathiya* but this is not obligatory in a conjoined phrase like this. Still, the sentence will not have the ridiculous and embarrassing meaning of the English sentence because, in Kannada, the verb comes at the end—after the object. So what we read is: *shubhashayagalannu sweekarisi*. Nothing embarrassing about that. The same situation, I believe, obtains in Hindi.

But when the sentence is literally translated into English—leaving the word *wife* without a possessive marker—we get the embarrassing interpretation because what we process first is: *Please accept my wife.*

The optionality of the possessive marker in Kannada / Hindi creates no problem because, under linear processing, we associate *shubhashayagalannu* with *sweekarisi* (since Kannada / Hindi are verb-final languages). The same linear processing creates an embarrassment in English when there is no possessive marker on *wife* because we associate *accept* with *wife* (English being a verb-medial language, with the object following the verb).

Moral: Beware of directly translating from the mother tongue into English. You may, in some situations, end up offering more than what you intended.

'please be rest assured'

An Indianism. The correct form is: *be assured / rest assured.*

Of the two, *rest assured* is the more common. It means 'be certain that....' *Rest assured that everything possible will be done. / Rest assured that the matter will be settled to your entire satisfaction. Be assured* means 'be confident that....' *Be assured of the consistent quality of our products and services.*

As can be seen, the two phrases are subtly distinguished. With *rest assured*, the meaning may be paraphrased as 'have no fears'. With *be assured*, the meaning is *have no doubts*. Both phrases are formal. IE has managed to combine both into an ungrammatical mess.

pleonasm

Tautology is repetition; pleonasm is superfluity—using additional words to convey a meaning already expressed, e.g., *I saw it with my own eyes.* Of course, you cannot see with somebody's eyes; nor can you see except with the eyes.

1. This example illustrates one class of pleonasms: a bodily activity is explained further by mentioning the organ performing it. *To hear with the ear; to speak with the tongue; to kick with your foot; to shout with a loud voice; to love with (all) your heart.* A similar expression is not possible with other activities. *She pricked her fingers—with a pin?/with a needle?* So *she pricked her finger with a needle* is not pleonastic.

2. Another type of pleonasm is seen in the phrases in normal print in the following: *A vacation at Ooty* is more *preferable to a visit to Bombay. Your suggestion is* equally *as important as his. With a rising middle class, the shops are* more especially *stocked with imported goods. Order has been restored but people* continue to remain *restive.*

3. The grossest form of pleonasm is seen in sentences where a word or phrase in one part of the sentence is explained elsewhere in the same sentence. In the following examples, the pleonastic phrase is shown in brackets. *The motion was passed unanimously* (by all the members present). / *You should not prejudge an issue* (in advance). / *It was an inadvertent mistake* (due to oversight). / *An audacious move* (quite bold and striking). *A galaxy of distinguished individuals* (who have earned name, fame, and recognition for achievement) *in their respective fields* (*Traveller's India*, Vol. 4, No 2, 2000).

4. Finally there are a number of stock expressions (rightly named *Siamese twins*) which are pleonastic or even tautological. Among these are: *hue and cry, kith and kin, spick and span,* etc. See SIAMESE TWINS.

Tautology is condemned because it is a mere repetition; *to revert back* says no more than *to revert; if in case* is not different from *if* or *in case.* But pleonasm is not a repetition: given A, there is another expression B which, in the context, is related to A but elsewhere is not a synonym. *Continue to remain* is a pleonastic phrase but elsewhere *continue* and *remain* do not mean the same thing; *more especially* is pleonastic but *more* does not mean *especially.*

For this reason, pleonasm is sometimes justified on rhetorical grounds: it can add force, emphasis. *Hear attentively the noise of his voice, and the sound that goeth out of his mouth* (Job, 37:2).

Ceremonial prose and legal prose are also pleonastic. The Royal patent creating a peer has, as Fowler puts it, 'a splendid prodigality of words'. Here is an excerpt: *advance, create, and prefer him to the state, degree, style, dignity, title, and honour of his rank, and guarantee that he shall enjoy and use all the rights, principles, pre-eminences, immunities, and advantages appertaining to it.* For an amusing example of legal English bristling with pleonasms, see the citation in my *Current English* (OUP, 2001, 2003).

In the absence of any registral or rhetorical justification, pleonasm is a fault of style.

police

The word *police* is frequently incorrectly used in Indian English. Here is a recent example: *You wouldn't call police an unconcerned lot* (*The Hindu*, 18 December 2001, p. 3).

Police is always used with the definite article *the*. And agreement is with a plural verb. *The police were called.* If you want to convey a singular idea, the word is *policeman*. *A policeman turned up unexpectedly.* Policeman is a countable noun. It can go with singular or plural verbs, as the case may be, and be modified by words indicating number. *Two policemen were standing at the street corner.*

political correctness

The NODE (1998) defines *political correctness* in this way: 'the avoidance of forms of expression or action that are perceived to exclude, marginalize or insult groups of people who are socially disadvantaged or discriminated against'. The expression originated in America in the 1980's and is now in use in Britain also.

The taunts and insults now shunned in the name of political correctness were there all along in India. For the British in India, the natives were all *coolies;* the educated ones among them (mostly clerks) were *baboos;* and their English *Baboo English*. The NODE now records only one meaning of *baboo* (also spelt *babu*), 'a respectful title or form of address for a man, especially an educated one'. That is the meaning the word has in the local languages. For the British, it had a different meaning. The *baboo* was a grovelling, flattering fellow to be treated with contempt; his English an object of ridicule (see *Hobson-Jobson*).

With the collapse of the Western powers after World War II and the end of the colonial days, things began to change. The rise of the Black Power movement in the USA (1960s and 1970s) and the spread of Women's Lib. contributed to a change of outlook. Centuries old terms of abuse, insult, and contempt got replaced by neutral expressions. *Negro, nigger* (in America) first gave place to *blacks*, then to *Afro-Americans*. Even expressions like *the gentle sex, the fair sex* came to be resented by women.

The range of political correctness is wider than what is indicated by the NODE definition. At the level of nations and nationalities; across classes and social groups within a nation; and finally as it touches disabled, handicapped, individuals—at all these levels we now find a flood of politically correct expressions.

Rivalry between the English and the Dutch in the fifteenth and sixteenth centuries—they were both seafaring, colonizing people—led to a remarkable crop of derisive expressions against the Dutch. *Dutch courage* (inspired by drinks), *Dutch leave* (absence without permission), *go Dutch* (where everyone pays for himself), *double Dutch* (gibberish). The English did not spare other nations either. Apart from such abusive terms as *Jerry* (for a German), *Chink* (a Chinese), *yellow peril* (Asian, especially Chinese threat to the West), there were satirical expressions like *Chinese fire drill* (a state of utter confusion) and *French leave* (to be absent without permission). Now all this has changed. Many expressions are quietly dropped or replaced. Earlier dictionaries, for example, list many more 'Dutch' expressions than the present ones. Compare the entry against *babu* in the COD (1990) with that in the NODE (1998).

In the area of gender, women in the advanced countries have taken exception to hundreds of words in the language: gender marked words like *actress* and *poetess* are anathema to them; whole dictionaries have been compiled on non-sexist lines (see NON-SEXIST LANGUAGE).

Political correctness as it relates to individuals handicapped in some way or other has drawn on euphemisms to get over the situation. The blind became *the visually handicapped*. Now they are *visually challenged*. *Challenged* is the right word now for all physical, mental disabilities; *lunatics* and *idiots* are now *mentally challenged*. The poor were first dignified as *the economically backward*; now they have become *the weaker sections*. (They are not called *the financially challenged* possibly because they have to be distinguished from persons in debt.) Doddering old fellows became *senior citizens* and the fatsoes *obese* (a medical term). Medicine has also come to the aid of the impotent. They are now persons suffering from *ED* (*Erectile Dysfunction*).

The earlier, politically incorrect, terms for blacks (and other nationalities) and women are now denounced as *racist, sexist*; hurtful terms like *idiot* and *lunatic* are *ableist*. 'Affirmative action' (measures designed to help blacks come up in society); 'women's empowerment' (measures to advance the cause of women) have become keywords of today.

As these examples show, politically correct expressions have a way of becoming 'incorrect' and so new expressions have to be coined. The Mahatma sought to give dignity to the lowest in the Hindu social hierarchy by calling them *Harijans*. This word is no longer acceptable. The abbreviations—SC, ST (Scheduled Castes / Scheduled Tribes) have replaced it.

Since the whole idea of being politically correct is to avoid giving offence or to cover up unpleasant facts, no wonder the military has spawned a host of such terms: *collateral damage* (destruction of civilian life and property) came into use in the Gulf war; the Vietnam war produced *pacification* (destruction of villages after evacuating the inhabitants), *defoliation* (destruction of forest cover).

The emergence of politically correct expressions within a society marks a conflict between liberals and conservatives. The conservatives are angry and bewildered why they can't call a spade a spade. Why should idiots be called *mentally challenged* and doddering old fools *senior citizens*? They are particularly angry at expressions conferring some dignity on groups within a society which were oppressed in earlier times (blacks in America; women everywhere; people in the erstwhile colonies, for example). As a reaction, some of them have come out with terms mocking the new politically correct phrases, e.g., *vertically abridged* (= short).

preposition with 'marriage'

There is no dispute when the word is used as a verb. As a verb, *marry* can be used transitively or intransitively. Used transitively, naturally there is no preposition. *Prince Charles married Diana.* When it is used intransitively *marry* takes *to*: *Charles was married to Diana.*

When used as a noun, too, *marriage* is followed by *to*. *Her marriage to Tom didn't last long.*

In IE (Indian English), *marriage with* is very common. *You are invited to the marriage of X with Y.* But if you had *You are invited to X's marriage...*, *with* would not seem to be so inevitable. Even those who use *with* would not, I think, quarrel with *to* here.

price/value/worth

Reviewing a book on the Gujarat riots, a writer says: '...unfortunately the 457-page paperback edition worth Rs 295 brought out by Penguin publications does not narrate anything new.' *Worth Rs 295*? Or, 'priced Rs 295'?

Here we see a confusion between *price* and *worth*. Rs 295 is the amount for which the book is offered for sale. So that is the *price* of the book. *Worth* can be used in several senses but two are relevant for present purposes:

1. The amount of money against which an article can normally be exchanged. *This necklace is worth Rs 30,000.* But it may not be its sale price. Price depends on such factors as: cost of production/manufacture; dealer's/retailer's profit/taxes that may be levied on it, etc. So there is usually a difference between the intrinsic worth of an object and the price at which it is sold or bought. In a distress sale, the price will be far less than the actual worth of the object. Hence the expressions: *an excellent bargain, good value for the money.* And when the commodity/object is in short supply, the sale price will be much higher than what the object or commodity is really worth (= would normally fetch).

Some more examples to show the correct use of *worth*: *The thieves broke into the house and stole one lakh worth of jewellery./This porcelain jar is worth more than what you think./It is a rare manuscript worth its weight in gold.*

2. *Worth* can refer to the value of the total assets a man has—stocks, shares, cash, properties, jewellery, etc. *The Sultan of Brunei is reputed to be worth $40 billion.*

Now for *value*. *Value* and *worth* share a common meaning—the amount for which something (an object, commodity) can be exchanged. But they differ in their grammar. *Worth* is a predicative adjective. *This ring is worth Rs 5000. Value* is a noun. *The value of this ring is around Rs 5000.* But in the second sense of *worth*, the two are not equivalent. You can say: *The Sultan of Brunei is worth....*' But you cannot say: *'The value of the Sultan of Brunei is....'* You have to say something like: *'The estate of the Sultan of Brunei is valued at....'*

Finally, *value* can be quite personal. An old building may have no *value* for an apartment builder. It is fit only for demolition. But for the children who were born and brought up there, its *value* is inestimable. 'It may mean nothing to you but it is very *valuable* to me' is not a contradiction in terms.

'pride of place'

The question is: Why not *place of pride*?

Pride here has to be taken in the sense of 'the best state or condition: the prime'; *the pride of youth*. Then the meaning (of the phrase in question) would be 'the best or most prominent section of the place': *In my study, an African mask occupies the pride of place on the wall facing the door.*

pronoun concord

Professor Sondhi himself was among the few in the academic community to have openly associated themselves with the Bharatiya Jan Sangh.

This (a quote from the editorial of a national daily) illustrates a subtle point of agreement. On a first reading, it may appear (to some) to be ungrammatical, lacking in pronoun concord. One may be tempted to substitute *himself* for *themselves. Professor Sondhi was among the few...to have associated himself with the Bharatiya Jan Sangh.*

A moment's reflection will show that it cannot be so. We should ask: 'What is the subject of the phrase beginning with *to have openly associated themselves with...*'?

Clearly the subject of this infinitival structure is: *the few* (the few to have associated themselves with the Bharatiya Jan Sangh). The full underlying structure would be: *the few + the few had associated themselves with the Bharatiya Jan Sangh.* This can be converted into: *the few who had associated themselves with the....* And then (after the dropping of the relative pronoun *who*): *the few to have associated themselves with the Bharatiya Jan Sangh.*

The sentence quoted at the beginning is equivalent to: *Professor Sondhi was among the few...who had associated themselves with....* There is no problem here. The phrase *the few* is plural; hence a plural reflexive (*themselves*) is needed. But when the subject of the infinitive is omitted, we tend to take *Professor Sondhi* as the (understood) subject of the infinitive. Since *Professor Sondhi* is singular, we feel that the reflexive pronoun should be singular.

To test the correctness of the analysis proposed here, consider the following pair: (a) *Professor Sondhi was the first to have associated himself with the BJS.* (b) *Professor Sondhi was among the first to have associated themselves with the BJS.* Sentence (a) can be paraphrased as: Professor Sondhi associated himself with the BJS. He was the first to do so. Sentence (b) can be paraphrased as: Some X number of persons were the first to associate themselves with the BJS. Professor Sondhi was among them.

Still on the subject of pronoun concord, consider the following: *Everyone thinks they have the answer./Has anybody brought their camera?/ No one could have blamed themselves for that.* (Examples from Quirk et al., *A Grammar of Contemporary English.*) The subjects *everyone, anybody, no one* are singular. But the pronouns referring to them in the sentences are all plural. How come?

It should be pointed out straightaway that these are informal statements. English has no third person, gender-neutral, singular pronoun. In the first sentence, a grammatically correct version would be: *Everyone thinks that he has the answer.* But then one may object that by using *he* we have left out all references to women while the subject *everyone* includes both men and women. A 'politically correct' alternative would be to write: *Everyone thinks that he/she has the answer.* But this is cumbersome. For this reason, in formal contexts, the preferred version of the sentence we have been discussing is: *Everyone thinks that he has the answer.* In the other two sentences also, the referring pronouns will have to be *his, himself.*

The device of using a third person plural pronoun to get over the problem of the gender-specific *his/her*, etc., becomes quite awkward in cases like: *Either he or his wife is going to change their attitude.* The conjoined subject phrase cannot have plural reference. It has to be singular. The use of *their* makes the sentence sound quite awkward (besides being ungrammatical). It would seem, then, that the effort to achieve a gender-neutral language has some grammatical limitations. At least in some contexts, *he* (and related forms) must be taken as the 'unmarked' form when the sex of the antecedent is not determined (as with *everyone, anybody,* etc.) See NON-SEXIST LANGUAGE.

pronoun reference

Toni Morrison's genius enables her to create novels that arise from and express the injustices that African Americans have endured. Is this sentence correct or incorrect?

That was the question set by the College Board in one of its examinations. The answer expected by the Board was 'Correct'. But a high school journalism teacher seems to have pointed out that the sentence was incorrect. Reason? The pronoun *her*, according to her, refers to *Toni Morrison's* (and not Toni Morrison). The Board promptly withdrew the question.

Reporting this, the *New York Times* in its editorial section (*Editorial Notebook*, 25 May 2003) expressed anguish and dismay that: 'the College Board experts, specifically focused on composing a grammatically correct sentence, wrote an error into it.'

The writer goes on to point out that 'the first three words *Toni Morrison's genius* are understood as the *genius of Toni Morrison*, and thus the true antecedent of 'her' is, correctly, Toni Morrison.' That reading has at least some commonsense on its side.

But this will not do. The Board agreed with the teacher rather hastily and threw out a good question. The editorial writer, too, had failed to see that the sentence was, in fact, quite grammatical.

The antecedent of *her* is not *Toni Morrison's,* as claimed by the teacher. The antecedent is *Toni Morrison.*

The subject of the Board's sentence is: *Toni Morrison's genius.* The 'head' of this noun phrase is *genius.* This is modified by the possessive modifier *Toni Morrison's.* The structure of this phrase is: *Toni Morrison + possessive.* The pronoun refers to the noun *Toni Morrison.* A pronoun does not always need an antecedent. *Look at him* can be said of a man working in a field. But if there is a noun in the same sentence, matching in features with a pronoun, the pronoun can refer to the noun—under certain conditions. But not in the minimal clause. *John loves him.* Here *him* cannot refer to *John.* To get that meaning, we should say: *John loves himself,* i.e., we should use a reflexive pronoun.

Nor can a pronoun refer to a noun further down the sentence. *He knows that John is a clever guy; he* cannot refer to *John* here.

But supposing a matching noun occurs in a preceding sentence or a clause. *John is an intelligent man. He knows what to do and when/John thinks that he will win.* In these cases, *he* can be construed as referring to *John.*

As can be seen, the relation between a pronoun and a noun (which we want to interpret as its 'antecedent') is not quite straightforward. A fairly complex theory has to be set up to account for all the facts. (See, for example, Chomsky, *Lectures on Government and Binding.*)

The point for us to note now (without going into further details) is: If it is the case that a pronoun cannot refer to a noun in the same simple sentence (i.e., when the two are connected by one verb/verb phrase, e.g., *John admires him/John has deceived him*), how can *her* refer to *Toni Morrison* in the sentence: *Toni Morrison's genius enables her....*This is not a complete simple sentence but here, too, there is a single verb. The facts would be the same if we had: *Toni Morrison's genius has deserted her.*

Reference is possible here because Toni Morrison is not the subject of the sentence. If we had *Toni Morrison enables/has enabled her...*the pronoun would not refer to *Toni Morrison.*

Toni Morrison is part of the subject phrase, *Toni Morrison's genius.* It is for this reason that we can interpret *her* as referring to *Toni Morrison.*

This is exactly as in *Beckham's admirers worship him*, where we understand *him* as referring to *Beckham*.

Moral: Even educated native speakers need a dose of grammar to be sure of themselves.

proverbs

Proverbs embody traditional wisdom. *If wishes were horses, beggars would ride. If the cap fits, wear it. It is easy to be wise after the event. Misfortunes never come singly....*

But many of the old proverbs are rarely encountered today. The changing language has made some words and expressions obsolete. So there would be little point in quoting something which either is not understood or strikes one as odd. To this class belong proverbs like: *If physic does not work, prepare for the kirk.* ('Physic' in the sense of 'medicine' and 'kirk' in the sense of 'church'—a Scottish word—are not in use in Standard English today.) *If thou dealest with a fox, think of his tricks. He that wipes the child's nose kisseth the mother's cheek.* (The pronoun form *thou* and the verbal forms in *-est* are obsolete.) In other cases, the patterning, the structure has rendered some proverbs unfashionable. Typical of this class are proverbs beginning with a relative clause headed by a pronoun: *He that will not stoop for a pin shall never be worth a pound. He that would the daughter win/Must with the mother first begin.* Here is one which combines all the points noted above. *He that walketh with one eye and looketh with the other, I will not trust him though he were my brother.*

These points of language and style apart, changes in lifestyles and values have made many proverbs out-of-date. *If the beard were all, a goat might preach.* With the decline of religion and the steep fall in church attendance, this proverb has lost much of its force. Time was when, in the western world (as with us till a few years ago), it was incumbent on a girl to get married. In that context, the saying: *If one will not another will and so are all maidens married* gave a sense of relief and hope. But not any longer. Single women far outnumber married women in the West today.

Nevertheless all-time truths not tied down to a particular social, cultural context are as popular today as ever provided the language is not old-fashioned. To this category belong: *It is a wise child that knows his father* (sixteenth century). *Jack of all trades master of none* (eighteenth century). *Lawmakers should not be lawbreakers* (fourteenth century). *Look before you leap* (fourteenth century).

Each generation makes its own proverbs. Naturally these proverbs reflect life as it is led around the time and, therefore, have an immediacy of appeal. In the industrial society with machines ruling our lives, a proverb like: *If anything can go wrong, it will* (Murphy's law) is eminently apt. Cf also: *If it ain't broken, why fix it? Ours is a tough, competitive world. It is no place for you if you are not a fighter.* And so: *If you can't stand the heat, get out of the kitchen.* Further, *It is a rich man's world. If you have to ask the price, you can't afford it* (attributed to J.P. Morgan. When somebody who wanted to buy a yacht similar to his and wanted to know how much it cost in annual upkeep, Morgan is said to have told him this.) The American oil billionaire Paul Getty once remarked: 'If you can actually count your cash, you are not really rich.'

People's perceptions have changed over the years. Proverbs which, at one time, sounded eminently sensible, no longer do so. *If you run after two horses, you will catch neither.* This is old world wisdom. But today's saying has it: *If you can't ride two horses at once, you shouldn't be in the circus.* The man who said this—an Independent Labour Party MP—said this in the context of his political career but it can be easily used in other contexts as well.

Many 'proverbs' of today are variations of old ones. *Behind every great man there is a woman.* That is a well-known saying. Here is a modern version: *Behind every great fortune, there is a great crime. He who laughs last, laughs best.* Yes. How about this? *He who laughs last probably didn't get the joke. Silence is golden.* Right? Now read this: *The less you say, the less you have to retract. The end does not justify the means.* That is, *getting the job done is no excuse for not following the rules. Necessity is the mother of invention.* But also: *Necessity is the mother of strange bedfellows. Trust in God but keep the power dry*—was said in the context of battles. More in tune with today's world we have: *Trust everybody but cut the cards.* The medieval philosopher, Occam, proposed a principle which is now at the heart of all scientific explanations: *Entities should not be multiplied.* It is for this reason that God has no place in scientific theories. A modern wit has, at a lower level: *When stupidity is a sufficient explanation, there is no need to have recourse to any other.*

Sayings of this type apart, there are new ones, absolutely original ones, providing insightful observations on contemporary life. *Never mistake endurance for hospitality,* cautions a wise owl. And here are some cynics speaking out some bitter truths: *A lot of people mistake a short memory for a clear conscience. It is always easy to see both sides of an issue you are not* particularly concerned about. *If two men agree on everything, you may be sure that one of them is doing the thinking.* And why is experience valuable? *Experience enables you to recognize a mistake when you make it again.* And now for some wholesome bits of advice: *If you can distinguish between good advice and bad advice, then you don't need any advice. Never ask a barber if you need a haircut.* And finally an encouraging word for those facing difficulties: *A path without obstacles usually leads nowhere.* Now for some proverbial statements especially relevant for contemporary life: *When packing for a vacation, take half as much clothing and twice as much money.* What sensible advice! *The biggest plays occur when you are out buying beer.* How true! And in every work situation, *People who work sitting down are paid more than people who work standing up.*

Isn't it everyone's experience when standing in a queue that *the other line moves faster?* And when you travel by plane, haven't you found that *when the plane you are on is late, the plane you wanted to transfer is on time?*

Most of these modern 'proverbs' are taken from a remarkable publication, *Murphy's Law*, brought by Andrews McMeel Publishing, Kansas City, Missouri. As many readers will recall, Murphy shot into fame with his 'Law': *If anything will go wrong, it will* (see my *Current English*, 2002). In the wake of Parkinson's Law (*Work expands to fill the time allotted to it*) and the Peter Principle (*An employee tends to be promoted to his level of incompetence*), numerous 'laws', 'principles', and 'rules' have erupted and Murphy's is one of them. The publication referred to above is a desk calendar with one such 'law' or 'principle' on each page. It is a novel publication with much to recommend it. No matter how you feel when you wake up in the morning, one look at the desk calendar will make you smile. Let's look at some more of them.

A successful leader is one who knows how to delegate responsibility. But how many could have put it this way? *When moving a pregnant cat, pick up the cat and let her take care of the kittens.* The manager should also keep this in mind: *Don't get mad—get even.* And always be optimistic: *We are making progress. Things are getting worse at a slower rate.*

It is a natural step from business to economics. What have our modern sages to say about this 'dismal' science? *Among economists the real world is often a special case.* Only those who have tried to follow modern economic theory can savour this principle.

As for politicians, here are some core observations: *No matter what they are telling you, they are not telling the whole truth. No matter what they are talking about, they are talking about money.* The stupidity of this tribe as a whole is well expressed by this maxim: *When a politician gets an idea, he usually gets it wrong.*

It is often said that what strikes one about a proverb is its insight into life. True. But equally striking is the way the thought is expressed. Proverbs are models of a type of writing: brief, often witty, and always brilliantly structured. Pope's definition of wit aptly characterizes them: *What oft was thought but [never] so well expressed.* Proverbs, maxims, laws, rules, principles—no matter what they are called—they are all models of effective writing in miniature. For this reason, this style of writing is much favoured in the field of advertising, leading, in turn, to more proverbs.

pun

Pun is a humorous play on words. It may be on the different senses of a word or on different words having a similar sound. *A psychiatrist on a hike fell into a depression* is of the first type: *He is so much given to the wearing of jeans, it looks as though it is in his genes* is of the second type. In between there can be any number of variations depending on the cleverness of the punster. The suggested pun may require a word to be broken up into a phrase to become apparent. *That pack is dark; this Pakistan* (pack is tan). The reader may have to think up the word which fits the context: *Old doctors never die; they just lose their patience* (patients); a word may be broken up and the pun based on its relation to the original word: *What is an ig? An Eskimo house without a loo.* The other word needed to understand the pun may not even be mentioned. The reader has to work it out: *Pacavi* (Latin; 'I have sinned'. Message apparently sent by Gen. Sir Charles Napier after he had conquered Sind.)

Because puns are just based on words and not on the interplay of character and situation (as in comedy, for example), they are looked down upon as a low type of humour. But when one considers the ingenuity of some of the punsters, one cannot but agree with Fowler who wrote: 'The assumption that puns are *per se* contemptible betrayed by the habit of describing every pun not as a pun but as *a bad pun* or *a feeble pun* is a sign at once of sheepish docility and desire to seem superior. Puns are good, bad, and indifferent, and only those who lack the wit to make them are unaware of the fact'. The pre-eminent American punster, Richard Lederer (from whom some of the examples given above are taken) has this in a bold defence of puns: 'Punning is largely the trick of compacting two or more ideas within a single word or expression.... Punning surprises us by flouting the law of nature that pretends that two things cannot occupy the same space at the same time. Punning is an exercise of the mind at being concise.'

There are puns at all levels to amuse everyone from a schoolboy to a scholar. For me, the best puns are those where there is an interplay between a physical or literal sense and a figurative sense and both senses are apt and relevant to the context. I now cite a few such specimens. The first one is based on a report in an American newspaper.

'Ms Ellen Felber is a gifted teacher who has developed novel techniques to teach her exceptional children. One of the techniques involves letting the children take a cake and then, on the icing, to print novel messages like "saying *no*". Children (even gifted ones) are liable to a variety of abuses and should learn, early on, how to say *no*. Ms Felber's way helps them to do it easily. She has literally cooked up a memorable way to teach her children. Thanks to Ms Felber, her students find "saying *no*" a piece of cake.'

Here is another example. Read the verse and then read the title again. HE NEVER LETS YOU DOWN: *Providential care is nowhere seen so much as in this. / When things get out of shape and friends forsake / Scenting a crisis / There still remains an ultimate hope / In the unmistakable rope.*

A farmer rebuking his son who has returned from studies in an agricultural college and has turned out to be a great womanizer, asks: '*In college did you learn / Anything other than / How to sow wild oats?* And then there is the cashier whose coat was in tatters. Caught stealing money he is reported to have protested: *I was only lining my pockets*—verses from Kay S. Wye (1988, 1997). Here is an epitaph on a dentist: *Stranger! Approach this spot with gravity! / John Brown is filling his last cavity.*

The interplay between the physical and the figurative meanings can vary over a range. All that is required (to make the lines effective) is that the lines suggest (even if they do not directly admit of) both the interpretations. In the first example (a piece of cake), we have a figurative sense as also a direct, physical application of the words. The case of the cashier *lining my pockets* has mainly a figurative meaning, although in the context of a tattered coat, a physical sense (of mending or stitching) is not ruled out.

Another class of brilliant puns exploits a seeming contradiction. *Before it's in fashion, it's in Vogue.* Since *to be in vogue* is *to be in fashion*, how can it be in vogue before it is in fashion? Well, *Vogue* is the name of a very famous fashion magazine. So nothing can be in fashion before it is publicized in

Vogue. Thus, if you want to know what is the current fashion, read *Vogue*. Another wordplay, this time exploiting a seeming tautology is: *Make time for Time* (ad. for the *Time* magazine).

Indeed the commercial advertisers have exploited pun in ways that are truly remarkable. *Who cares what people think? We do* (advertisement by a market survey group playing on the literal and metaphorical meanings of the *wh-* question). *How do you stop a charging rhino?* asks another ad. Before you can collect your wits, comes the answer: *Give it an American Express*. This may sound at first bizarre, incomprehensible. But a moment's reflection on 'charging' in the context of American Express makes the point clear. Visa is ever attacking and making fun of American Express. *They* [at a resort] *will take a lot of trouble to make your stay comfortable, but the one thing they will not take is American Express*.

One final point. Both ambiguity and pun admit of more than one interpretation. But with pun, the double meaning is intended and jocular; further, ambiguity may arise from more sources than word meanings.

punctuation

This is a complicated subject. Its main purpose is to aid comprehension by marking the text with a set of marks, the punctuation marks. Some marks of punctuation—the question mark, the mark of exclamation, for example—are governed by clear principles. But in the case of many other marks, the author's intent of how he wants the text to be understood guides his marking. Further there is an element of convention also here. The major publishing houses, whether of newspapers or books, have their own set of conventions in respect of some punctuation marks. These uncertainties apart, problems arise in the punctuation of particular types of texts. This can be appreciated if one looks at any scholarly text—a grammar book for example. Here I can do no more than mention some basic facts as they relate to the punctuation of ordinary texts.

1. Capital letter

(a) This is used for the first letter of the word beginning a sentence. *The Golden Gate bridge is in San Francisco.*

(b) A sentence enclosed in brackets within another sentence does not begin with a capital letter. *The girl (she looked quite cheerful) was selling flowers near the temple.* But an afterthought or aside presented separately begins with a capital letter, even though enclosed in brackets.

(c) Quoted sentences begin with a capital letter, *She looked around and said, 'This is a nice place.'*

(d) Capital letters are used with names as shown below: Names of persons (*Pranav, Roopa*), nationality names (*Indian, Englishman*), names of days and months (*Monday, January*), names of institutes (*the Mythic Society, Oxford University*), names of countries and geographical names (*America, India, the Pacific, Mount Everest*), titles of books (the Ramayana, the Holy Bible), names of newspapers (*The Hindu, The New York Times*), films, television programmes, etc.

(e) With designation of rank and relationship used as titles: Queen Elizabeth, President Bush, Swami Vivekananda, Dr Johnson, Professor Amartya Sen, Sir C.V. Raman, the Bishop of Bangalore, Aunt Amelia, Uncle Kiran. When used by themselves as names of designations, they are in small letters: a professor, bishop, etc.

(f) Names formed from initials are in capitals: AIR, BBC, NATO. Note the style in academic degrees: B.A., M.A., M.S., Ph.D., M.Litt. (On the use of stops here, see below).

(g) with the names of periods of history: *the Middle Ages, the Renaissance*; and also when used as adjectives: *a Renaissance painting*. But when used in a general sense, they begin with a small letter: *a renaissance in classical music* (= a revival).

(h) Names of languages begin with a capital letter (*English, French, Hindi*); but names of academic subjects are in small letters: *physics, chemistry*, except when studying for courses in a university, etc. *He got a first class in Economics. I wish I had studied Mathematics.*

(i) Names of roads, streets also begin with a capital letter: *MG Road, Commercial Street.*

(j) Prefixes with proper names begin with a small letter: *anti-American feeling, pro-British rally, un-Christian teachings, non-Islamic religions*. But with names of organizations prefixes begin with a capital letter: *Non-Aligned countries, Anti-Apartheid organization.*

2. Full stop

(a) To mark the end of a declarative sentence: *Asia is the largest continent.*

(b) A sentence ending with an abbreviation having a stop does not need another stop:

The place was littered with books, magazines, pictures, tapes, cassettes, etc.

Contrast the above with: *The room was a mess (littered with books, cassettes, pictures, etc.).*

(c) To indicate omitted material in a quotation, three stops are used; if the omission occurs at the end of a sentence, one more stop is used to mark the end of the sentence.

(d) The full stop with abbreviations: The general tendency in British English is to omit stops in abbreviations. Still stops are found in some cases, and in others usage varies.

(i) No stops are found in abbreviations consisting entirely of capital letters: BBC, GMT, TV, COD (*The Concise Oxford Dictionary*), TLS (*The Times Literary Supplement*), UNESCO, NATO, etc.

(ii) Stops are found with a person's initials: *H. W. Fowler*; military ranks: *Col. Roberts, Gen. Franks;* no stops are used with familiar titles like: *Mr, Mrs, Ms, Dr*; but *Prof. Chomsky.*

(iii) Abbreviations standing for academic degrees used to be marked with stops: *B.A., M.A., Ph.D.* There is now a tendency to omit the stops: *MA, PhD.*

(iv) Abbreviations for the periods of the day have stops: *a.m., p.m.;* also names of months: *Jan, Feb,* AD, BC marking historical time now appear without stops.

(v) No stops are used after *1st, 2nd, 3rd,* etc.

3. Comma

The comma makes for a clearer understanding of a sentence which, otherwise, could have been somewhat confusing. It is used:

(a) between adjectives appearing before a noun: *a long, straight, dusty road.*

(b) In groups like *a fine old gentleman,* no commas are found. This is because *old gentleman* is viewed as one unit. This is modified by the adjective *fine.* No commas separate an adjective and the noun it modifies.

(c) to separate items in a list: *coffee, tea, sugar and biscuits.*

There is some question whether a comma should be used before *and* in a sequence like the one above. In some cases, it will help avoid misreading if a comma is placed before the last *and* in a sequence.

Some of the leading builders in Bangalore are: Raheja, Prestige, Brigade, and Larsen and Tubro. Larsen and Tubro is one company; without a comma after *Brigade,* a reader might get confused.

(d) Within a sentence, parenthetical matter is set off by commas: *You can, if you wish, leave now. / The situation, unfortunately, turned for the worse.*

(e) No commas should separate a subject from its verb: *Sheela and two of her friends are coming for lunch.* But when the subject is long and complex, a comma is required.

(f) A noun phrase in apposition is set off by commas: *Ramanujam, the great mathematician, was born in Chennai. / Delhi, the capital of India, is a historic city.*

(g) A non-restrictive relative clause is set off from its antecedent by a pair of commas: *The man, who was evidently in a hurry, pushed his way through the crowd. Bombay, which is the financial capital of India, produces more films than Hollywood.*

But a restrictive relative clause, i.e., a clause which identifies the antecedent is not set off by commas: *The timepiece which is on the table is a gift from my sister.*

(h) Participial phrases opening a sentence are set off by commas: *The authorities arriving, the ceremony began. Considering everything, it was a wise decision.*

(i) An adverbial clause opening a sentence is separated from the main clause by commas: *When I was a boy studying at St Joseph's, I used to play in this park. If you drop the glass, it will break.*

No commas are needed if the clause follows the main clause: *I used to play in this park when I was a boy. The glass will break if you drop it.*

(j) To mark off quoted material from the rest of the sentence: *She said, 'It's time to go home.'* (On the use of colon here, see SEMICOLON.)

(k) To mark the omission of a main clause verb in the rest of the sentence: *As a Christmas gift we bought Pooja a watch, Raju, a pocket radio, and Sarita, a bracelet.*

(l) Commas and coordinated clauses: Coordinated clauses connected by *and, but, or* are separated by commas, unless the clauses are very short. *Rajesh left for Bombay last night, and Sudhir is coming from Delhi next week. Tara's parents want her to learn Hindustani classical music, but I don't think she is keen on it. I looked for the book but could not find it.*

(m) A subject clause or an object clause is not separated from the verb by a comma: *That John went to the party surprised Mary. I didn't know that he had settled down in Germany.*

4. Colon

(a) To introduce speech or quoted material: *It was Bacon who said: 'Knowledge is power.'*

(b) To introduce a clause which, in the context, explicates the main clause statement: *I want to say something: Let's get the job over as quickly as possible. It was not easy to persuade him: he had rejected all earlier suggestions.*

Or a clause which is in the nature of a result or effect: *It started raining: so I took a taxi.*

(c) To introduce a list of items: *This is what we found in the drawer: two floppies, a couple of pens, a diary, and a writing pad.*

(d) To introduce the subdivisions of a subject: *Articles: the Definite Article.*

(e) In plays after a character's name, to introduce his words , or when quoting a famous line or speech: *Caesar: Cowards die many times before their death. As Parkinson said: Work expands to fill the available time.*

5. Semicolon

The semicolon marks a stronger break than the comma but not so strong as the full stop. It is used:

(a) to separate two sentences which are complete in themselves but are so closely related that together they express a complete idea: *Religion should be more than a dogma; it should be a way of life. To err is human; to forgive divine. Nehru was a visionary; he was also a practical man.*

(b) To separate items in a list where the members to be separated already have commas in them: *Before you go on a hiking expedition make sure that you have a good, sturdy backpack; a light all-weather jacket; a pair of sturdy, knee-length boots.* Contrast this with: *Take with you a backpack, a torchlight, an insect repellant, and a raincoat.*

(c) To separate a sequence of clauses: *You can enter a foreign country provided that you have a valid passport; that you have an unexpired visa; that you furnish proof of having enough funds to support yourself there; or that you produce a letter from a sponsor willing to support you.*

6. Quotation marks (inverted commas)

(a) To indicate direct speech or quotation. In British usage single quotes are used: *She said: 'It's time to leave'.*

The closing quotation mark comes after any punctuation mark needed for the quoted material; the final punctuation of the sentence containing the quotation comes after the quotation mark: *He shouted: 'Fire!' He asked, 'Can I go now?'*

(b) If a quoted sentence is broken up (by the reporting verb and its subject, for example), each part of the quotation is enclosed within its own quotation marks; any punctuation indicating the break is placed within the quote marks: *'Come in,' she said, 'Make yourself comfortable.'*

(c) A quotation within a quotation is put in double quotes: *She asked: 'Do you know what "litotes" means?'.*

(d) To enclose words/phrases used as words/; to give the meaning of a word/expression; with titles of articles: *Amphibian* means *'living both on land and in water'. To kick the bucket* means *'to die'. George Orwell's article, 'Politics and the English Language', was published in 1946.*

7. Brackets and dashes

Brackets and dashes are both used to mark off parenthetical matter. A casual remark or aside in the middle of a sentence is marked off by dashes, as in (i) below additional information (in the course of a narrative or description) is enclosed in brackets, as in sentence (ii):

(i) *When I was in Mysore—that was a long time ago—I used to attend the debates in the Maharaja's College quadrangle.*

(ii) *We entered the auditorium (It was a fairly new building). At the end was a blue-black curtain forming a backdrop.*

8. Punctuation in sentences with parenthesis

(a) A parenthetical statement in the nature of an aside or comment (see example (i) above) does not begin with a capital letter. But a parenthetical statement giving additional information as a comment, if a full sentence, begins with a capital letter. (See example (ii) above.)

(b) The parenthetical phrase/sentence is punctuated as required: *It was in 1943 (or was it?) that I first heard of the phrase 'Quit India'.*

(c) Any punctuation mark that would have appeared at the point where the parenthesis begins (if the parenthesis was not there) will appear after the parenthesis: *In those days before World War II (as I've heard my father say), a family of four could live comfortably on Rs 40 a month. Sir C.V. Raman made his great discovery when he was in Calcutta (as you perhaps know).*

9. Question mark

(a) Used to mark a direct question: *Where did he go?* Not used after an indirect question: *Ask Sheela if she is coming to our bridge party next Sunday.*

(b) A request with the force of a question has a question mark: *I wonder whether I can borrow this book for a week?* And statements implying a question: *You didn't see him at all yesterday?* (This will have a rising intonation.)

(c) Enclosed in brackets after a piece of information to express some doubt about the correctness of it: *This manuscript dates back to the fifth (?) century.*

10. Exclamation mark

This is used after a sentence expressing a strong feeling (anger, disgust, joy, etc.): *What an ass! I hate you! Stand back! Fire! Tell me another!*

11. Italics

(a) To indicate that a word is being used as a word and not as indicating a thing:

We walked along the river for some time.

'In the above sentence *we* is a pronoun; *river* is a noun.' 'I wonder what *abracadabra* means.'

(b) For foreign words not fully absorbed into English:

'Apropos your letter what does *ipso facto* mean?' (The first word—from French—) is now part of the language; but not the second.)

12. Apostrophe

(a) To indicate possession (among other things):

(i) In nouns not ending in *s* (whether singular or plural), the apostrophe is placed before the *s*: *John's bike, children's toys.*

(ii) In singular nouns ending in *s*, usage varies: *Charles' friends / Charles's friends.*

(iii) In plural nouns ending in *s*, the apostrophe is placed after the *s*: the boys' team.

(iv) With places of business understood as such without a headword: *the tobacconist's; the butcher's; Macy's.* In many cases there is no apostrophe: *Selfridges, Harrods.*

(b) To indicate the missing letter(s) in contracted forms: *I'm surprised. He's not here. I haven't seen him. He's gone out (has). I'd know it (would). She won't tell me (will not).*

(c) Plurals of letters, abbreviations, and numbers are usually written with a small *s* and no apostrophe: *MPs, 1960s.* But *Dot the i's and cross the t's.*

(d) No apostrophe is used with the possessive pronouns: *its, yours, theirs, ours, whose.*

q

'queer the pitch'

This means 'to spoil someone's chances of doing something; especially maliciously or secretly'. So you can't say: *George Bush queered Saddam's pitch.* There was nothing secret or malicious about Bush's plans. But now that Bush is again contesting the Presidency, some people are trying to *queer* his pitch by raking up the question of his service in the National Air Guard in the 1970s. Clearly this is being done maliciously. Nearer home our politicians have always *queered the pitch* of their rivals in power by quietly engineering defections, manipulating cross-voting, or (if they are partners in power) by withdrawing support.

Queer, as verb, means 'to spoil, ruin someone's plans, arrangements, etc.'. As an adjective, it meant 'odd, strange': *a queer fellow*. In the last century it started getting used, both as adjective and noun, to refer to homosexuals. *A queer* was an offensive term. Then the homosexuals started calling themselves *queer* to take the sting out of the word. But it is still an offensive term referring to homosexuals. So think twice before you call someone *queer* (when you are in England!).

The history of *queer* parallels that of *gay*. Even as recently as the 1990s, *gay meant 'light-hearted and cheerful'*. This is the first meaning given in the COD (8th edn) with the example *a gay life*. Now *gay* refers only to homosexuals. The older, earlier meaning survives only in literature.

question tags

Which of these is correct?: (a) *I don't think he will come, will he?* (b) *I don't think he will come, do I?*

Generally speaking, the tag is on the main clause statement. In the usual cases, there is just a statement followed by a tag. *He is rich, isn't he? He will come, won't he? She doesn't mean it, does she?*, etc.

But a tag can also be formed on a subordinate clause when the main clause has a verb like *suppose* and *think*. *I suppose they mean business, don't they?* Such being the case, the tag in (a) is correct.

Can there be a tag on the main clause which has a dependent clause following it? Yes, there can be. *I didn't say he would reply, did I?* But what we have in (b) is a semantic absurdity. The speaker is seeking confirmation of what *he* thinks! How can he expect the listener to confirm what he thinks? Consider also: *I believe there are no ghosts, do I? I suppose he is just marking time, do I?*

Quirk, et al. (GCE) suggest that when a main clause is followed by a sub-clause, no tag is possible on the main clause. They give this example: *I suppose you are not serious, don't I?* But this is absurd for the reason given above. A perfectly grammatical tag is possible on the main clause even when there is a following sub-clause (as shown above).

r

rain-rains

Rain is an uncountable noun; you cannot use it preceded by a numeral. You cannot say: *We had one or two rains last season*. It has to be *two or three showers (of rain)*. But we can use it in the plural with a word like *some*. *The plants were washed away by some heavy rains*.

The rains without any qualification refers to the rainy season in the tropical countries; in India, the monsoon. *The rains come in June*.

refute/reject

It is quite common these days to read in the newspapers headlines like: 'India refutes Pak charge that the 13 December attack on Parliament was stage-managed by Indian agents.'

To *refute* is to show by elaborate analysis that what is asserted or imputed is false and cannot hold water. This would involve collecting evidence, analysing it, and then showing that the evidence does not support the charge or, more conclusively, disproves it.

But what is usually done is *rejection*, not *refutation*. The two countries routinely charge each other with committing some atrocity or other. Then promptly the country accused of committing the atrocity rejects it (the charge).

relative clause

1. Have you finished reading the book *which I gave you last week?*

The *underlined* clause in the above sentence refers to the noun (more strictly the noun phrase) *the book*. It describes or identifies it; 'which book?' *The one I gave you last week*. Such clauses are called relative clauses. The noun phrases to which they refer are their antecedents. And where the clause identifies (or defines) the antecedent, it is called a DEFINING RELATIVE CLAUSE.

Now look at this example. *My mother, who lives in Mysore, writes short stories*. The clause *who lives in Mysore* refers to *my mother*. This, too, is a relative clause. But the clause does not identify or define the antecedent noun. It doesn't answer the (absurd) question *which mother?* It gives some additional information about *my mother*, the antecedent. It is a NON-DEFINING RELATIVE CLAUSE.

Defining relative clauses are also called 'restrictive relative clauses'. Non-defining relative clauses are also called 'non-restrictive relative clauses'. Some more examples:

(a) Defining (or restrictive) relative clauses: *Who was the man who first ran a mile in under four minutes?* / *That's the girl who came first in the Higher Secondary exam this year.* / *Bangalore is a city which is much talked about in the US these days.*

(b) Non-defining (or non-restrictive) relative clauses: *Calcutta, which was once the capital of India, is a very big city.* / *My niece, who is an animal lover, has a small zoo in her house.* / *The match, which was abandoned because of heavy rains, was never very exciting.*

Non-defining clauses are set off from the rest of the sentence by a pair of commas. In speech, this is marked by a clear break.

2. The choice of the relative pronoun depends on the antecedent. Persons are referred to by *who (whom),* non-persons and inanimate objects by *which.* *That* can be used for all antecedents. (But not in non-defining clauses: *the Bible, which* (not: *that*) *is the world's most widely circulated book.*) The possessive is *whose* (in all cases). Some examples: *The cheetah which escaped from the zoo has been caught.* / *Qutub Minar, which is in Delhi, is a historical monument.* / *Women's equality with men is an idea that is gaining ground everywhere these days.* / *The sun, whose rays give us light and warmth, is a very small star.*

We will now note certain properties of defining relative clauses.

3. The relative pronoun refers to the antecedent. But within the relative clause it has its own function.

Subject: *The parcel which came yesterday.* (= the parcel came yesterday).

Object: *The movie which we saw yesterday* (= we saw the movie yesterday).

Indirect object: *The girl to whom you sent a gift* (= you sent a gift to the girl)....

It may have other functions, e.g., adverbial of place, time, etc.

Have you seen the place where the accident occurred?

Do you know (the time) when the plane is landing?

4. It is not possible to drop the relative pronoun in a non-defining relative clause. But it can be omitted in a defining relative clause under certain circumstances.

(a) The relative pronoun (we may call it the *wh-* word) can be omitted so long as it is not the subject of its clause: *The movie which we saw yesterday was an old classic. The movie we saw yesterday....* (The subject of the clause is *we; which* is the object of the verb *saw.*) *The girl to whom you spoke is my neighbour's daughter. The girl you spoke to....* (*to whom* is the indirect object).

(b) A subject relative cannot be omitted: *The parcel which came yesterday was a gift from my sister. Which* is the subject of the relative clause, so you can't omit it.* *The parcel came yesterday was a...*

A relative pronoun in the possessive form also cannot be dropped: *I spoke to Ravi whose brother I had met in the US.* (*Whose brother* is the object of *met*. But we can't omit *whose* as it is a possessive. So the object phrase cannot be omitted here.)

There are some constructions where a subject relative can be dropped in informal speech and writing. *This is the best book there is on the subject.*

(c) When the relative pronoun is a prepositional object there are two possibilities. The preposition can be moved along with the relative pronoun. *The man to whom you spoke is a cousin of mine.* Or, the preposition can be left behind: *The man who you spoke to is a cousin of mine.* Or, the relative pronoun can be left out: *The man you spoke to....*

In informal speech and writing, the second construction is preferred. The form *whom* is not very popular these days. But in a formal situation, the relative pronoun is retained: *The party to whom we gave the contract....* In this situation (i.e., when the relative pronoun appears with the preposition), the object form is obligatory.

5. Relative clauses with no expressed antecedent:

Take what you like. The meaning is: 'Take anything that you like'. *I don't remember what* (= the things which) *she said.* Since *what* already includes a possible antecedent, there can be no expressed antecedent. **Take that what you like.*

Other such words are: *whatever, wherever, whenever, where, when.* *You can do whatever* (= *anything which*) *you like.* / *The wind blows wherever* (= *anywhere that*) *it likes.* / *You should be ready to go whenever they call you.*

With *where* and *when*, an antecedent can be supplied: *Can you tell me* (the time) *when I should call again?*

6. The relative clause is a noun modifier and can occur in contracted forms also. *A man to watch* can be viewed as the shortened form of *a man who should be watched.* Similarly *a time to dance* can be related to: *a time when we can (or should) dance;* and *a point to observe* is *a point which one should observe* or *which should be observed.*

In some cases, the 'reduced clause' can appear before the noun. This is so with phrases like *the sleeping child* (= the child who is / was sleeping;

the burnt houses (= the houses which were burnt); *the abandoned woman* (= the woman who was abandoned). But there are restrictions on when this sort of reduction is possible. *The boy who came* cannot be turned into *the came boy*; or *the man you talked to* into *the talked to man*. See also 'AGOG VILLAGERS', 'CONCERNED CLERK'.

remember–forget

Both the verbs can be found in two different constructions: v + *ing*, v + *to-* infinitive. Let's first look at *remember*. *I remember meeting her at a book fair. Remember to post the letter.*

As you can see, with the -*ing* form, the reference is to the past; with the infinitive, to the future.

The same distinctions are found with *forget*. *I can never forget my first day in college. Don't forget to invite Rajesh for the party.*

It may appear that the distinction made above is contradicted by a sentence like: *I forgot to post the letter.* But it is not so. At the time of forgetting, the action had yet to be done. The same analysis applies to *I remembered to write the address in capital letters.*

repeated subject

Here is an interesting construction: *Those who want to take up serious, advanced practices, they must follow the ancient [yoga] texts.*

The point to note here is the repetition of the subject of the sentence in the form of *they*. To whom does the pronoun refer? It refers to *Those who....*

This sort of repetition would be justified if the preceding structure were so long as to leave the reader in some doubt as to what the subject is. *Those who want to take up advanced practices...and are prepared to spend a lot of time and energy with a total disregard of...they must follow the ancient texts.* Otherwise there is no need to repeat the subject by means of a pronoun. The subject is also repeated with justification in cases like this: *John, he is a wonderful fellow./Mary, she is a darling./Mauritius, it is a wonderful place.* This type of construction is, technically, said to involve 'Left Dislocation'. There is also 'Right Dislocation'. *He is an excellent worker, John./She is a real darling, Mary.*

Going back to the sentence we started with, here is another example of the same type (from the same source). *The soul, according to his Karma, he may go to the higher region or the lower region.*

restrict/refrain

The exorbitant expenditure incurred for each call restricts and refrains flow of easy communication between [Hosur and Bangalore]. (Letter to *Deccan Herald*, 27 June 1998.)

Restrict and refrain? Quite possibly in the speaker's language, this is a fixed phrase meaning something like 'limit, discourage from'. But there is an interesting confusion behind this collocation.

Restrict implies a context in which A restricts B's freedom to act in some way. *He was placed under house arrest and his movements were restricted.* *Refrain*, on the other hand, suggests no such external agent. You refrain from doing something. You are not refrained from doing something by anybody. It is possible that somebody may impose conditions on you which, in turn, force you to *refrain* from doing something. But the person directly and immediately involved in not doing something is you. 'A' can restrict your freedom to act; then (out of fear, respect, or whatever) you may *refrain* from doing something.

It can now be seen why *restrict and refrain* is an odd, actually impossible, phrase.

retronyms

Time was when a guy played a guitar and that was that. Just a guitar. But when the electric guitar came on the scene, the old guitar could not remain just a guitar. It became the *acoustic guitar.*

Books have been with us for a long, long time. But when paperbacks appeared, the other type of books had to be distinguished by a suitable modifier. They became *hardcover books.* *Book* has remained a cover term but when you buy a book the price depends on whether it is a *hardcover* or *paperback.*

Mail or *post* is the term still in common use with many in India. But for many in the West (and for quite a few in India), there is also *e-mail* and *voice-mail.* For such people, *You have some mail today* is confusing. Is it *e-mail, voice-mail,* or just what the postman (or *mailman*) brings? In any case, what is it that the postman/mailman brings? It is *hard mail.* Some imaginative computer men have suggested a more appropriate term: *snail mail.* Journal editors ask for a *soft copy* (via e-mail) followed by a *hard copy* (the manuscript).

Acoustic guitar, hardcover books, hard copy—these are all examples of *retronyms.* A *retronym* is a noun which once could stand by itself but now has a modifier tagged on to it (to distinguish it from a later coinage). Here are some more examples: *manual typewriter* (after the invention of the *electronic typewriter*), *ground war* (after the development of *aerial warfare*), *natural languages*, i.e., human languages (after the development of artificial languages like *computer languages*). A recent *retronym* is *wet shaving products* (after the wide popularity of electric shavers).

The development of *retronyms* is not always a straightforward matter. A *steam engine* (i.e., an engine making use of steam power) was originally a *fire engine*. *Steam engine* in the sense of a locomotive came into use around 1815. Initially both the terms were in use. The OED has this citation: '...*powerful locomotive steam engine for the purpose of drawing...coal wagons*'. Soon *locomotive* alone began to be used. But with the invention of the diesel engine (in 1894) and its use in locomotives, *steam engine* came back into use.

A similar development can be seen with *watch*. Watches carried about one's person were simply *watches*, although, in fact, they were carried in pockets. Occasionally the term *pocket watch* was used. (OED has a citation dated 1696.) But it was only after the coming of *wristwatches* (in the 1890s) that *pocket watch* came into regular use.

In these cases we see how a so-called *retronym* is a revival of an expression in occasional use earlier.

In the cases discussed till now, the original term is still retained as a cover term: *watch, locomotive, war, typewriter, mail*.... But in some cases, the original term retains its specific meaning and does not develop into a *retronym*. We now have *veterinary doctors* (and, in the U.S. *lawn doctors*, specialists who take care of your lawn). But *doctor* without any further modification is understood as one who treats human patients (although confronted with Ph.Ds and D.Ds one may be forced to say: 'He is a medical doctor').

Generally speaking, a *retronym* will not arise if there are distinct words/expressions for a set of related but distinct concepts: *house, flat, bungalow, mansion, palace*. Terms expressing man-woman relationships also show the same behaviour. In the West, you have *wife, girlfriend, live-in partner*. In view of the increasing recognition given to gay couples, *domestic partner* has emerged as a cover term. But *wife* remains as it was without any modifiers. But there may be a cultural slant in this. With us, *dharmapatni* is in common usage. Does this suggest that having a mistress was quite common with our ancestors? Or is it, as with *suputra,* a conventional, stylized modifier?

S

same

We find no merit in these petitions and so dismiss the same. Is the use of *same* here correct?

 Same is generally used as an adjective: *They are of the same age./We have lived in the same house for twenty years.* The meaning here is one of identity. A slightly different variant meaning is: 'not different from'. *I have bought the same car as yours. Old men who are bald all look the same.* And then there are some stock phrases where *same* has the same meanings as distinguished above (*What you say comes to/amounts to the same as what he has said./We are in the same boat* (= unfortunate situation); or has specialized meanings: *And in the same breath he said...*(= immediately after)./*We are on the same wavelength* (think alike, have the same views). *Same* is also used as a pronoun. But here there are two different cases, one of which is viewed with some disfavour. The totally acceptable construction is seen in: *I would do the same/say the same again.* Here, clearly, a following noun (e.g. *thing*) is understood. We have the same use in the common, informal exchange: *Happy New Year. (The) same to you.* There are several exchanges of this type where *same* appears with or without *the.* A clearly pronominal use (i.e., where it replaces or stands for a previously mentioned noun) is seen in commercial English: *To repairing the chair, Rs 300. To polishing the same, Rs 50.* In this usage, the article *the* is not usually found.

 Now for the sentence we began with. Clearly this is a case where *same* is used as a pronoun; *the same* here stands for *the petitions.*

 At an earlier stage of the language, *the same* was freely used in this way. Thus in the Bible: *But he that shall endure unto the end, the same shall be saved* (Matthew 24: 13). But some time in the nineteenth century, this usage disappeared. The use of *same* as a pronoun is now restricted to commercial English and legal English, apart from the stock phrases mentioned above. Outside these two domains *same* should not be used as a pronoun. *I borrowed some books from the library but forgot to return the same by the due date.* Change this to *forgot to return them....* That is, in ordinary usage, use a regular pronoun (*it, they* as the case may be) instead of *the same.*

satisfying/satisfactory

A government notification (as reported in the newspapers) reads: *You have submitted the report on time, completing the work in a satisfying manner.* Satisfying or satisfactory?

There is a sense of satisfactory which means 'passable but not really good.' Parents are only too familiar with this comment in their children's report card: *Character and conduct satisfactory.* In a parent–teacher meeting, the teacher may tell the parent: *Sudha's English is excellent. Performance in Maths? Oh, well, satisfactory.* A Confidential Report which rates the performance of an officer as *Satisfactory* actually condemns him as unfit for promotion.

Perhaps it is this sense of the word which prompted the government to say *in a satisfying manner.*

But *satisfying* cannot be used in such contexts. You can speak of *a satisfying meal.* You can also use the word in contexts where you are personally pleased at the turn of events. *After all he'd put me through, it was very satisfying to see him begging for once.* (LDCE,1995)

In the absence of any personal gratification of the senses, *satisfying* would sound odd.

Then what is the solution?

You can take away any negative association that may be with *satisfactory* by saying: *completing the work in a thoroughly satisfactory manner.*

As a matter of fact, there are contexts where *satisfactory* is used without any suggestion of *not as good as it should be. The result of the experiment was satisfactory. / We want a satisfactory explanation of your lateness* (ALD, 1989). You cannot ask an officer to give a *satisfying* explanation of his conduct.

search/search for

Searching a woman named Josephine Tay was not easy. I looked for her in Charing Cross and Leicester Square.

To *search* means 'to make a physical examination of a person, place, etc. looking for something concealed, hidden'. What is *searched* is the person/place. Customs officials are known to *search* persons suspected of smuggling in undeclared gold, drugs, etc. The police routinely *search* persons in their custody.

Search for means to look for, to find out; say, a missing person. So Josephine was not *searched*. The writer *searched for* her all over London. He looked for her, as he correctly puts it in the second sentence.

seasonal, seasonable, seasoned

All these adjectives derive from *season*. In *seasonal* we have the suffix *-al* meaning 'of the nature of', 'belonging to': *seasonal changes in temperature, educational facilities, fictional characters*.

In *seasonable*, the suffix is *-able*; cf *knowledgeable, objectionable*. *Seasonable weather* is weather as expected for the season. In the case of *help, advice,* etc., the meaning is 'right', 'appropriate to the occasion', e.g., *seasonable advice.*

In *seasoned* we have the suffix *-ed* added to the verb *season*. Depending on the context, the meanings can be as in: *seasoned wood* (fit for use having been exposed to weather) *highly seasoned sauce* (flavoured with salt, pepper, etc.), *a seasoned politician* (well-experienced politician).

sequence of tenses

'The army will be withdrawn once the situation *became* normal'—DD 9 p.m. news, 2 November 1997

Here we have the use of a past form (*became*) which may be logical but not grammatical. Of the two events, withdrawal of the army and the situation becoming normal, the second one should take place first. Once it takes place, it will be a past event and so, we feel, should be in the past tense (*the situation became normal*).

But it is not so. The rule of sequence of tenses requires that all tense forms in a complex sentence be the same (with some exceptions). *Will* (in: *the army will be withdrawn*) is in the present tense. So the next clause will also have to be in the present tense. *The army will be completely withdrawn once the situation becomes completely normal.*

Does this mean that in a situation like the one analysed above, a past tense is not possible?

A past tense would be possible in the second clause if the first clause also had been in the past tense. *The army would be completely withdrawn once the situation became normal.*

severe–acute

The respiratory infection which swept across China and some other South Asian countries sometime ago was named SARS (Severe Acute Respiratory Syndrome). Do we see a tautology here? *Severe, acute*—are they synonyms?

No. *Severe* has several meanings. The one relevant now can be seen in such expressions as: *severe damage* (to a building), *severe congestion of* the lungs, *severe shortage of food grains.* What is common to all these is a sense of being 'critical'. There is an impending crisis (unless things are handled very carefully).

Acute, in the medical sense, means 'developing very fast'; 'quick onset and rapid development'. The rapid onset and development lead to a critical (*severe*) condition. The COD's definition: 'coming sharply to a crisis'.

The respiratory condition is *severe*; it is reached suddenly and rapidly (*acute*).

In ordinary, non-medical, usage, the two words are often used interchangeably. A serious shortage in the supply of food grains can be described either as *severe* or *acute*. We are concerned here only with the stage reached.

This does not mean that in: *a severely damaged building*, you can say: *acutely damaged building*. *Severe* can combine the meanings of 'extensive' and 'critical'; *acute* usually suggests 'intensity'.

But in the case of pain, there is not much difference between *severe pain* and *acute pain*. So there is no hope of getting relief from a toothache by calling it *severe* instead of *acute*.

The opposite of *severe* (in the medical sense) is *mild*; that of *acute* is *chronic*.

shoot/shoot at

Sometime ago there was a news report about a daring dacoity in broad daylight on Residency Road: *Architect and aide shot at, robbed* proclaimed one headline. *Duo shot, Rs 9 lakh robbed near bank* screamed another paper.

Is it *shot* or *shot at*?

In the present case it is *shot*. This implies that the men were actually hit by the gunmen's bullets. And, in fact, that was the case. The architect was wounded in the chest.

To shoot at does not convey this meaning. You may *shoot at* something but miss it. But you cannot say *I shot him but missed*. If you *shot* him, that's it. You have *shot* him, possibly dead.

This choice (with/without the preposition) is not available with other verbs of this type. There is no choice between *hit/hit at*. *I hit him*. Not: *I hit at him*. There is *hit out at* (= try to hit). But this phrase is most often found only in transferred (= figurative) meanings. *Jayalalitha has hit out at the Karnataka government's handling of the Veerappan affair.* Similarly with the verbs: *kick, beat*. If you kick someone, you have *kicked* him. But you may *aim a kick at someone* and miss.

'should have been'?

'Perhaps if this should have been a war, they would have succeeded.' (A naval officer in a private conversation).

Here we see a typical Indianism—the use of *should have* in place of the past perfect. The correct phrase is: *if this had been a war*. But some of us feel that this does not bring out properly the hypothetical nature of the situation. In sentences like: *If you went there, you would know,* a future result contingent on a hypothetical situation is correctly expressed by a simple past in the *if-* clause and a modal (*would*) in the main clause. Where the reference is to the past, the past perfect is needed in the *if-* clause.

The situation we are discussing (technically, *if-* clauses of rejected condition) presents problems to non-native speakers everywhere. Here is a sentence I heard on South African TV (a long time ago) when there were race riots in Sweto: *If proper precautions should have been taken* [the death toll would have been less].

Siamese twins

The phrase entered the English language, thanks to the Siamese men, Chang and Eng (1811–74) who, despite being joined at the waist, led an active life. Today perhaps they would have been separated surgically; but not in the nineteenth century. Sir Ernest Gowers in his 1965 revision of Fowler's *Modern English Usage* (1926) introduced the expression *Siamese twins* to characterize certain two-member phrases (connected by *and* or *or*) which always go together. Many of these are merely tautological. Such are *alas and alack, bits and pieces, gall and wormwood, heart and soul, jot or title, leaps and bounds* (*the country is progressing by leaps and bounds*), *lo and behold* (to introduce an event/development which, though surprising, could have been predicted). *The new deadline came and lo and behold, work on the International Airport began*); (in any) *shape or form, sort or kind*. The terms in these phrases can also be used separately: *There isn't a jot of evidence* (to support your view); *accept life's gall* (bitter, cruel situations) *without blaming others*.

Some other paired terms can't be used independently. Either one of the terms is used in an archaic sense and would not now be understood by itself or the combination has acquired a sense different from that of the components. Among these are: *fair and square, hue and cry, kith and kin, might and main, odds and ends, part and parcel, spick and span*. These are more or less pleonastic.

In yet another group, the terms consist not of synonyms but of associated ideas: *bill and coo, flotsam and jetsam, hum and haw, thick and fast, ways and means, loud and clear, nuts and bolts, spit and polish*; or of alternatives or opposites: *cut and thrust, fast and loose, hither and thither, by hook or by crook, thick and thin, to and fro*.

Some are legal expressions: *aid and abet, let and hindrance, null and void*. The classification is not exhaustive nor are the lists complete. The point to note is that these are fixed expressions. As already noted, some are tautological and some pleonastic. But with the exception of a few (*leaps and bounds, ways and means, by hook or by crook*), they are not condemned as cliches.

some/any

A tricky point of English usage concerns the use of *some* and *any*. *Any* is usually found in negative and interrogative sentences. *Is there any coffee left? Have you seen any of them? I don't have any problems with her*. *Some* is found in positive contexts. *Here are some friends of Jane's*.

There is a further context for *any*: conditional sentences. If a sentence is, or can be interpreted as, a conditional, *any* is possible. *If anyone calls, tell him I'm not at home*.

The distinction between *any* and *some* noted above is what is discussed in grammar under: assertive vs non-assertive. These are technical terms. In ordinary usage, a sentence like *He denied having any knowledge of the crime* would be regarded as making an *assertion*, asserting something. But in grammar, 'assertion' has the specific meaning of making a positive affirmation. There is no such affirmation in *He denied having....* Hence it is non-assertive. Hence also, we find the use of *any*. Questions, too, are non-assertive. Hence we find *any*, and not *some* in questions. *Have you read any fiction recently? Is there any coffee left?*

In apparent contradiction to what has been said above, *any* may be found in positive sentences and *some* in interrogative sentences.

I'll show you a trick. Give me a coin. Any coin will do. Similarly: *Is there some coffee left?* What is the explanation?

Any is used in affirmative sentences in the sense of 'no matter which/who/what'. This directly follows from the fact that *any* is a non-assertive word. As for *some* appearing in questions, there is a difference between *Is there any coffee left?* And *Is there some coffee left?* The question with *any* has a negative expectation. The speaker is prepared for a negative answer. (*Sorry. There's no coffee left.*) But the question with *some* suggests a positive expectation on the part of the speaker. He expects to hear something like '*Yes. There is a little coffee left.*'

Now consider this sentence. *We need any sort of help from weapons to money but we need help* (a high Nepalese dignitary as reported in *Deccan Herald* (9 December 2001). Supposing it had been: *Any sort of help will do— from weapons to money.* This is fine. The meaning of *any* is indifference; no matter what. But with *need*, a positive statement has to follow. *We need all sorts of help—from weapons to money.*

some verbs
(say/tell/hear/listen)

There are some closely related verbs which, nevertheless, are distinct and have different contexts of use, e.g., *say* and *tell*. *He said, He told*, both are possible. But in *Tell me* you cannot have *Say me.* And, while you can say *I told him*, you cannot say *I said him.* It has to be *I said to him.* In the construction *Say what you will*, you cannot have *Tell what you will.* These distinctions are not always observed in Indian English. Because it is *I said to him*...some people say *I told to him.* Some months ago I was with the Principal in a prestigious school. She was quite bitter and outspoken about the poor knowledge of English of her colleagues. Her assistant (who was on the other side of the partition) came to her with a file. She briefly looked at it and said: '*Tell to him to see me tomorrow.*'

Another such pair is *hear* and *listen. Hear* stands for a physical activity. You *hear* when sound waves impinge on the drum in the inner ear. But it is not always the case that this is registered in the brain. (Most often this is what happens in a classroom.)

You *listen* when you pay attention to what you *hear.* There is also another meaning of *listen*: you act on the basis of what you *hear.* When a father shouts: *Listen to me. Brush your teeth after breakfast*, he means that they should show by action that they have heard him.

The distinction between these two words has been beautifully brought out in a recent advertisement by a very famous hospital in New York City: *We turned a child who couldn't hear into a typical 2-year-old who doesn't listen.* A deaf child was brought to them. They operated on its inner ears and made her *hear*.

specific/specified

Specific (adj.) has to do with the particular as opposed to the vague or general.

Specific instructions/proposals/aims: It can also mean 'for a particular purpose'. *The money is given for the specific purpose of providing midday meals to school children.*

Specified means 'expressly so stipulated, mentioned'. *The contract specifies that you will get a royalty of 10 per cent.* / *The school regulations specify the colour and style of the uniform.*

Occasionally there is some confusion in the use of these terms. *The job has to be done in the specific* (wrong)/ *specified time.*

'strove as they did'

A sentence like: *He tried very hard but could not succeed* can be reformulated in this way: *Though he tried very hard, he could not succeed.* The choice between the two is a matter of style. The second one is more formal and literary.

There is one more variant of the sentence. *Try as he might, he could not succeed.* This is even more literary and rhetorical.

Notice the tense of the verb *try*. In the sentence we started with, it is in the past tense; in the variant now being discussed, it is in the present tense. The sense of past is now shown in *might*.

This is important. The sentence: *Tried as he may/might, he could not succeed* is ungrammatical. The fronted verb must be in the present tense. Observe also: the adverbial *very hard* is missing but its force has been retained.

Consider now this (authentic) sentence: *Strove as they did, the Indians could not inject that element of pace in their workouts....*' (From a report on an India–Pakistan hockey match, *The Hindu*). Here we have a double past tense: *strove, did*. This is inadmissible. This should read: *Strive as they might, the Indians could not inject....*

The construction is possible with other verbs. *He ran very fast but he could not catch up with his competitor. Run as he might....* Also: *Though he ran very fast....*

A somewhat similar construction is available when the clause contains a form of BE and a predicate adjective. *He is poor but generous. Though he is poor, he is generous. Poor though he is, he is generous* (see my *Current English*, 2002).

structure of the verb phrase

The English verb phrase has a fairly simple structure but students and others have considerable difficulty in getting it straight. Research done at the CIEFL some decades ago showed that this was the one area in which most students entering college had problems. A more recent experience of going through more than a dozen M.Phil dissertations at a deemed university in the South confirms that even graduates have the same problem.

To understand the structure of the English verbal group, we should see what elements go into it. In the simplest case, we have just a verb and TENSE. *She laughed. The baby cried.* This may be analysed as Tense (past) + v. In *she works in a factory*, the structure of the verbal group is Tense (present) + v.

Rajesh is studying in the library is also in the present tense. But it tells us something more. It shows that the action is continuing, going on, at the time of speaking. The verbal group here is in the PRESENT PROGRESSIVE (or CONTINUOUS) tense. In *Rajesh was working in the library* we have the verbal group in the PAST PROGRESSIVE.

If you look at the phrases *is working/was working*, you will see that in both cases the verb has the suffix *-ing* attached to it. You will also see that in one case we have *is* and in the other case we have *was*. These may be analysed as the present tense and past tense forms of BE: present + BE = *is*; past + BE = *was* (in the singular; in the plural it would be *are, were*).

Why do we have BE here? BE is a carrier of what is called ASPECT. English has two aspect phrases; one of them is found with BE and expresses the PROGRESSIVE (continuous) aspect. We use this aspect phrase when we want to indicate that an action is going on at the time of speaking. The full form of the progressive aspect phrase is: *be- ing*. So we represent *is working* as: Tense + *be- ing* + v. Tense is attached to *be* resulting in *is*; *ing* is attached to v resulting in *working*. So we get *is working*.

Now look at the sentence: *He has finished his work.* How do we analyse *has finished*? *Has finished* expresses another aspect of the English verb: the PERFECT aspect (in this case the present perfect). The perfect aspect is expressed by *have -en* (where *en* is a symbol for the past participle form of the verb. So *has finished* can be analysed as: Tense (present) + have -en + v. As before, tense gets attached to *have*, resulting in *has*; *en* gets attached to *finish* resulting in *finished*. And so we get *has finished*.

The analysis till now can be stated in this way. Structure of the verbal group: Tense + (Aspect) + v.

We have enclosed aspect in brackets to show that it is an optional element. Clearly there are verbal groups without aspect. *He came. She left.* The verbal group here contains only tense and verb.

Now look at this: *Rajeev has been working all day.* How do we analyse this? Clearly it contains not only tense (present) but both the aspects, perfective and progressive. The structure of the verbal group is:

Tense	Aspect	verb
Present	+ have -en+ be -ing +	*work*

As before, *tense* is attached to *have* (= *has*), *en* is attached to *be* (= *been*) and *ing* is attached to the verb (= *working*) resulting in *has been working*. Note the order of the elements: first, tense; then aspect. If both the aspects are present, the perfect comes first; then the progressive. It is *has been working*; not *been has working* or anything else. Note also: if one member of aspect is present, the other member should also be present: *is working*, not *is work* or just *working*. *He is work*/*He working* are impossible. It is *has written* (say, a letter) not *has wrote* or *has write* or just *written* (**he written a letter*).

There can be one more element in the verbal group as seen in *He may come tomorrow.* We see no aspect phrase here but there is tense (present). What is *may*? May is one of a handful of verbs which help convey certain meanings not conveyed by tense, aspect or even by the verb itself. Tense locates an action on a time scale—present or past (English has no future tense. See EXPRESSING FUTURITY); aspect presents an action as completed (*has typed*) or continuing (*is typing*). But quite often, the speaker wishes to express such meanings as: whether an action is *likely to happen*, or *certain to happen*; whether it is *necessary to do something* or *it has to be done*; whether one is *able to do something* or *not able to do it*, etc. These are meanings which express the speaker's attitude towards an action or event. Such meanings are called MODAL meanings. The verbs which express them are MODAL VERBS.

So we may analyse a phrase like *may have been working* as: modal + perfect + progressive +verb. What about tense?

Tense is an obligatory element of all verbal groups which help make complete sentences. Without tense, we can only have incomplete phrases, not sentences. *He to come* is not a sentence because there is no tense. *He came* is a sentence because it contains past tense.

Now *he may have been working* is a sentence. It makes good sense. Where, then, is tense?

We assume that tense is in the modal verb. We analyse *may* as *present + may*. But the modal verbs show no change of form. Some modals are analysed as containing a past tense. *Might, could, would, should* may be regarded as the past forms of *may, can, will,* and *shall*. But *must* and *ought to* which are also modal verbs have no other forms. So the modals are either in the present or past tense but have no other forms like the regular verbs.

There is one more element that can occur in the verbal group. In *the letter was written by Suman,* the verbal group is *was written*. The verb (*write*) is in the past participle form (*-en*). We saw earlier that where there is *-en* there should be *have*. But there is no *have* here; only *be*. Does it mean that there are two structures *have -en* and *be -en*? Indeed it is so. *Have -en* marks the perfect; *be -en* the PASSIVE. It is possible to have both structures as in *The letter has been written* (= *present + have -en + be -en + write*).

The presence of *be -en* means that the verb is in the passive voice. If it is not there, the verb is in the ACTIVE VOICE. On comparing the sentences *Suman wrote the letter / The letter was written by Suman,* we notice that the object of the active sentence has become the subject of the passive sentence; the original subject appears at the end of the passive sentence in a *by-* phrase (called the agent phrase). And the passive verb phrase contains *be -en*. Quite often the *by-* phrase is omitted. *He was admitted to the hospital.* By whom? Not mentioned (see PASSIVE).

So the possible elements in a verbal group are: tense, modal, aspect, the passive marker, and the verb itself. Of these, only tense (and the verb) are obligatory, if the sentence has to make 'complete' sense. It is possible to construct a sentence with the verbal group containing all the elements. *He may have been being questioned by the police.* But such sentences are very rare.

The elements of the VP can appear only once in a simple sentence; there can't be more than one tense or more than one progressive or perfective phrase. *Did you saw it* is wrong precisely because there are two past tenses here (in *did* and in *saw*). *Do you have any girlfriends?—Not now. I did had some years ago* (actual conversation in a TV serial). It should be: *I did have* or, if no emphasis is needed *I had. I have had my lunch already* has only one tense (the present as seen in *have*); *had* is the past participle of *have* and not its past tense here. *Have had* is a present perfect phrase with the main verb *have. Will you join us for lunch?—Thanks, no. I have already had my lunch. Going, going, gone*—is not a case of two present progressives and a past perfect. It should be viewed as the abbreviated form of: *It is going. It is going. It is gone* (Auctioneer's cry). Finally: *Go see what she is doing* is not a case of two main verbs in one verb phrase. It is equivalent to two: *Go and see.* The verb *go* admits this sort of conjunction without *and. Go tell your mother/Go look for it,* etc.

subsequent/consequent/pursuant

I was sitting in a lawyer's office the other day (Don't ask me what I was doing there!) and could not help overhearing a young lawyer dictating something to his clerk. '...Mr X was transferred, subsequently his family had to move out of town.' He didn't like this. He corrected it immediately. 'Pursuant to Mr X's transfer, his family moved out of town.'

But was it *pursuant to* or *consequent upon*?

The three words: *subsequent, consequent, pursuant,* establish a relationship between two events, A, B. *Subsequent* relates the events on a time scale: A and then B. *He was posted to Ahmednagar. Subsequently he was transferred to Nagpur.* This is a purely temporal relationship. *Consequent* implies a resultative relationship. B because of A. *He was handed a charge-sheet. Consequently he had to defend himself. Pursuant* implies that something was done as per *instructions given. Pursuant to your order dated 9 February... I am reporting for duty....* The relationship here is one of 'acting as directed'. B is done as per instructions in A.

Now going back to the case we began with. If somebody was transferred and his family had to shift residence, it was as a consequence of the transfer. The officer has moved pursuant to the transfer order; the family has moved as a consequence of this.

Note also: *subsequent* and *consequent* have the adverb forms: *subsequently* and *consequently*. No such form exists with *pursuant*.

subside/allay

Judicial pronouncements are not to be scrutinized, it may be said, for grammatical solecisms or incorrect use of words. And yet this may not be a correct view either. After all, law and language go together.

The greatest precision is expected of legal documents. I remember reading, years ago, a discussion in one of our high courts on the correct interpretation of a modal verb. I think it was *may*.

Now here is a sentence—I reproduce as I found it in a newspaper—from a recent Commission Report: *'Apprehensions entertained by the minorities should be subsided with the guaranteeing of fundamental rights to minorities.'*

Subside is an intransitive verb. *The flood waters have begun to subside/* (= to recede, to go down)./*The storm has begun to subside./He waited till the applause subsided* (= died down). It cannot be used transitively, as in the citation given above. (To see that the verb is used transitively, consider the active form of the sentence. *Guaranteeing of fundamental rights will subside the apprehensions entertained by the minorities.*)

This apart, apprehensions are *allayed*.

suggest/imply

Most dictionaries gloss *imply* as *suggest* and *suggest* as *imply*. Both the words share a certain core meaning but in actual usage it will be found that the two words are not freely interchangeable.

Suggest, of course, has several meanings not relevant for present purposes. *I suggest that we go for a walk.* Here *imply* is obviously impossible. The relevant case is a sentence like: *Are you suggesting that I am a liar?*

Suppose someone has said something about you which broadly hints that you have not spoken the truth. You can then say: 'Your statement suggests that I am a liar.' Or: 'Your statement implies that I am a liar.'

We can now see that the distinction between *suggest* and *imply* is quite a subtle one. Implication is a logical relation between sentences. (A implies B.) It is, in a sense, a passive relation. *Suggest*, on the other hand, is a more active relation.

The speaker's words may often suggest nuances which are not possibly implied logically; tone, demeanour, gesture may all contribute to suggesting something. In these cases, *suggestion* is a broader, more vaguely defined term than *implication*.

The same distinction may be found when there is no speaker before you in person. It may be a piece of text, a record of what happened or what someone said. *This* (the text) *suggests, this* (the text) *implies*...are not always the same thing. One may not always see an implication—it may require some analysis to see what a text implies. But when you say

This suggests, the suggestion is that it is something readily apparent to all. With these comments in mind, consider now this remark (*The Hindu*, 9 August 1996, magazine section, p. viii), *It* [that is, blaming the teacher] *is not really going to solve the problem, as the following story implies*. Or, should it be: *as the following story suggests?*

t

take care

We tend to use the verb *take* more extensively than the British. A very common construction among us is as in: *I take coffee in the morning*. The Standard BE, construction would be: *I have coffee in the morning. Take*, in BE is more likely to be found in the context of, say, medicine: *Take two tablets in the morning and one in the evening*. Coffee or tea is not the only thing we 'take'. *We take breakfast, we take a bath, we take a nap*. In all these cases, Standard English uses *have*.

Observe now that the actions mentioned above are of a habitual nature. But taking medicine is not, with most people, a habit. But supposing the speaker is a diabetes patient on regular insulin injections. He will say: 'I have my shot around eight in the morning.' It is a habitual act with him.

The distinction made above between habitual and other activities needs to be refined. You may be in the habit of catching a particular bus (say at 9.30 in the morning) to go to your office every day. Is this now a habitual action? Whatever it is, you 'take' or 'catch' a bus (at 9.30 a.m.). You don't 'have' it. To *take leave of someone* is another common expression with us. Thus a junior lecturer after meeting his professor will say, deferentially: 'Sir, may I *take leave of you?*' In this particular context, this may not be inappropriate. Senior persons (among us) expect a degree of formality and respect from younger people. But in other cases this expression is best replaced by things like: 'I should be leaving now.' 'I think I better be going now.'

Take up is another phrase used by us in contexts not found in British English. This *takes up too much room* (say, a piece of furniture) is correct. But: *Who will take up this job?* is not. The correct form is: *Who will take on this job?* Again: *We have taken up numerous schemes in the current year*, is IE. Better choices would be: *initiated/undertaken*. We have *initiated several new projects*.

Take up, besides the meaning already given, has these meanings in Standard English: interrupt or question (*to take up* a speaker); absorb (a sponge *takes up water*); become interested in, pursue (*take up* the study of Mathematics) among others.

tautology

Tautology is the repetition of the same idea, in whole or in part, concealed in different words. Here are some examples: No matter what you do *the end result* is the *same*. Please go through the proofs and *revert back* to me at the earliest. *If in case* you cannot come, give me a ring. The phrases in italics are tautologies.

Tautological expressions may be classified into: (a) phrasal, (b) non-phrasal, and (c) sequential.

(a) The example sentences given above contain phrasal tautologies. This is, by far, the most common. Here are some more examples: *Resultant effects, sum total, real/actual/true facts, old adage, an armed gunman, a new recruit, the reason why*; and verb + particle phrases like: *reply back, return again and cancel out* etc. These are tautologies in all varieties of English. The Americans are particularly fond of *exact same*. Burchfield (1998) has noted the common (uneducated!) tautologies in the use of acronyms: *HIV virus* (human immunodeficiency virus), *LCD display* (liquid crystal display), etc. (But it can be plausibly argued that these are no longer tautologies. *HIV* and *LCD* have acquired the status of names. Cf Microsoft's announcement on its Windows 2000 as: *Built on NT Technology*. Initially NT stood for 'New Technology'.)

(b) In the non-phrasal tautology, the repetitive word appears, not in the modifier position of the tautological phrase, but elsewhere in the sentence. There is *no cause* for *undue alarm*. Merit and merit *alone* is the *only* thing that should count. In view of the holiday season, *additional* trains have been *added*. *Both* Vajpayee *as well as* Advani are secularists at heart. Let's meet at *10 a.m.* tomorrow *morning*.

Undue alarm says nothing more than *no cause for alarm*; the meaning of *as well as* is already there in *both; morning* is already there in *a.m.; earlier* is implicit in *already*.

(c) The grossest form of tautology is where a second clause repeats the meaning of the first. The clause is presented as indicating the result or consequence of the action indicated in the previous clause. This is typically Indian. He *put in his papers* and *resigned*. India and Pakistan should *bury the hatchet* and *make peace*. Your final exams are fast approaching. You should *burn the midnight oil* and *study hard*. This type of tautology is what I have called 'sequential'.

The tautologies illustrated at (a) arise from a habit of propping up every noun with an adjective; or of supporting a verb with an adverb, a habit reinforced by the fact that English is rich in verb + particle constructions (e.g., *look up, come in, hand over*, etc.). A moment's reflection will show that the adjective is unnecessary; the adverb, pointless. But the habit of thinking in set phrases makes this scrutiny impossible.

The tautologies of the second type are partly due to carelessness, and partly due to sentence structure. The writer who says that *merit and merit alone* should be the *only* consideration has forgotten that he has put in *alone* by the time he comes to *only*; and also if he had said *should count*, the matter would have ended there. But having put in *be*, he has to continue and end on an emphatic note. So he brings in *only*.

The tautologies of the third type (the sequential) arise from sheer ignorance. The writer is not aware of the meaning of the idiom he has used; he has only a vague idea of what it means. So he makes his thought clear by a repetitive phrase. These are typically IE tautologies.

Tautologies of the first type (the phrasal) have sometimes been defended. Wilson Follett (1996) has argued that *personal friend* is not a business acquaintance; *old adage* is a set phrase and we should not quarrel with it; *cancel out* is more emphatic than just *cancel* (see *CE*).

But no defence can be found for such phrases as *revert back, reason why, exact same*, etc. or for the tautologies of the second and third type. The best advice is: Just avoid all forms of tautology.

Tautologies of the types discussed above should be distinguished from repetition for rhetorical purposes, as in these lines from Coleridge: *Alone, alone, all all alone/Alone on a wide, wide, sea* ('The Rime of the Ancient Mariner').

Now for some IE tautologies. The most famous is *suppose if* (and its equivalent *if in case*). These are frequently found in speech and the other tautologies listed earlier, in writing. I can cite here only a few of them and one or two not listed earlier: I am *enclosing herewith* an application form. *As soon as he heard the news, he returned back immediately./We have postponed the meeting to a later date.* Now for some citations....His philosophy and vision *transcended beyond* the mere coverage of news and views (*India Post*, 21 November 2003); '...non-existent figment of a perverted imagination' (A prominent politician as quoted in *The New Indian Express*, 3 February 2004).

that–how

Subordinate clauses are often introduced by the word *that*. *The Greeks thought that the world is flat.* But this is so only when the clause corresponds to a declarative sentence. If what is subordinated is a question, it will not be introduced by *that*. *Tell me how you did it. I wonder what he thinks of us.* The way Reported Speech (or Indirect Speech) is taught in schools has led to a peculiar construction. So much emphasis is put on the verb *say*, as the reporting verb, being followed by *that* (*He said that....*) we find such sentences as: *To make our case strong we have to show that how Sharma made money and then gave it to the killers* (as reported in *The Times of India*, 15 October 2002). Correction: omit *that*.

'that' in indirect speech

Supposing you are quoting someone's views on a subject, say, Advani on cross-border terrorism. You can say: 'The Deputy Prime Minister says that unless cross-border terrorism stops there can be no talks with Pakistan.' Notice the clause-introducer *that*. But suppose you are giving your own view of the matter which, let us assume, is the same as the Deputy Prime Minister's. You will say: 'As the Deputy Prime Minister says, unless cross-border terrorism stops there can be no talks with Pakistan.' Notice the clause-introducer *that* is now missing.

The first sentence is an indirect quotation. You are reporting what the Deputy Prime Minister said. So the reporting verb *say* is followed by *that*. But in the second sentence you are not reporting anyone's statement. You are expressing your own views which happen to be the same as that of the Minister's. Hence there is no *that*.

This distinction is not always observed in Indian English Here is a citation. *As Morita points out that unlike Americans who prefer building their walls with bricks,* [sic] *Japanese prefer building their wall* [sic] *with stone.* There are several mistakes in the sentence not relevant for us now. Confining ourselves to the question of *that*, notice that the sentence cannot be taken as quoting Morita. In that case, *as* would be uncalled for. The presence of *as* forces us to interpret the sentence as expressing the speaker's corroboration of what Morita says. If so, *that* has no place in the sentence. The correct version would be: 'As Morita points out, unlike [the] Americans who prefer to build their walls with brick, [the] Japanese prefer to build their walls with stone.'

'the likes of him'?

Some time ago *Time* magazine carried the handsome face of the basketball superstar Michael Johnson on its cover. Below it was the single line comment: *We may never see his likes again.*

This comment seems to have generated a lot of discussion. Shouldn't it have been *his like again?*

It is generally assumed that *likes* has a pejorative sense (Cf *I will have nothing more to do with the likes of you*) and when no such sense is intended, the phrase is *like of*, that is, the singular form is used. Thus the LDCE: *the like of somebody/something*, 'something similar to someone or a particular person or thing, or of equal importance or value'. *He gave a superb performance, the like of which has never been seen since; the likes of* (spoken)...*used to talk about someone you do not like: I'd never vote for the likes of him.*

The distinction made in the LDCE is not a recent development. More than sixty years ago, Henry Cecil Wyld in *The Universal Dictionary of the English Language* (1932) noted: 'that which resembles, is of the same nature as, is equal or equivalent to something else': *We should not look upon his like again'.* As for the plural forms: '*not for the likes of me* (colloq.) such a humble, unimportant person'.

Going still further back we find that a distinction was made in the plural depending on whether *likes of* was followed by a first person pronoun or second/third person pronouns. In the very first edition of the COD (1926), the Fowler brothers have, besides the two usages I have quoted from Wyld, this: *the like of you* (coloq.), persons so distinguished as you'.

There are, then, these cases to be considered: (1) *like of* + singular third person pronoun, *the like of him*, (2) *likes of* + first person pronoun, *the likes of me*, (3) *likes of* + second person pronoun, *the likes of you*, (4) *likes of* + third person pronoun singular, *the likes of him*, and (5) *likes of* + third person pronoun plural, *the likes of them*. In (4) and (5), instead of a pronoun, there could be names: *the likes of John; the likes of John, Henry, and Arthur.*

It would seem that in respect of (1), current usage is what it was all along. We need go no further back than Shakespeare for a supporting citation. Hamlet, speaking about his ghostly father says: '*He was a man, take him for all in all; I shall not look upon his like again.*' Not a trace or shadow

of any disparaging sense here; on the other hand, it is brimming with
reverence and admiration.

As for (2) *the likes of me*, common sense would suggest that this can
only have a self-deprecating sense, unless one is an egotistical fool.

As for (3) *the likes of you*, there is a strong disparaging sense here.
The same goes for (5) *the likes of them*. We see here that the neutral or
even positive tone recorded in the COD (1926) has now disappeared in
these cases. But, according to *Webster's Dictionary of English Usage*, in
case (5) if we have a list of names, instead of a pronoun, no suggestion
of any disparagement is found. 'It often implies that the list which follows
is regarded as being in some way impressive or surprising. Disparaging
connotations are rare': '...*goblets and bowls coveted by the likes of The
Smithsonian and The Metropolitan Museum of Art*'. '*The likes of* is appropriate
and inoffensive in such contexts.'

This leaves us with case (4): The *likes of him; His likes* chosen by the
Time's editors is a paraphrase of this.

Safire, who has noted the controversy raised by the *Time's* cover-
line, grudgingly admits that there may be a case for the *Time's* usage.
But this final observation on the whole question is summed up as follows:
'You could say, with a sneer in your voice, "Thank goodness we won't be
seeing the likes of him"', because that plural of *like* is part of a colloquial
put down. But you cannot run somebody down with *the like of him* because
that *like* is comparative not pejorative; it means 'we may not see anybody
like him again' (as reproduced in *Frontline*, 28 August 1998, p. 73).

This is unexceptionable. Indeed, Safire's 'okaying' notwithstanding,
there is little to justify the *Time's* cover-line.

Why should there be such a drastic difference in the interpretation
of the phrases: *the like of him/the likes of him*? Why should the singular
form (*like*) suggest respect and admiration while the plural form (*likes*)
has only contemptuous overtones?

The singular form presents the person in question as unique,
unmatched. So the possibility of meeting another such person is very
unlikely. On the other hand, the plural suggests that the person in question
is so ordinary and contemptible that there are plenty like him. Excellence,
being a rare quality, is not easily found again; but mediocrity (coupled
possibly with mendacity) is there everywhere. The speaker expresses
his firm resolve to keep his distance from the crowd. *I shall have nothing
more to do with the likes of you.*

If men of excellence are aplenty, there is no reason to assert that we will not meet them. It is only when they are few and far between, extremely rare, that we can express doubts about meeting them. And in the most deserving case, there is just one man. One Michael Johnson (Magic Johnson, as he is called) and after him it is doubtful if we will meet anyone like him again.

the rich
(adjectives as nouns)
Adjectives which can be used with human nouns and refer to qualities shared by groups can be used as nouns: *the rich, the poor, the weak, the mighty*, etc. As can be seen, there is invariably the definite article *the* in these cases: *a rich* is impossible.

Used in this way (with *the*), they convey a generic sense and refer to all such people. Agreement is with a plural verb, naturally. *The rich have no idea of the sufferings of the poor.*

This point (about agreement) is not always observed in Indian English. *When the going gets tough, the tough gets going (The Times of India,* 28 December 2001). This should read: *the tough get going.*

'there' in IE
The restriction noted on 'indefinite' subjects in Standard English (see Introductory 'there') is not found in IE. Sentences like *Twenty boys are in the classroom./A man is standing outside* freely occur.

But with proper names, IE has a peculiar construction. Something similar to the English 'dummy', *there* is found but at the end of the sentence:

A. I'm afraid our team is rather weak.

B. What do you mean? Ramu is *there*, Krishnan is *there*, and David is *there*.

The explanation seems to lie in the felt 'deficiency' of existential sentences. A sentence like *Twenty boys are in the classroom* is semantically 'complete'. But *Ramu is* is not. The meaning is not as in *God is.* The predicate is completed by *there.* The meaning of *there* here is not adverbial.

thought–thinking
I have heard a number of people say: 'At that time, the *thought* was..../'Yes, we did it like that.' The *thought* then was...'. I am sure, many will agree with me that the word needed here is *thinking* not *thought*.

The distinction between *thought* and *thinking* is a subtle one. *Thought* has a much wider context of use than *thinking: Eastern thought, Indian thought*: the collective set of ideas of the East or Indian thinkers on a subject (philosophy, religion, etc.); *A history of European thought in the nineteenth century, the tradition of western thought*, etc.

One can also speak about the characteristic way a person, group, or people think: *His thinking is always self-centred.*/*Orthodox and religious groups are getting more and more isolated. Their thinking doesn't appeal much to younger people.* The reference here is not to any specific set of ideas or beliefs but the way one *thinks*. An orthodox religious man may have, for example, a negative attitude towards many of the things that the young people of today like.

The distinction till now is: *thought* as a collection of ideas: *thinking* as a way of looking at things.

Thought can also refer to a sudden idea you have on a problem: *We were wondering what to do. Suddenly Ramesh had a brilliant thought* (idea). (In the plural) *Have you any thoughts on the matter?*

Thought in this sense ('an individual act of the mind') is very common: *Late in the night there was a sudden knock on the door. Her first thought was to shriek.*

Thought can also refer to the act of bringing up something before the mind and examining it: *I know I have promised to take you on a holiday. But don't pester me now. I haven't given a thought to it.* (Or *I haven't given much thought to it*). Thinking (noun) is not used in this context. If used, it has to be as a verb in the progressive form: *I have been of late thinking about it.* So while *thought* appears in a past perfect context, *thinking* (verb) appears in the present progressive.

Thoughts can be used in a collective sense to refer to one's hopes, plans about some project, idea. *He has given up all thoughts of building a house/of going abroad.* *Thinking* cannot be used here. It can only be used as a verb and have a future reference. *I am thinking of building a house/of going abroad.*

We have now distinguished four meanings of *thought* (noun): (1) the collective ideas of a group of thinkers on various subjects (*Western thought*); (2) a spurt of ideas on a given problem, topic (*any thoughts on this?*); (3) the act of bringing up something for consideration (*I haven't given much thought to going on a holiday*); and (4) a collective sense including hopes, aspirations, etc. on some project, activity.

In senses (3) and (4), *thinking* (verb) can be used (with the difference noted above).

Now what about the sentence we began with—*At that time the thought was.../ The thought then was*. You will notice that this case is not covered by any of the meanings elicited above. (If you think that meaning (2) given above covers this, think again). The meaning here is 'opinion or judgement' (COD). The word here is *thinking. The thinking then was....*

This apart there are a number of phrases where only *think* appears: *think for yourself, think twice* (over something; 'give careful consideration to it'); *think aloud* ('speak one's thoughts as soon as they occur'); and, of course, *think again. Thought* would sound odd in these cases. Note also *to put on one's thinking cap.*

Similarly there are some phrases where only *thought* (noun) is possible and *thinking* (noun) cannot be used: *give thought to something, thought-provoking* (of a piece of writing, an author), *thought-reader, thought transference* (telepathy), *thought police* (of Orwell).

'threaten with life'

Senior BJP leader and Rajya Sabha member Shatrughan Sinha was threatened with his life by anti-socials in Patna on Sunday (UNI report, *DH*, 18 March 2002).

You *threaten* somebody with something. *The Boss threatened the Accounts Manager with dismissal. / TDP has threatened to withdraw support to the Vajpayee government. With* can also be used in a literal sense: *He threatened her with a knife / gun.* But how can you *threaten someone with his life?*

The news report should have read: *Shatrughan Sinha's life threatened.* Or *Sinha receives threats to his life.*

to be conscious/to be in one's senses

There is a distinction between *to be conscious* and *to be in one's senses.* To be (fully) conscious, is to be aware of what is going on around you, to be able to see, hear, speak, think, etc. The term (in a medical sense) is often used of patients. *He has come out of the anesthesia. He is now fully conscious. / We have given only a local anesthesia. He won't feel any pain but he will be fully conscious* (during the surgery).

To be in one's senses does not have the same meaning. The phrase is often used as in: *Who in his senses would agree to such a proposal? / Are you in your senses? How can you talk like that?* This is equal to: *Are you out of your mind?*

To get the meaning associated with patients undergoing surgery (with a local anaesthesia), we should say something like: *He is in full possession of his senses.*

The point is of some relevance in the context of the recent surgery undergone by the Prime Minister. Some newspapers reported that the operation would be under regional anaesthesia and 'the Prime Minister would be *conscious* throughout'. Others said: 'The PM will be in his senses during the operation.'

The question: *Are you in your senses?* is not a polite inquiry calling for any factual information. It is a sign of exasperation, incredulity. A suitable answer would be: *Shut up, I know what I am doing.* Or, *Get lost. Mind your business.* The question may also express great concern and solicitude. In that case, an answer would be: *Don't worry, I know what I am doing.*

In any case, it would be an insult to say that Mr Vajpayee was in his senses during the operation. Mr Vajpayee has always been a man of great reasonableness and equanimity and was never out of his mind.

Now let's distinguish between: *to be aware of* and *to be conscious.*

One meaning of *conscious* we have already seen in the previous discussion. It has another meaning: *to notice.* In this sense, it has no direct reference to *one's senses. All the time I was conscious of being watched./I am keenly conscious of my own drawbacks.*

In this sense, *aware* can replace *conscious. I was aware of being watched./ I am aware of my drawbacks.*

(In the earlier sense discussed above, the synonym for *conscious* would be *awake.* Throughout the operation, he was *conscious/awake* (not: aware). There are two negative forms of *conscious,* matching the two senses distinguished above. *Throughout the operation he was totally unconscious* (meaning 1)./*I am not conscious of any regulation prohibiting this action.* (meaning 2). It may be possible, but not desirable, to use *not conscious* in the first sentence. (The sentence will have to be drastically recast.) It is not possible at all to use *unconscious* in the second sentence.

'to graduate, postgraduate...'

'...to graduate, postgraduate, doctorate, and post-doctorate in computer sciences....'

This may be a jocular use. (It is taken from a humorous piece on the Indian community in the USA) But it is well to note that only *graduate* exists as a verb. *I graduated from UCLA in 1969. To graduate* means slightly different things in Britain and the USA. If you *graduate* in Britain, you have at least secured a first degree (B.A./B.Sc) from a university. In the USA, elementary schools and high schools hold *graduation* ceremonies. One who completes a course of studies in a high school is said to have *graduated*. This apart, a *graduate student* in the USA is one who is doing his M.A. or Ph.D. He is in a *graduate school*. A student studying for an M.A. or a Ph.D. in a British university would be a *postgraduate student*. In the USA, a *postgraduate* is one who is studying after getting a Ph.D. In both the countries, a *doctoral* student means the same thing: one working for a Ph.D. The term *post-doctoral* also is current in both the countries.

Finally note that there are no verbs corresponding to the words *postgraduate, doctoral* and *post-doctoral. Graduate* can be a noun, adjective, or verb (a graduate, a graduate student, to graduate); *postgraduate* can be a noun or adjective (a postgraduate at Edinburgh; postgraduate studies); *doctoral* is an adjective; *doctorate* is a noun, not a verb (a doctorate from Harvard), and *postdoctoral*, an adjective only. In the USA, a *post-doc* is used as a noun—to refer to someone studying after getting a Ph.D.

'totally'

Totally there were 170 students in the school which has only one teacher (*The Hindu*, 2 April 2002).

This is an Indianism which has, surprisingly, gone unnoticed in discussions on Indian English. The Standard English equivalent is: *in all. In all there were 170 students.*

The fact that hundreds of adjectives are converted to adverbs by the addition of -*ly* must be at the root of this Indianism. (It is interesting to note that the same people who say *totally* also have the adjective *strengthy*—on the analogy of such conversions as *wealth—wealthy, health—healthy, stealth—stealthy*....)

Totally means 'completely, wholly'. *Several buildings were totally destroyed in the earthquake./That's a totally different matter.*

'troubleshooter'

The district administration will conduct another flag march on Thursday to sound a warning to troubleshooters (*The Times of India*, 14 March 2002). A *troubleshooter* is one who has the ability to face a difficult situation and resolve the crisis. How, then, can the administration send 'a warning to trouble-shooters'? Obviously the reporter is under the impression that a *troubleshooter* is a *troublemaker*. (In an extended sense, one who can fix/repair gadgets is also a troubleshooter.)

'turn seventy'

In Standard English, this expression, when used of a person, can only mean that he/she has completed age seventy. But we find it frequently used in our newspapers in the sense of 'entering the seventieth year'. A mistake. It was recently reported of Mr Deve Gowda, the former Prime Minister, that he had turned *seventy*; the Kannada papers said that he had entered his seventieth year. Another report says (*Deccan Herald*, 29 June 2002) *Narasimha Rao turns 82*. Has he completed eighty-two years or is he stepping into his eighty-second year?

U

'under process'

An Indianism which seams to be gaining ground. A judicial dignitary said the other day (on *Star TV*); *The matter is under process.*

We have phrases like: *under consideration/under examination/under scrutiny*. Then why not: *under process*?

Unfortunately there is no noun *process* with the intended meaning. We have *a chemical process, a photographic process, the process of digestion...* More generally, *process* refers to the series of steps that have to be gone through in getting something done. *Reforming the educational system is a long and slow process.* In legal parlance, *process* refers to a summons. But the sense of *process* I have noted is a different one. It is the noun equivalent of the participle phrase *being processed*; the matter (a proposal or whatever) is being studied, examined.

Rather than condemn it as an Indianism, we should, perhaps, welcome it as a legitimate extension of the usage of the word. It is well-established in American English.

undone

They feel tense so long as there is something undone.

We frequently use the word *undone* to mean 'unfinished', 'not completed'. But *undone* (the past participle of 'undo') has this sense only in the specific context of some work, job. *He has left his homework undone* (NODE); *left the job undone* (COD). Otherwise the meanings of *undone* are (1) 'come loose, unfastened': *My shoelace has come undone.* (2) 'ruined':

My God, this is terrible. I am undone. (This sense is somewhat archaic.) (3) 'reverse or change': *The first priority of every government is to undo whatever good programmes the previous ministry had initiated./What has been done can't be undone.*

It is clear that the writer could have achieved his intended sense if he had said: *They feel tense as long as some work remains undone.*

unhappy yokings

I take this opportunity to thank you for your kind help and cooperation extended to me in the past and expecting the same in the future also. (From the manager of a finance company to the investing public.)

This sentence, as you will see, exemplifies a typical structural mistake not confined to self-made finance company managers. There are two conjoined phrases here. The first one, *kind help and cooperation* is fine. Two nouns (more strictly, noun phrases) are joined by *and*. Although the first noun phrase has an adjective qualifier *kind* and the second noun phrase has no such adjective, this does not matter. What matters is the head of these phrases. In both cases we have nouns: *help, cooperation.*

But in the second conjoined structure—the heads here are verbs— we don't have parallel structures. In the first conjunct (we refer to structures conjoined as *conjuncts*), we have the verb *take*. And in the second we have *expecting.* These two are different in form.

Suppose we had *expect* in the second conjunct. The two conjoined structures would now be parallel: *I take...I expect.* (Of course the subject *I* is missing in the second conjunct but this can be easily reconstructed.)

Partnership Summit 2000 began with much fanfare:...aptly described as the biggest, boldest and comprehensive...(DH News Service, 5 January 2002). Something odd here. What is it?

A faulty conjoined structure again. We have a set of adjectives here. But while the first two are in the superlative degree, the last one is not. It is in the positive degree. See for yourself how quickly matters are improved if we change it to: *most comprehensive.*

There is increased incidence of cancer in smokers and who take alcohol in excess (The Hindu, 8 June 1997). Here we see *and* used to connect a noun (technically a noun phrase), *smokers,* and a clause. The two are different. No wonder the sentence sounds odd.

Suppose you add *those* after *and*. The sentence now reads: *There is increased incidence of cancer in smokers and those who take alcohol in excess.*

This is fine: because the conjunction now connects two noun phrases (a relative clause is a noun phrase. If the reference in the sentence is just to one group, remove *and*. Now there is no conjoined structure).

Finally, consider this. *According to Professor S.C. Sharma, Head of the Mechanical Engineering Department at RVE College and who helped Rani pursue studies at the pre-university and degree levels*.... As it is, the sentence is bad. The sentence is exactly like the previous one. The only difference is: the reference is to just one person. You can remove *and*, put a comma after RVE College. You will find the sentence is good. But now there is no conjoined structure. If you want to retain the conjunction, you must make the conjuncts parallel.

Suppose you say: 'Professor S.C. Sharma, who heads the Mechanical Engineering Department and who helped Rani....', now the conjuncts are both relative clauses, and connect parallel structures.

School grammars define a conjunction as a 'joining word'. It is nowhere made clear that the structures conjoined must be parallel. The closer the parallelism, the better the conjoined phrase. But, alas, even accomplished writers fail to notice this. *Muslim opponents of the Pakistani idea were dissuaded, sidelined, or (like Sir Sikander Hyat Khan in Punjab and Allah Bux in Sind) died*...(Tharoor, p. 130).

unless/if not

Michael Swan (*Practical English Usage*) has some interesting comments on the use of *unless* and *if not*. He first notes some cases where the two are interchangeable. *Come tomorrow unless I phone. / I'll take the job unless the pay is too low. / I'll be back tomorrow unless there is a plane strike*. In these cases, it is possible to have an alternative construction with *if not*. *Come tomorrow except if I phone* (or: if I don't phone). Swan comments: '*unless* can be used instead of *if not* when we refer to exceptional circumstances which would change a situation'. (In the first sentence, the exceptional situation is my telephoning.)

But (says Swan) in sentences like the following, *unless* is not possible. *My wife would be very upset if I don't get back tomorrow.* 'We do not use *unless* to refer to something negative that would be the main cause of the situation we are talking about. If the speaker does not get back that will be the main cause of the situation that we are talking about.'

Fine. Now consider the sentence: *They won't release the child unless you pay the ransom.* This is a case where *if not* cannot be used. *They won't release the child if you don't pay the ransom* does not mean the same thing as the sentence with *unless*. The sentence with *if not* raises an objection to a suggestion of not paying the ransom. No such implication is found in the sentence with *unless*.

Clearly the facts are a little more complicated than presented in Swan.

The different cases are: (1) where either *unless* or *if not* can be used and (2) where no such alternation is possible. Here we have (*a*) where only *if not* is found and (*b*) where only *unless* is found. In (*a*) emphasis is on the content of the main clause: *My wife will be upset if I don't get back tomorrow*. In (*b*) emphasis is on the condition precedent: The ransom has to be paid.

'until...not'

Until the forensics don't come nobody is moving. (English dubbing in the Hindi Serial, *Astitva*.)

Here we see a typical Indianism—a negative in an *until* phrase. *You can stay here till the lights are turned off* means *You can stay here as long as the lights are not turned off*. The negative force is already there in *till*; there is no need to buttress it with *not*. It is ungrammatical. *She won't come till you call her* is English. *She won't come until you don't call her* is Hindi(?).

use/utilize

In the relevant sense, *utilize* is a more complex idea than *use*. In addition to the basic meaning found in *use*, *utilize* involves the additional meanings of: finding a use for something and then using it effectively. *To utilize solar energy for heating/to utilize every inch of available space/to utilize garden waste as organic manure.*

Use has figurative meanings not found with *utilize*: *use one's position to gain some advantage/use a person to serve one's ends*, etc.

W

was the picture hanged or hung?
(irregular past participles)

Many are under the impression that the past form of *beat* is *bet* (as in *set*). It is not. The past is spelt and pronounced the same way as the present: *beat* (rhymes with *seat*).

In a few cases where the past and the past participle forms are the same, there are alternative spellings: *burnt/burned; learnt/learned; dreamt/*

dreamed. The forms in *-ed* are the regular forms; the forms in *-t* are the irregular forms.

In British English, the irregular forms are preferred. *They burnt down the cottage. / We have burnt all the trash. / I dreamt a strange dream. / I have often dreamt of flying like a bird*. The forms in *-ed* may also be found in British English. It has been suggested that the forms in *-ed* are more likely to be used when the action indicated is of a prolonged nature. *He learnt his lesson. / She learned a lot about life from her mother* (ALD). The Americans prefer the regular forms: *learned, dreamed, burned*.

Both in American and British English, when the participle appears before a noun, modifying it like an adjective, the form in *-t* is used: *a spoilt child, a misspelt word, spilt milk* (examples from ALD).

Many past participles can be used either after a verb (a form of BE or HAVE) or before a noun, without change in form: *The leaves are fallen—the fallen leaves; the cloth is torn—the torn cloth; the chair is broken—the broken chair;....* But in a few cases, we have two separate forms: one for the position after the verb and another for the position before the noun. *The ship has sunk—the sunken ship; his head has been shaved—a shaven head. The man is drunk—a drunken man. The meat has been roasted—roast meat*. With the verbs *light* and *mow*, there are two forms available in the position after the verb. *The candles are lighted* (or *lit*). *The lawn is being mowed* (or *mown*). But before a noun, the forms are: *the lighted candle, the mown lawn*. With *melt*, the form after the verb is *melted*. *The lead has melted*. But: *molten lead* (or *melted lead*).

There are cases where one form of the past participle is used in a literal sense and the other in a figurative sense. Of someone who has lost a member of his family, you can say *he is bereaved*. But a man who has been continuously unlucky and has no hope, the phrase is *bereft of all hope*. *A swollen river* but *a swelled head* (= conceited; *a swollen head* is also possible). Cf also: *He was bound hand and foot. It is my bounden duty. He was beaten black and blue*. But *dead beat* (thoroughly exhausted; a colloquial expression). *The tube is bent*. But: *He went down on bended knees* (to propose). In a few cases, where the 'base' form of the verb has more than one meaning, there will be two different sets of past / past participle forms. This is so with *bid, hang, knit*. For example, *bid* can mean 'to bid at an auction'. The past and past participle forms are *bid/bade*. In the sense of *tell, invite*, the forms are *bade/bidden. Do as you are bidden. He bade farewell to his sweetheart. Hang* can be as in: *Hang this picture on the wall*. With this meaning, the past and past participle forms are: *hung*. But a condemned man may be *hanged*.

Although it is *put-put-put*, with *input*, *output* we have: *inputted*, *outputted* (computer language).

'were' in place of 'was'

Were is used in place of *was* in *if-* clauses denoting a condition not likely to be fulfilled or a state of things contrary to reality. *If I were a millionaire, I would go on a cruise to the Bahamas. / If we were angels, we would be in the sky blowing trumpets. / If I were you I would talk to her.*

This is also the case where the sub-clause is introduced by *as if, as though. He talks as if he were the owner of the place.*

A lexical verb in this construction would be in the past form. *He talks as if he knew all about it....*

Were (and not *was*) is also used after *I wish. I wish I were living in London* (an unrealized or unrealizable desire). This does not mean that after *I wish*, only *were* is possible. *I wish* must be followed by the past form of the verb chosen. *I wish I knew the answer.* If BE is chosen, it must be *were* and not *was*.

I mentioned above one condition for the choice of *were* (against *was*): the *if-* clause or the clause after *I wish* must express a state contrary to fact, i.e., a state (or desire) which is not realized or cannot be realized. There is another condition: the reference must be to the present. As the examples make clear, the speaker is not talking about past events.

'whatever...that'

...a point to be noted is that whatever changes that have occurred in the Indian economy and society since 1991 cannot be wholly attributed to globalization.

Suppose we omit *whatever*. The sentence will now read '...a point to be noted is [that changes that have occurred...since 1991] cannot be wholly attributed to globalization'. This is perfectly grammatical. The bracketed portion is the subject of the predicate *cannot be wholly attributed to globalization*. The subject contains a relative clause: *that have occurred...since 1991*. The antecedent is *changes*.

Suppose we omit *that* in the original sentence. We now get '...a point to be noted is [whatever changes have occurred...since 1991] cannot be wholly attributed to globalization'.

This, too, is grammatical. As before, the bracketed portion is the subject of the predicate: *cannot...globalization*. Again the subject contains a clause:

whatever changes have occurred...since 1991. It may not be immediately clear what type of clause it is. It is in fact a relative clause: *whatever changes = any changes that*. Since *that* is already there (in *whatever*), the structure *whatever changes that have occurred* sounds odd. It is ungrammatical.

Because of the perfectly grammatical *changes that have occurred*, we are tempted to write *whatever changes that have occurred*. But with *whatever* you cannot also have *that*.

Consider finally the structure '*...a point to be noted is that whatever the changes that have occurred...since 1991...*'. This is grammatical. *Whatever the changes* is an abbreviated clause equivalent to: 'Whatever may be the changes'. *What* changes?...*the changes that have occurred since 1991*. We have here an explicit relative clause introduced by *that*; *the changes* is the antecedent.

To summarize, we have these constructions: (1) *whatever changes have occurred*, (2) *changes that have occurred*, (3) *whatever the changes that have occurred*, and (4) *whatever changes that have occurred*. The first three are grammatical; the last one is not.

what is good English?

Matthew Arnold is reported to have said: 'People think that I can teach them style. What stuff it all is. Have something to say and say it as clearly as you can. That is the only secret of style' (quoted in Gowers). Nothing can be simpler. But one small question remains: 'What do you do to make sure that what you say has been said 'as clearly as you can?' Much earlier Swift had this to say: 'Proper words in proper order maketh the true definition of style.' This is certainly more specific. It talks about words (which is what we are concerned with); they should be *proper* and in *proper order*. But what is *proper*?

Clearly one-liners won't do.

Fowler (1926) approached the problem by looking at the qualities one would generally associate with a piece of good writing. He wrote: 'Anyone who wishes to become a good writer should endeavour, before he allows himself to be tempted by more qualities, to be direct, simple, brief, vigorous and lucid.' He went further. He answered how these qualities could be realized.

The general principle may be translated into general rules in the domain of vocabulary as follows:

Prefer the familiar word to the far-fetched.

Prefer the concrete word to the abstract.

Prefer the simple word to the circumlocution.

Prefer the short word to the long.

Prefer the Saxon word to the Romance.

These rules are given in order of merit, the last is also the least.

In his much-discussed essay, 'Politics and the English Language', in *Collected Essays* (1946), George Orwell sums up his discussion with these six elementary rules:

(1) Never use a metaphor, simile, or other figure of speech which you are used to seeing in print.

(2) Never use a long word where a SHORT word will do.

(3) If it is possible to cut out a word, always cut it out.

(4) Never use the passive where you can use the ACTIVE.

(5) Never use a FOREIGN PHRASE, a scientific word or a JARGON word if you can think of an everyday English equivalent.

(6) Break any of these rules sooner than say anything outright barbarous.

Orwell is more specific about what words not to use. Fowler's point about the 'familiar' word is elaborated under Rule 5. He also warns against the use of cliches (Rule 1). And, by stressing the use of the active over the passive, he makes a point for *directness.* These things become readily intelligible when we remember the context in which Orwell wrote his essay. Politics was corrupting the language. The half-truths, euphemisms, and cliches of political speech and writing were to be opposed and exposed.

Gowers (1954), reviewing Fowler's and Quiller-Couch's recommendations (Quiller-Couch: *On the Art of Writing*), offers these rules:

(1) Use no more words than are necessary to express your meaning, for if you use more you are likely to obscure it and to tire your reader. In particular, do not use superfluous adjectives and adverbs and do not use roundabout phrases where single words would serve.

(2) Use familiar words rather than the far-fetched, if they express your meaning equally well; for the familiar are more likely to be understood.

(3) Use words with a precise meaning rather than those that are vague, for they will obviously serve better to make your meaning clear; and in particular prefer concrete words to abstract, for they are more likely to have a precise meaning.

As can be seen, Gowers' first rule elaborates on Orwell's third rule (on brevity); his second rule is Fowler's first rule; and his third rule expands Fowler's second rule. Fowler's last rule (on the use of Saxon words) is ignored by both Quiller-Couch and Gowers.

I don't think anything more can be said on this question of style and the choice of words. Perhaps a summation may be in order.

It is well to remember what aspect of style we are concerned with here. In the words of Gowers: 'What we are concerned with is not a quest for literary style but to convey our meaning without ambiguity and without giving unnecessary trouble to our readers' (p. 85). With this limited goal in mind, what are the qualities that we would like to see in a piece of writing (apart from its being grammatical)?

(a) It should be *brief* and *direct*. This means there should be no circumlocution and long-windedness; no tautology, pleonasm, periphrasis, or padding. It also means that, as far as possible, sentences should be in the active and not in the passive voice.

(b) It should be *clear* and *precise*—no ambiguity or equivocation; concrete words to be preferred to the abstract, as far as possible; the familiar to the far-fetched. All jargon should be avoided; the words chosen must be such as correctly express the intended meaning.

(c) It should be *fresh* and not *stale*. Avoid all cliches, and worn out metaphors and other figures of speech. Your writing should show that you have thought over and carefully chosen your words and are not echoing some readymade phrases.

The points made above are all in terms of *composition*. This is necessary because while some aspects of good writing may be characterized in terms of words (prefer the short word to the long), others cannot be. The injunction against stale writing cannot be given in terms of words. It is not words that are stale but phrases and expressions. But given a set of features characterizing a piece of composition, most of what needs to be said about words follows. If writing has to be brief and direct, one should prefer the short to the long one, wherever possible; if it has to be clear and precise, in a large number of cases, the words have to be necessarily concrete.

The brief comments against each specification are meant to give an idea of how they translate into the choice of words. The comments are only by way of suggestions—they are not intended to be exhaustive. I feel it is futile to attempt to list everything one would like to say about the choice of words. Keeping in mind the essential qualities of a piece of good writing, given above, and with the guidance given therein, a writer should be able to resolve on his own many questions that arise concerning the choice of words.

See also: AMBIGUITY, CLICHE, JARGON, PADDING, PLEONASM, PERIPHRASIS, TAUTOLOGY; DIMENSIONS OF A WORD.

'what I will do'

The other day I overheard a doctor say (he was speaking into his mobile): *What I will do, I will now go to Rajajinagar....*

What I will do is not English. It is a plain translation from the mother tongue: *naanu eenu maaduttheene endare....* The Standard English phrase would be: *Tell you what. (Tell you what, I will now go to...).*

There is no need to point a finger at the young doctor. We are all, all the time, translating from the mother tongue into English. The most famous (and the most widespread) is: *Do one thing.* We have also phrases like: *I take coffee in the morning* (for *I have...*) / *What is your brother doing now?... Nothing. He is keeping quiet* (say: *Nothing. He is still unemployed*)./ *We are not on talking terms now* (say: *not on speaking terms*)./*He is at the backside of the house* (say: *at the back of the house. Backside* is the part of the anatomy on which you sit.)/ *When I asked him a question he just blinked (kannu kannu bitta).*

This habit of translating from the mother tongue/regional language can reach unbelievable limits. A lawyer friend vouchsafes to having heard: *English comes to me* (English *nanage barutthe*). And many will agree that they have heard (perhaps themselves used) the phrase: *No asker, no teller* (*keeluvarilla, heeluvarilla*; meaning: 'totally irresponsible; no accountability'. (used especially of the workings of government offices.)

'what we do and why we do'?

Training manuals prepared by state institutes which have been set up for various purposes provide an (as yet) untapped source for the study of Indian English. Recently I had an opportunity (?) to go through a booklet on budgeting prepared by the State Institute of Health and Family Welfare, Jaipur in 1996. I present here one among several interesting constructions I found in this eminently helpful booklet: *'...a process of questioning what we do and why we do...'.*

What and *why* are *wh-* words. If you can say *what we do,* why can't you say: *why we do?*

Though apparently similar, the two questions are structurally different. In *what we do*, the object is being questioned: *We do what?* In the second question, the reason for doing something is questioned. *We do it for reason x.* The questioned element, *reason*, is represented by *why*. But since the object is not being questioned, it must appear in its place: *why we do it*. The correct form, then, is: *a process of questioning what we do and why we do it.*

'whether–no'

Commenting on the gross violation of the building code in the construction of buildings in Bangalore, a reader writes: '*The way certain buildings are built would make anyone wonder whether there are no rules at all...*'.

Whether introduces an alternative. *I wonder whether he is coming* means *whether he is coming or not*. *We will know next week whether we will be called for the interview or not.*

But the phrase '*no rule*' in the sentence cited above shuts off this possibility.

To get the right meaning (of an alternative being available) we should use *any*. *I wonder whether there are any rules at all*. This means: 'there may be some rules but this is very doubtful', i.e., the chance of there being no rules is greater. This is exactly what the writer wishes to say.

The distinction between *no* and *any* is one of assertion vs non-assertion. Cf *I am not sure whether anybody asked that question* (non-assertion). *I am sure nobody asked that question* (assertion). See SOME/ANY.

worth one's salt

The phrase *worth one's salt* means that someone is competent at his job, deserves what he earns. *Mr X is an able administrator. He is worth his salt.*

The phrase is more often found in contexts where the point is not just to assert that someone is competent but to say that such a person would or would not say something or do something that would bring him discredit in the eyes of his colleagues. *No scientist worth his salt would subscribe to such views* (say, vodoo, black magic, etc.). *No scientist worth his salt would approve of a university course in astrology.*

The phrase *worth his salt* may also be found in sentences beginning with *any*. *Any scientist worth his salt would tell you that you cannot entertain such beliefs. Any scientist worth his salt would know that genetic engineering is here to stay.*

It should now be clear that *worth his salt* cannot be used to mean just 'competent' without suggesting further what a person so described would not do, or say, or know. What he will or will not do, say, or know are things which follow directly from his being a person *worth his salt*.

Such being the case, it is difficult to see the point of using the phrase in a sentence like: *No scientist worth his salt could predict the earthquake in...* *Gujarat.* The sentence would have read well without the phrase *worth his salt.* If some emphasis were needed, the sentence could have read: *Even the most competent scientist could not predict the earthquake in Gujarat.*

y
'yeoman service'

The phrase *yeoman service* is frequently used by us when referring to the outstanding service done by some person in his official or personal capacity. Pandit Nehru is often eulogized for his *yeoman service* to the nation as the first Prime Minister of the country; distinguished professors on retirement are lauded for their *yeoman service* in building up the department and securing for it a place in the world of higher learning/research.

The phrase, however, means no more than 'useful, efficient service'; 'long and loyal work'. It carries no suggestion of anything outstanding or superlative. This is the meaning given in the OED: 'good, efficient, or useful service such as is rendered by a faithful servant of good standing'. *The society has done yeoman service during the ten years of its existence* (OED). The honorary secretary of a society, a devoted middle-level worker of a political party, a competent teacher who has laboured long and hard in his/her school or college...these and such others may be singled out for this praise but not persons like Nehru, Indira Gandhi, Vajpayee, Radhakrishnan, or C.V. Raman.

The etymology of the word is uncertain but the best guess is that it developed from earlier forms standing for *young + man.* In later times, the word came to stand for a landholder who had certain rights and privileges (like serving on juries). The term was also used to refer to a servant in a royal or noble household. 'In current usage, apart from the phrase *yeoman's service,* the word survives in such expressions as *yeoman of the Guard* (= a member of the British Sovereign's bodyguard).

Select Bibliography

Amis, K. (1998), *The King's English*, NY: St. Martin's Press.

Ammer, C. (2001), *Dictionary of Cliches*, E.P. Dutton.

Collin's Cobuild English Dictionary. (1990), ed. J. Sinclair, London: Harper Collins.

Follett, W. (1996), *Modern American Usage*, New York: Hill and Wong.

Fowler, H.W. (1926), *A Dictionary of Modern English Usage*, Oxford: Oxford University Press.

—— (1965), 2nd edn, revised and ed. Sir Ernest Gowers, Oxford: Oxford University Press.

—— (1998), 3rd edn, R.W. Burchfield, Oxford: Oxford University Press.

Gowers, Sir Ernest (1951), *Plain Words—Their ABC*, London: Her Majesty's Stationery Office.

—— (1986), *The Complete Plain Words*, revised and ed. S. Greenbaum and J. Whitcut, London: Her Majesty's Stationery Office.

Greenbaum, S. and J. Whitcut (1988), *Longman Guide to English Usage*, England: Longman.

Lederer, R. (1989), *Anguished English*, NY: Dell Publicity.

—— (1994), *Adventures of a Verbivore*, New York: Pocket Books.

Leech, Geoffrey and Jan Svartvick (1975), *A Communicative Grammar of English*.

Lehman, R.A. (1968), *A Handlist of Rhetorical Terms*, Berkeley and Los Angeles: University of California Press.

Lowth, Robert (1775), *Short Introduction to English Grammar*.

Mallai, Amulya (2003), *The Mango Season*, New York: Ballantine Books.

Mulvaney, J. (2002), *Diana and Jackie*, New York: St Martin's Press.

Orwell, G. (1968 [1946]), 'Politics and the English Language', in *Collected Essays, Journalism and Letters*, eds Sonia Orwell and Ian Angus, London: Secker and Warburg, Vol. 4. pp. 127–40.

Oxford English Dictionary (1989), 2nd edn, Oxford: Clarendon Press.

Oxford Dictionary of Collocations (2002), Oxford: Oxford University Press.

Partridge, E. (1940), *A Dictionary of Clichés*, London: Routledge.

_____ (1999), *English Usage and Abusage*, 3rd edn, revised Janet Whitcut, London: Penguin.

Quirk, et al. (1972), *A Grammar of Contemporary English*, New York and London: Seminar Press.

_____ (1985), *A Comprehensive Grammar of English*, London and New York: Longman.

Rees, N. (1985), *Dictionary of Cliches*, London: Cassell.

Safire, W. (1980), *On Language*, New York: Times Books.

_____ (1990), *Language Maven Strikes Again*, New York: Doubleday.

_____ (1997), *Watching My Language*, New York: Random House.

Strunk, W. and E.B. White (1979), *The Elements of Style*, 3rd edn, New York: Macmillan Alyn and Bacon.

Swan, M. (2003), *Practical English Usage*, Oxford: Oxford University Press.

Tharoor, S. (2003), *Nehru: The Invention of India*, New York: Arcade Publishing.

The Concise Oxford Dictionary (1990), 8th edn, Oxford: Oxford University Press.

The Economist Style Guide (2002), 7th edn.

The New Oxford Dictionary of English (1998), Oxford: Oxford University Press.

The New Shorter Oxford English Dictionary (2002), 5th edn, Oxford: Oxford University Press.

The Oxford Guide to English Usage (1993), 2nd edn, Oxford: Clarendon Press.

Trask, R.L. (2001), *Mind the Gaffe*, London: Penguin Books.

Webster's Dictionary of English Usage (1989), Springfield, Massachusetts: Merriam-Webster.

Wood, F.T. (1962), *Current English Usage*, revised edn [1981], ed. R.H. Flavell and L.M. Flavell, London: Macmillan.

Wyld, H.C. (1932), *The Universal Dictionary of the English Language*, new edn, [1936], London: George Rutledge and Sons.

Yadurajan, K.S. (2001), *Current English*, New Delhi: Oxford University Press.

Zandvoort, R.W. (1962), *A Handbook of English Grammar*, 2nd edn, Longmans.